DEMOCRACY AT THE BALLPARK

DEMOCRACY AT THE BALLPARK
SPORT, SPECTATORSHIP, AND POLITICS

THOMAS DAVID BUNTING

Published by State University of New York Press, Albany

© 2021 State University of New York

For information, contact State University of New York Press, Albany, NY
www.sunypress.edu

Library of Congress Cataloging-in-Publication Data

Name: Bunting, Thomas David, author.
Title: Democracy at the ballpark : sport, spectatorship, and politics / Thomas David
    Bunting, author.
Description: Albany : State University of New York Press, [2021] | Includes
    bibliographical references and index.
Identifiers: ISBN 9781438485676 (hardcover : alk. paper) | ISBN 9781438485683
    (ebook) | ISBN 9781438485669 (pbk. : alk. paper)
Further information is available at the Library of Congress.

10 9 8 7 6 5 4 3 2 1

In memory of Richard C. Post,
a good ballplayer and citizen.

CONTENTS

ACKNOWLEDGMENTS

I first want to thank my wife, Ann Sojka. Without her, this project would not exist. She supported me in graduate school, read way too many drafts of these chapters, and helped me believe in myself on many a hopeless day. I hope I have been able to return some of the favor and look forward to our next adventures. Thank you for your courage, intelligence, kindness, and for pushing me to do more. I love you.

I also want to thank the rest of my family. My dad, Dave Bunting, spent countless hours playing baseball with me and came to all of my events near and far, from games, to concerts, races, and beyond. I know you died inside a little when I quit baseball in tenth grade, and I hope this book is sufficient atonement. It would be hard to imagine a more supportive person than my mom, Sue Godbold. I am forever grateful for all of her love, support, and understanding as I went on my ill-advised academic journey. You helped me find a reason even in the seemingly terrible things. Thank you to Val and Mike Krist for bringing me to Tigers games and to Elliot for brightening a difficult year just by being there. I am grateful for my stepparents, Tom Godbold and Ann Bunting, who treat me like their son. I am also thankful for my expanded family, including Janice Kritchevsky, Chris and Ellen Needham, Jasper, Miriam, and the Sojkas, Karole, Paul, Abbie, and Phil.

I have been lucky to have a great group of friends to support me throughout this project as well. Thank you to Joey Costanzo for listening to me try to translate democratic theory into language normal humans use. Thank you to Tyler Klifman for being the best roommate and friend a guy could ever want. I also want to thank John and Ayanda Crispin along with Leah, Olivia, and Noah for giving me a family in graduate school. Thanks to Jacob Ahern, Griffin Bohanon, Andrew Borgman, Keegan Boyle, Marcus Breidinger, Lakin Brown, CJ Holmes, Luke Klifman, Krista McCoy, Chris Reznich, Kareem Seifeldin, Kyle Vaughn, Dave Walsh, Annie Wildfong, Jim Yost, and others for years of friendship and giving me a life outside of academics.

Thank you to my many friends and colleagues who helped at various stages of this project. Thank you especially to Brianne Wolf for being a friend every step of the way during our parallel journeys. Thank you to Meg Rowley for being immediately on board with a project bringing together political theory and baseball. Thank you to Evan Crawford, Sean Dunne, Rob Gingrich, Katelyn Jones, Richard King, Rebecca LeMoine, Michael Promisel, Jeff Rice, Rachel Schwartz, Christine Shea, Ben Toff, and Logan Vidal. Thank you also to the great community of folks over at Bless You Boys on SB Nation who helped rekindle my baseball fandom and supported my writing.

I owe a debt of gratitude to the many great teachers who helped me on my way. Thanks especially to Rick Avramenko for all his help through the years with this project and others. I will never be able to repay the time, energy, and support he gave me. He encouraged me to do the stupid brave thing instead of the boring safe thing, and I will never forget that. Thank you to Daniel Kapust for all of his support and advice through grad school, this publishing process, and for paying me to watch Maple when I was a broke kid. Thank you also to the other great faculty at University of Wisconsin, especially Helen Kinsella, Michele Schwarze, and John Zumbrunnen. Finally, thank you to all the other wonderful teachers who helped shape my academic journey, including Tobin Craig, Ron Dorr, Kristina Eggenberger, Waseem El-Rayes, Folke Lindahl, Sue Nichols, Eric Petrie, and too many others to list.

I will be forever thankful to SUNY Press for giving this project a shot and their constant professionalism and helpful feedback throughout the process. It has been a joy working with SUNY, and they have been invaluable in shaping this book into its final form. Thank you especially to Michael Rinella for his work ushering this project forward. Thank you to Diane Ganeles for all of her work as production editor. Thank you to Michael Campochiaro for marketing help. I owe a great deal of thanks to John Wentworth for copy editing this book and providing the illusion that I am a better writer than I am. And finally, thank you for the work of the anonymous reviewers and their essential feedback.

An early version of chapter 3 originally appeared in the journal *Democratic Theory* as an article titled "Breaking Barriers and Coded Language." Thank you to the editors at *Democratic Theory* for allowing me to re-print portions of that article here, and thank you to their readers for their valuable suggestions.

I am grateful to my many students throughout the years, especially students who took my sports courses at the University of Wisconsin, at Shawnee State, and with KIIS in Greece. Students are what makes this job worthwhile, and the countless conversations in class no doubt shaped the direction that this project ultimately took.

Thank you also to everyone in the discipline who gave me helpful feedback at conferences on different chapters of this project. There are far too many to name, but those conversations and words of encouragement made a difference and justified the airfare.

The final years of this project were marked by loss. While I have dedicated the book to the memory of my grandfather, I want to acknowledge the other loved ones my family lost and to honor the memories of Robert and Cora Joan Bunting, Dick and Beverlee Post, Louise Godbold, Jeff Godbold, Evelyn Kritchevsky, and John Sojka. They are desperately missed and live on in our memories.

Last but never least, thank you to Humphrey and Yanni for being perfect, judgment-free companions as they watched me write this book, occasionally reminding me it might be time to take a walk. You are both good boys, always.

INTRODUCTION

This project began in 2014, and by the discontented spring of 2020, when colleagues would ask about the project, I would quip that the book made more sense back when we had democracy and baseball. That spring, it looked like the baseball season could be cancelled amid the COVID-19 pandemic and the botched response by an impeached president and administration that demonstrated a constant disregard for both laws and norms. As of this writing in November 2020, we saw the conclusion of a shortened baseball season riddled with indifference toward the health of the players and spectators. Joe Biden is President-elect, yet President Trump and many of his Republican colleagues refuse to acknowledge this defeat. It seems we do have baseball and democracy, each flawed and facing uncertain futures.

The main argument that I advance in this book is that our politics and our everyday pastimes are not separate. It should not be surprising, then, that both of these institutions, baseball and American politics, face similar problems. Wealthy baseball owners and elite politicians (who often receive donations from said owners) view their power as a means to wealth and more power. However, American politics is not primarily about leaders, just as baseball is not primarily about owners. Nearly 160 million people voted in 2020, and baseball derives its meaning far more from fans than owners, or even players. Nobody is compelled to follow baseball—they do so freely. Consequently, America's pastime is democratic, shaped by the people and not the few. However, saying that baseball is democratic does not necessarily mean that baseball is always good or healthy for democratic life. If, in baseball, democracy shines its clearest, we must admit that we do not always like what we see shining.

To understand a concept like democracy at the ballpark, it is imperative to keep these tensions in mind. Democracy is fundamentally about possibility. As a regime built on equality and liberty, democracy is a goal and a promise that is often unrealized. The history of American democracy is largely a history of failing to live up to the founding ideals set forth in the Declaration of Independence and the Constitution. Inherent in the democratic world is the possibility that democracy undermines itself, whether through the tyranny of the majority or the selection of a populist or authoritarian leader.[1] True moments of democracy can be rare, and people are not often brought in to participate beyond relatively infrequent events like elections and mass protests. As a result, everyday venues for politics in social life like sport are valuable windows into democratic life.

Baseball illuminates democratic politics by acting as a metaphor: sporting events and the way spectators and fans engage with them are representative and symbolic of how people view social and political issues. Taking sport seriously as a metaphor for politics explains why baseball's value to democratic life lies in its potential. Many times, anti-democratic visions of America have found support in the baseball world. However, baseball has also been a testing ground for projects more radically democratic than any politician could advance. The game reflects the people who care about it, for better and worse. Democracy at the ballpark suffers from the same drawbacks as democracy at the ballot box. To embrace such a concept, one must ultimately have faith in people, in fans, in citizens.

Taking baseball seriously as a political venue recognizes the importance of humble, small, everyday ways of thinking about politics. The game is quotidian, and surely most people participating in constructing baseball into a mass spectacle do not do so as a political statement. Going to a baseball game or following baseball through media is an average, everyday act. However, in these everyday acts, what people truly care about shines through. Democracy does not always unfold on the grand stage of routinized politics; it instead resides and grows in the small spaces, in the routine.

Given the high stakes of the current polarized political climate in America, one may rightly ask why a political scientist or theorist would choose to study something as seemingly frivolous as baseball in times as momentous as these.

The full answer lies in the rest of the book, but briefly I see in baseball a different possibility for American life and politics. Baseball reveals a different mode of being together than what national politics offers. Baseball provides a model of mutual respect between those that disagree. In baseball, there are not enemies, but rivals. Baseball requires respect for rules and norms. Fans of opposing teams have more in common with each other than they do with those who do not follow the sport. The game gathers not only those with similar goals and desires but unites those with opposing wishes as well. Patience, care, attention, time—the game demands all of these, and much more. Fandom requires vulnerability and teaches people how to handle both success and failure. In short, the sport offers endless instruction in arts necessary for any successful democracy.

That these lessons are learned in the relatively low-stakes environment of something diversionary and fun like a sport only makes them more important. Democracy requires spaces where people can learn such lessons voluntarily. The alternatives are a lack of civic preparation or state-run programs that hamper democratic liberty, a cure worse than the disease. Democracy at the ballpark is not a cure all, the only, or even the best way of improving democratic life. Democracy at the ballpark presents the possibility of a different way of being together; it is a reminder of what we share, how freedom fosters things we love, how investment in something seemingly small can change one's life, and how caring about the stories we tell through sports can change our horizons.

This is a story about small things that matter. Throwing a ball very hard and hitting it with a stick is absurd. The physical acts that make up a game of baseball are often improbably silly. Yet, these acts are meaningful and taken seriously because people have decided they matter. Paying attention to that decision, why people decided baseball matters, what people see in the game, and how this relationship evolves, reveals much about the democratic mind and our own politics. This project explores these worlds of meaning that most political science and theory ignores.

• • •

To make this argument, this book is divided into five chapters. The first chapter on spectatorship serves as a background for the rest of the project to understand how watching something like a baseball game matters for democratic politics. Spectatorship is a large and meaningful part of our everyday lives and allows realms like sport to serve as a metaphor for politics and a potential site of political action and change. Far from being diversionary or connected to tyranny, spectatorship allows spectators to foster independent judgment and empowers the viewer. This chapter will examine critics of spectatorship to show that these critics miss that spectatorship is not essentially dangerous by nature but has potential to be a valuable part of democratic life as well. Sport and baseball is only one such arena that demonstrates spectatorship provides a political platform to other areas of everyday life outside of formal, elite politics.

Chapter 2 examines the relationship between baseball and community. This chapter examines different theories of community to understand the practical experience of being at the ballpark (or watching elsewhere) to show how baseball brings people together. This explication of being at the ballpark is the ground for an analysis of how this type of event can be the basis for building community. I show how teams can be desirable for building community if harnessed correctly by serving as reflections of their community and sites of displaying local concerns. I also examine how teams that focus exclusively on business and economics can actually undermine local community through exploitive practices such as holding cities hostage for exorbitant amounts of tax money. Spectatorship thus provides possibility for community that can be harnessed or undermined. I conclude by theorizing baseball spectatorship as a meaningful type of community that, although fleeting, has a resilience that outlasts the games themselves.

Chapter 3 examines baseball and equality, focusing on how baseball can both illuminate inequalities and exclusion, while also being a platform for contesting exclusion. I argue that baseball is one important way that Americans can watch the democratic dynamic of inclusion and exclusion in their everyday lives. I examine how who plays baseball, and thus who the crowd watches play, is significant toward understanding the American dynamics of inclusion and exclusion. I focus primarily on race in the sport, and then endeavor to show what baseball can reveal about gender and sexual inequality. I argue that these dynamics both reveal much about the nature of inclusion and exclusion, and show that inclusion and incorporation of groups entails more than simple legal equality. Baseball often reinforces existing inequalities but can sometimes challenge how fans see these inequalities: the sport can incorporate new groups into a team-based "we." In short, I argue that, at times, baseball can be a mechanism for political and social change.

Chapter 4 addresses baseball and public virtue. The chapter examines contemporary virtue theory and ancient writings on the connection between virtue and athletics to understand how sport mixes with visions of virtue. I argue that while the state often has difficulty promoting virtues, baseball both reflects and teaches important social and political virtues. To make this argument, I look at the experience of playing baseball in Little League to argue that this experience teaches what I am calling

"Little League virtues." These virtues provide a basis for understanding how spectatorship can later reinforce these early lessons. I then show how spectatorship of eras of morality, heroes, and villains can reveal and influence politics around virtue. Looking at the history of the game and its moral concerns is like reading the rings in a tree of American morality. I examine patriotism at the ballpark, which is a striking example of how public virtue is expressed or manipulated through baseball. And, finally, the chapter concludes with a reflection on recent cheating scandals and what happens when the sport abandons any pretense of virtue.

Chapter 5 deals with the drastic change in sport and baseball from a pastoral game to an industry shaped by technology. I argue that baseball reveals a broader shift toward technological thinking. To understand this paradigm shift, I draw on writers like Martin Heidegger, Jacques Ellul, Hannah Arendt, and Eric Voegelin to argue that this shift toward technological thinking in sport is important because it indicates that such thinking has penetrated into democratic consciousness even in its everyday pleasures. As to how the shift manifests itself in the game, I trace the rise of technology in baseball, showing the continued desire for quantitative rigor brought into a realm usually believed to be the domain of chance, fate, and skill—the realm of the baseball gods. I argue that this shift is significant and indicates a drastic change in sport from its ancient roots in the sacred and the holy into the scientific realm of analysis and precision. I examine normative questions about the desirability of thinking of sport and players in terms of efficiency and production and look at public perception of this new breed of baseball and the political dimensions of this response. Finally, looking at how technological thinking is resisted in the game, I argue, is helpful for thinking about combatting this thinking in other areas of everyday life.

The book's conclusion ties the chapters together to argue that examining baseball and politics shows that democracy is not confined to halls tread by elites and unseen by the masses. Instead, looking at baseball reveals how narrative and meaning emerge in everyday spaces. This ability to tell a story with sport, sport's potential and power as a metaphor, shows how sport can be inclusive and democratic. I argue that this relationship between baseball and politics is normatively good: it shows that civic life can flourish in many ways. Democracy can unfold wherever masses of people get together and inject something with meaning. The long history and present popularity of baseball shows that it is possible to have democracy at the ballpark complete with contestation and community.

CHAPTER 1

WHY SPORT SPECTATORSHIP MATTERS

In baseball, democracy shines its clearest.

—Ernie Harwell[1]

Sports are a part of the everyday lives of many Americans, but often thought of as a realm apart from more serious endeavors, such as politics. And yet, we often see sport and politics mingling. One such example came in the wake of 9/11 when, after a pause, baseball resumed and became a stage for a political spectacle. George W. Bush took the mound on October 30 for game three of the World Series in New York City to throw out the first pitch. In the face of terrorist attacks, the president used the game to show that the American way of life was still alive by using the sport as a rhetorical appeal to American leisure and resilience.[2] Similarly, in the wake of the Boston Marathon bombing, the ballpark again became a political stage, this time with the baseball players proclaiming the strength and value of their community in the face of terrorism.[3]

Beyond using sport for political messaging in extreme moments, sport also reflects everyday political issues. Recent incidents of domestic abuse in the National Football League have prompted mass discussion of domestic abuse and political life, spreading the discussion across news-papers, blogs, and televisions everywhere. Racial politics and sport have been connected as well from the groundbreaking integration of Major League Baseball (MLB) in 1947, to Willie Horton standing on top of a car in his Tigers uniform amidst the Detroit race riots, and to more recent protests and even strikes by NBA players in the wake of George Floyd's murder.[4] Further, research has shown that sports can highlight prevailing norms and views on gender, reflect social change and revolution, and serve a role in education.[5] These are but a few examples of how everyday politics emerge in sport.

In other words, sport can be political in extreme moments, manipulated by politicians, but it also shapes politics in the small moments, in the everyday unfolding of the sport. Sport does not become political when politicians notice; the latent political potential always resides in sport.

Despite the evidence that sport and politics are related, political science generally and political theory specifically have largely ignored this sphere of political life.[6] Analysis of sport has mainly been relegated to English, history, and sociology departments as political scientists ignore a field that is expanding in scope over the last century. Indeed, sports are a more popular phenomenon than ever, turning into an enormous business and entertainment industry in the twentieth and twenty-first centuries. Often, more Americans watch the Superbowl than vote.[7] One need not run through the statistics on massive attendance figures and revenue generated by different sports to grasp that in America sport occupies a massive part of our cultural, social, and political lives. On any given night, thousands of citizens gather together in public and private spaces to watch an athletic contest. Americans invest money, time, and emotional attachments in their teams, and in sports generally. And yet, we lack a coherent, contemporary political theory to understand this phenomenon.

SPORT AND POLITICAL THEORY

The suggestion that athletics and politics are entwined may elude modern theorists, but it is an ancient insight. In the Greek cradle of Western thought, politics were inextricable from sport. The Greek world centered on agonism and competition aimed at achieving distinction and excellence.[8] This agonistic urge pervaded their culture, and it is unsurprising that sport and athletics were praised and tied to Greek political life. Indeed, athletic and physical prowess was tied to virtue, education, religion, and politics.

Athletes certainly held a prominent position in the ancient world. Pindar's many odes sing athletes' praises for a variety of reasons. Athletic success indicated among other things that the athlete had toiled striving toward noble action, enjoyed the gods' favor, and possessed virtue.[9] Athletes were examples of what it meant to be a good Greek, something seen in the model of the swift-running Achilles. Even Plato's Socrates, a critic of the Greek tendency to overvalue athletics, admits that athletics and physical fitness are important toward achieving the good. Plato also portrays Socrates as strong, capable of handling much physical duress. In Plato's *Symposium*, Socrates's physical (and mental) strength is on full display when Alcibiades claims that Socrates took the hardships of war—including cold, hunger, and the chaos of battle—"much better, in fact, than anyone in the whole army."[10]

Part of the value that Plato and others see in athletics and physical *arête* (a term translated as excellence or virtue) is its role in education. *The Republic* features an extensive dialogue on education and the importance of balancing gymnastic education with music to create well-ordered souls in the guardians. Socrates states, "goodness of the soul develops excellence in the body's capabilities," and argues that the guardians, "our athletes," should be able to compete in the "toughest contests."[11] In *The Laws*, Plato's Athenian says that the rulers "should always be devising noble games to accompany the sacrifices" and that "prizes should be distributed for victory or prowess, and they should compose for one another poems of praise and blame that reflect what sort of person each is becoming both in the contests and in life as a whole."[12] Later on in *The Laws*, it is clear that games not only educate citizens, but also reveal character in a unique way. The Athenian claims that by playing games that have an element of danger, "it will in a certain way make apparent who has a stout soul and who does not"—preparing the "whole city to be serviceable in the true contest it must wage throughout life."[13] Even the rational Aristotle similarly linked gymnastic education with courage, and though he chastised Spartan practices in gymnastic education, athletics remain an important component of education.[14]

Aside from any educative functions, athletics also served a vital role in the religious life of the Greeks. The noted and oft-cited example of Patroclus's funeral games illustrates this point well. Athletic contests commemorated and consecrated the sacred funeral rite. The contests themselves are a communion with the gods, and the gods influence the contests.[15] The Greeks knew of no higher way to honor a fellow citizen and grieve than through holding the type of contest that gave their lives meaning. We see this phenomenon in American life as well, with local stadiums often dedicated to deceased, influential members of the community. For example, in my hometown of Alma, Michigan, the football field is called the Don Miller field, named after a former teacher, coach, and principal.

Because sport was such an important source of meaning, it is unsurprising that athletics themselves had a distinctly religious character. Wrestlers anointed themselves in oil, akin to a traditional religious rite and indicative of the sanctity of athletics.[16] Sandsone argues that athletics in the Greek world—and in many respects, today—represent a ritual sacrifice of energy.[17] Athletics united Greeks from different city-states through the cultic and widely popular nature of athletics, most notably at Olympia.[18] Though often at war with one another, the Greek city-states could set aside their political quarrels to share their common enjoyment of athletics and contests.

It is no surprise that since sport was so important to the Greeks, athletic prowess and political merit were also linked. For example, Alcibiades famously claims that his feats at horse racing demonstrate his fitness to lead the Athenians into war.[19] The attack on his merit did not come from a "political" angle, either. Instead, to undermine Alcibiades's reputation, there was a Spartan smear campaign on his athletic achievement. Xenophon claims that Agesilaus, "persuaded his sister Cynisca to breed chariot horses, and showed by her victory that such a stud marks the owner as a person of wealth, but not necessarily of merit."[20] By showing that the chariot race was indicative of wealth rather than *arête*, the Spartans hoped to attack Alcibiades's merits at their root. Other examples of political merit linked to athletics include the practice of giving free meals to Olympic victors, the portrayal of Homeric heroes as athletes, and the fact that to compete in athletics at all, one had to be of a higher, more noble sort than commoners or slaves who could not afford to participate in these often exclusive events that demanded extreme training.[21]

Later in Greece, sport was exploited politically as a manipulative tool with which to control the masses. Kyle notes that Philip and Alexander both "appreciated the political value of both winning and fostering games, and of using athletic festivals and sites as political forums."[22] Games were used for diplomatic purposes, as celebrations of victory, and to prevent political unrest. Although Alexander himself did not particularly enjoy the games—preferring drinking contests and dogfights—he recognized their cultural and political currency.

Writers often condemn Rome for its brutal sporting spectacles, including fights with wild animals and gladiatorial combats. They also held tamer events such as chariot racing, and in the Roman republic these events were used by politicians desirous of votes.[23] Despite modern reconstructions of Roman sport and spectacles, their brutality was not extremely different from that of the Greeks.[24] Roman games were also entwined within the Roman social fabric and were massively popular, well-attended social and political events.

However one looks at these sporting events of the ancient world, it is clear that they had deep social, religious, cultural, and political ties. The games were not simple diversions keeping citizens or competitors from more important, pressing matters. While sport and games generally are leisurely and fun, it is imperative not to assume that makes them unimportant. The importance of such activities is hard to overstate. For example, Johan Huizinga makes a compelling argument that the play instinct can be found in many areas of society and that play is itself a civilizing force.[25] For Huizinga, society and civilization is created only through play. Sport is a realm in which this play instinct is more overt, but it is present everywhere in society.

Further, this type of public event remains necessary (and certainly prevalent) in modern regimes based on self-government. Part of the reason athletics mesh with the democratic world is that they too require freedom. Athletic events in particular are a fitting means of spending one's leisure time if leisure is understood as a celebration and a festival—a break from the toil and work necessary for democratic life.[26] Athletics and sport stand out from work in that although they require much physical strain, they are pleasurable and voluntary.[27] Sport represents a different way for citizens to be together than offered by work or lesser forms of entertainment that reduce boredom but fail to fulfill spectators in a meaningful manner.

Rousseau, for example, highlights the importance of a similar kind of physical entertainment to republican life:

> What! Ought there to be no entertainments in a republic? On the contrary, there ought to be many. It is in republics that they were born, it is in their bosom that they are seen to flourish with a truly festive air. To what people is it more fitting to assemble often and form among themselves sweet bonds of pleasure and joy than to those who have so many reasons to like one another and remain forever united? We already have many of these public festivals; let us have more; I will be only the more charmed for it. But let us not adopt these exclusive entertainments which close up a small number of people in a melancholy fashion in a gloomy cavern, which keep them fearful and immobile in silence and inaction, which give them only prisons, lances,

soldiers, and afflicting images of servitude and inequality to see. No, happy peoples, these are not your festivals. It is in the open air, under the sky, that you ought to gather and give yourselves to the sweet sentiment of your happiness.[28]

Rousseau's proper form of entertainment is not isolating; it brings people together in a festive celebration under the open sky.[29] This type of leisure is appropriate for a system of self-governance because it fulfills the vital function of uniting citizens. The corporeal celebration and face-to-face interaction among citizens is vital, and athletic games and events are the locus of this interaction.

A key point to recognize is that athletic events both past and present are not solely, or even primarily, about the competitors. Sport requires not only athletic participants to have meaning, but spectators. What made the ancient Olympics linger in the modern memory was not that athletes competed in a serene and barren grove to prove who was faster, but that their feats were seen by thousands of spectators cheering on the athletes. Similarly, our athletic spectacles and events today derive their meaning not from the mere act of being played, but from the spectators who watch them and fans who preserve them.

For the spectators, the athletic events themselves are important, but not the only reason for attending; the games also give people a reason to be together and to engage with one another. Just as the Olympics brought people together and even connected different Greek city-states by appealing to a shared Greek identity, sport in democratic times has the potential to gather people in a common space. Sport is a means of uniting people and bringing them together as spectators and participants; in other words, sport's distinctive character is that it is inherently communal and political.

CRITICS OF SPECTATORSHIP

Once we understand that sport realizes its political potential through spectatorship, it becomes clearer why political scientists and theorists have ignored sport as a political venue. Instead of focusing on moments when citizens commune with each other under the open sky, much contemporary democratic theory focuses on the role of deliberation and reason in political life. Theorists have been wary of spectatorship for two main reasons: first, there has been a tradition of distrust of spectatorship in political life and, second, modern political theory has focused on voice as the center of democratic life.

Spectatorship has not always been ignored, but often actively rejected. There are very real and valid objections to spectatorship and its role in democratic life, normative and otherwise. The influence of spectatorship was questioned as early as Plato. Plato's allegory of the cave is largely meant to cast doubt upon appearances and warn against mistaking appearance for truth. Plato's shackled spectators passively consume images projected on the cave by puppeteers. These prisoners passively consume a fiction portrayed by actors. Plato tells us of a prisoner freed and forced to ascend out of the cave. It is interesting that the spectator becomes an actor not by his own agency, but is forced to leave the cave by an outside party. And once outside the cave, he adjusts and eventually watcher does sees the true light of the sun. The contrast is between the deceptive world of visual appearances and the deeper truth that one can reach through reason unmitigated. The eyes do not elevate; only the mind transcends illusion.[30]

This Ancient critique of spectatorship took on more immediate and troubling political significance in the twentieth century with the rise of fascism. The role of spectacle, aesthetics, and optics assumed new importance, especially in Nazi Germany. Leni Reifenstahl's films, for example, show the emphasis the regime placed on spectacle and spectatorship. The Nazi Olympics were similarly a venue for displaying the power of spectatorship. This very real connection between the aesthetics of spectatorship and fascism understandably made thinkers suspicious of spectatorship and mass crowds of spectators.

Crowds themselves are often thought of as dangerous. In *The Crowd*, Gustave Le Bon provides an account of how crowds transform people:

> The most striking peculiarity presented by a psychological crowd is the following: Whoever be the individuals that compose it, however like or unlike be their mode of life, their occupations, their character, or their intelligence, the fact that they have been transformed into a crowd puts them in possession of a sort of collective mind which makes them feel, think, and act in a manner quite different from that in which each individual of them would feel, think, and act were he in a state of isolation.[31]

A transformation occurs within the crowd that takes the individual out of themselves and changes them. Le Bon claims that crowds are impulsive, irritable, incapable of reason, driven by emotions, and lacking in judgment and critical thinking.[32] Of course, these traits are not only ill-suited for democratic life, but potentially destructive.

Others similarly show the transformative effect that crowds have on people. Elias Canetti describes a discharge in which everyone in the crowd becomes equal and shows the tendency that crowds have to be destructive.[33] The primary traits of the crowd, for Canetti, are that crowds want to grow, there is equality within the crowd, the crowd loves density, and the crowd needs a direction or goal.[34] These traits make crowds dangerous phenomena, especially given their relationship to power and their need for a direction or goal. For Canetti, crowds are vulnerable to manipulation and exploitation by someone able to command the crowd because those in the crowd are unrestrained and unreasonable.

As a result, many thinkers reject this form of being together. Guy Debord, for example, critiques spectatorship in *Society of the Spectacle*. Debord argues that quality of life diminishes with the rise of spectacle, and an authentic way of being in the world is replaced by an inauthentic representation in the form of spectacle. These spectacular images dull critical thinking and paralyze the viewer. Spectacle is a form of social control used by the ruling class. Debord writes:

> By means of the spectacle the ruling order discourses endlessly upon itself in an uninterrupted monologue of self-praise. The spectacle is the self-portrait of power in the age of power's totalitarian rule over the conditions of existence. The fetishistic appearance of pure objectivity in spectacular relationships conceals their true character as relationships between human beings and between classes; a second Nature thus seems to impose inescapable laws upon our environment. But the spectacle is by no means the inevitable outcome of a technical development perceived as natural; on the contrary, the society of the spectacle is a form that chooses its own technical content. If the spectacle understood in the limited sense of those "mass media" that are its most stultifying superficial manifestation seems at times to be invading society in the shape of a mere apparatus, it should be remembered that this apparatus has nothing neutral about it, and that it answers precisely to the needs of the spectacle's internal dynamics.[35]

In other words, the spectacle is a manifestation of political power and human relationships even though it conceals this fact. Further, the spectacle exists to perpetuate itself and to continue to bind people to the spell of images.

Modern political theory sought to reject this tyrannical vision of the spectacle and the illiberal influence of the World War II era by turning to voice. Democratic participation is thought of by many as intimately connected to the voice. Indeed, it makes sense to think of democracy in terms of voice—to think that we need to have a voice in our government, leaders should listen to that voice, and thus politics centers on discourse. Democratic politics focuses on debate and reason giving, and these are vocal acts that require speaking and listening in the public sphere.

Deliberative democracy has put theoretical heft behind these intuitive arguments. Jürgen Habermas, for example, aims to create intersubjective, rational discourse through institutions. He writes, "Discourse theory has the success of deliberative politics depend not on a collectively acting citizenry but on the institutionalization of the corresponding procedures and conditions of communication."[36] For Habermas, institutionalization of the rules of debate and deliberation in a constitution guarantees the possibility of public discourse. In other words, well-structured discourse creates rational, consensus-based politics. His ideal speech situation achieves consensus by excluding "all motives except that of the cooperative search for truth."[37] Though Habermas later backed away from this ideal speech situation, he consistently maintains an emphasis on "rational opinion and will formation."[38] He restricts public debate to the reasonable, that is, what can engender consensus, ignoring that this type of discourse excludes those who lack the time, resources, and necessary skills to engage in such demanding dialogues.[39]

John Rawls reverses this equation, arguing for reason that leads to rational deliberation culminating in consensus. Rawls claims his political liberalism substitutes what is reasonable in place of questions of truth, and free and equal citizens in place of philosophical conceptions of the person.[40] He seeks to create a society that is a "fair system of cooperation between free and equal persons. Justice as fairness starts from this idea as one of the basic intuitive ideas which we take to be implicit in the public culture of a democratic society."[41] The overarching goal is a just society in which citizens are equal and free. This concept of justice relies on reason. Rawls wants to "achieve a practicable conception of objectivity and justification founded on public agreement in judgment on due reflection. The aim is free agreement, reconciliation through public reason."[42] In other words, Rawls's justice and reason are not subjective or open to just any kind of debate, but can be objectively discerned and rationally explained in public deliberation in the original position underneath the veil of ignorance.

More recent work on deliberative democracy argues for more nuanced and complicated forms of deliberation. Still, fetishizing the deliberative aspects of democratic politics remains, with consensus as the goal. James Fishkin, for example, puts forth a more tempered vision of deliberative democracy, moving beyond Habermas's ideal speech situation.[43] Rather than imagining ideal deliberation, Fishkin engages alternatives to enhancing deliberation, including a nationally televised "deliberative poll."[44] More than Habermas, Fishkin shows a fondness for direct democracy, but like Habermas, he favors equality, non-tyranny and deliberation.[45] Amy Guttman and Dennis Thompson similarly endorse deliberative democracy in which free and equal citizens "justify decisions in a process in which they give one another reasons that are mutually acceptable and generally accessible, with the aim of reaching conclusions that are binding in the present on all citizens but open to challenge in the future."[46] The system thus values reciprocity, equal opportunity, and consensus, albeit temporary consensus. The underlying assumption is that either rational, liberal principles will not be up for democratic debate, or democratic debate will lead to rational, liberal politics. Further, all of these writers assume and believe that voice *is* and *ought to be* the primary mode of politics defined by deliberation.

The problem with this focus is that it demands much of citizens and ignores everyday modes of politics. While it may be healthy and good for democracies to engage in this type of deliberation, it is unclear that citizens have (or ever will) participate in these demanding types of dialogues that take time and energy. There is little evidence that this type of rational discourse actually succeeds in bringing people together as irrational forms of participation like sport regularly does. In other words, understanding democracy as rational discourse may itself be elitist and anti-democratic. Further, this concern with reason has made consensus a virtue of democratic life, despite the fact that democracy is by definition about disagreement and contestation. Put simply, although we may long for this type of varsity level discourse, it is doubtful that it will ever be an actualized everyday part of democratic life. In addition, this focus on voice overlooks other meaningful political relationships outside of voice, such as spectatorship.

REEXAMINING SPECTATORSHIP

Fortunately, recent work has begun to reexamine spectatorship and its role in democratic society. Under the rubric "plebiscitary democracy," Jeffrey Green in particular examines the relationship between democracy and spectatorship and argues that watching politics is a meaningful form of participation. Instead of locating public power in voice like many democratic theorists, Green argues for an ocular theory of power, writing, "The ocular paradigm recognizes *the leaders who are watched* as the ultimate medium wherein popular empowerment makes its impact felt."[47] In other words, it would be a mistake to reject political relationships that do not involve voice as anti-democratic—democratic relationships can be more varied and nuanced. Further, the exclusionary and demanding requirements of rationality are also not necessary for democratic life.

Green delineates the key differences between an ocular model of political empowerment and the vocal model, writing, "The ocular model understands the object of popular power to be the leader rather than the law, the organ of popular power to be the gaze rather than the decision, and the critical ideal of popular power to be candor rather than autonomy."[48] Green's model consequently values the spectacle and spectators (the leader in public and the gaze of spectators) over the outcomes (law and decision) and believes such a relationship requires candor. Spectator democracy thus recognizes meaningful political empowerment outside of deliberation. For example, if public deliberation is the sole focus of democratic theorists, we miss real-life power dynamics such as accountability before public eyes. Green also shows that spectacles and spectatorship can be democratic. By putting candor first, Green uses an ideal often sought in deliberative theory, but advances it beyond its narrow application. No one denies that candor is a desirable political good, but Green shows that there is candor outside of the deliberative sphere.

While groundbreaking in many ways, this work is not entirely without precedent. As Green notes, many writers have provided evidence for the value of nonverbal politics. Weber's writings on charisma certainly posit a political relationship beyond discourse involving a leader and followers or disciples.[49] Schmitt's anti-cosmopolitan political sphere defined by opposition between friends and enemies presupposes a conception of a *volk* that groups itself beyond reason and debate.[50] Machiavelli too recognizes the power and importance of political spectacle, notably in his discussion of Cesare Borgia and Remirro de Orco.[51] More contemporary work by those studying American politics has examined the importance of presidents going public and why these types of events matter.[52] The largest critics of this type of work have not countered that true power lies in the power of citizens and their voice, but that in fact the president has power without going public through use of executive orders.[53] In short, that participation and power exists beyond contemporary vocal models is clear.

Still, modern critiques of spectatorship and this ocular version of democracy continue. They argue that modern spectatorship is passive and anti-democratic. Nadia Urbinati, for example, claims that Plebiscitarian democracy is dangerous for democratic life:

> Plebiscitarian democracy in the audience style . . . is a post-representative democracy in all respects because it wants to unmark the vanity of the myth of participation (i.e., citizenship as autonomy) and to exalt the role of mass media as an extraconstitutional factor of surveillance (in fact, even more relevant than constitutional checks). It declares the end of the idea that politics is a mix of decision and judgment and makes politics a work of visual attendance by an audience in relation to which the basic question is about the quality of communication between the government and the citizens or what people know of the lives of their rulers.[54]

Urbinati thinks that this transformation effected by Green and others revives a form of politics that is related to totalitarianism. Indeed, spectatorship is often viewed as passive at best, and often it is viewed in much harsher terms—it creates apathy that makes citizens susceptible to influence by the powerful that ultimately ends in tyranny. Urbinati is skeptical that spectator democracy empowers people in any meaningful way. She argues that by keeping decision-makers separate from spectators that judge, the model is antithetical to democratic politics, not least of all because it emphasizes moments of inaction. Or, as Urbinati says, spectator democracy becomes "a celebration of the politics of passivity."[55] For Urbinati, this is part of a trend of what she calls "unpolitical democracy."[56] Sheldon Wolin is similarly critical of spectator democracy because the model elevates passivity and inaction rather than a more active and spontaneous kind of democracy.[57]

Others, viewing the rise of populism, find similarities between populism and this spectator model. While there is much disagreement around what exactly populism means, scholars generally agree that populists cast politics as a battle between the "true people" and corrupt elites. Populists are often hostile to classic liberal institutions such as the free press and seek to consolidate power, eroding institutions and norms based on passionate, irrational appeals. Most agree that these appeals are dangerous for liberal democracy, and some argue populism is by its nature hostile to democracy.[58] Certainly, these appeals are dangerous for democratic pluralism.[59] Often, sport is associated with populist politics in part because many European populists own soccer teams, but also because sport is thought to share a similar irrational, "us v. them" appeal that populists sell.[60] While it is understandable to associate populism with spectatorship, this overlooks the pluralism, disagreement, and agonism that goes hand in hand with something like sport spectatorship. Further, as democratic norms diminish, potential sites of resistance like sport become more essential. It is possible spectatorship could enable populist politics, but just as possible spectatorship could undermine such politics.

This connection between passivity, tyranny, and spectatorship is indeed a possibility of spectatorship, but not the *only possibility*. In fact, there is reason to believe that spectatorship is not a wholly passive activity. Jacques Rancière corrects some of these misunderstandings, and shows how spectatorship is an essential feature of all politics, even or especially in realms of life beyond routinized politics like the theater. Rancière recognizes the traditional paradox of spectatorship in the form of the theater: there is no theater without the spectator, but being a spectator is thought to be bad because viewing is the opposite of knowing and the opposite of acting.[61] For him, this traditional way of viewing the theater and, spectatorship in general, is problematic. It is problematic, first, because theater has the potential for being a communal site. He references that this has been the understanding of the theater since German Romanticism: the theater is a living community and a form of aesthetic constitution.[62] People come together in the same time and place and share a dialogue and event. However, he finds behind understandings of the theater as a site of community a presupposition that the theater is communitarian and wants to challenge how we understand this community.

In particular, he wants to challenge how we understand this community as a largely passive place. For Rancière, we need to break with this understanding and emancipate ourselves from the prejudice behind it. He writes:

Why identify gaze with passivity, unless on the presupposition that to view means to take pleasure in images and appearances while ignoring the truth behind the image and the reality outside the theatre? Why assimilate listening to passivity, unless through the prejudice that speech is the opposite of action? These oppositions—viewing/knowing, appearance/reality, activity/passivity—are quite different from logical oppositions between clearly defined terms . . . They are embodied allegories of inequality.[63]

In other words, these traditional oppositions are themselves emblematic of power relationships and existing inequalities. The myth that spectatorship is a passive activity is itself used to perpetuate power relationships and inequality.

How, then, does the spectator act? He writes, "The spectator also acts, like the pupil or the scholar. She observes, selects, compares, interprets. She links what she sees to a host of other things that she has seen on other stages, in other kinds of place. She composes her own poem with the elements of the poem before her. She participates in the performance by refashioning it in her own way . . . They are thus both distant spectators and active interpreters of the spectacle offered to them."[64] For Rancière, the oppositions between viewing and knowing, appearance and reality, and activity and passivity are not logical oppositions, but arbitrary constructs. The spectator *does act,* she acts like a pupil or scholar acts by observing, comparing, and interpreting. Spectators are not passive consumers; they too exercise judgment and gain knowledge, and ultimately their response co-constitutes the content of the event they watch.

Sport spectatorship also reveals the power of spectators, because without spectators the whole event crumbles. Similarly, if no one attends political rallies, the speaker will not have power. Power radiates *from the spectators*, not just the spectacle. In sport, spectatorship is itself a form of participation. People decide to pay to attend and support teams. Spectatorship entails an active construction and support for the sport itself. Rejecting this power dynamic from democratic theory is based on a misunderstanding of spectatorship. When we watch a film or a game, or look at a piece of art, we do not consume it—we interpret it. In sport, we not only use our judgment, we support the existence of the sport itself. The understanding that spectators are passive is, at its core, flawed.

Rancière relates this interpretive power to the emancipation of the spectator: "Being a spectator is not some passive condition that we should transform into activity. It is our normal situation. We also learn and teach, act and know, as spectators who all the time link what we see to what we have seen and said, done and dreamed."[65] In other words, when you enter a theater or baseball park, what you see is not consumed separate from the rest of the world that you inhabit. Indeed, spectatorship is the condition that we find ourselves in most of the time. Most of the time we are not on the stage, we are watching others. This is true literally and figuratively; we watch the events of the world, and our interpretation is itself action and grounding for all future action.

Further, it is clear that there is a link between the world of the theater that Rancière describes and modern sport. Richard Lipsky notes this similarity, writing, "The Sportsworld is a lived world, like those of literature and the theater, that is highly charged with human meaning. As a dramatic and symbolic world the Sporstworld has its own plots, scenes, characters, and settings."[66] Sport has a similar structure to theater (or to politics); there are stories, characters, settings, and more that encourage fans to interact, judge, and participate in the language of the world.

Other Marxist critiques about the passivity of sports fans are ill-founded. These critiques allege that, first, spectators are not doers; second, spectatorship diverts from politics; and third, spectatorship is a paralyzing catharsis. Drawing from data on sports fans from America and abroad, Allen Guttmann shows that people who watch sport or follow sport are much more likely to be active and do sports themselves.[67] Regarding the claim that spectatorship diverts from politics, he also finds the data do not agree. People who attend sporting events are also active in other social spheres, like politics.[68] Finally, the catharsis that the spectator experiences is not as some portray it—an energy release that makes citizens docile. This catharsis, instead of being paralyzing, is energizing, evidenced by phenomena such as college football games, which involve mass participation, celebration, and revelry.[69] Spectator violence similarly attests, albeit in a dangerous fashion, that the catharsis of sport is not antithetical to action.

Taking spectatorship seriously requires a humbler vision of what constitutes political engagement than that offered by prevailing models of democratic theory. Rather than demand active civic debate, it is possible to think about democracy existing in more informal ways. This more modest formulation of political life is especially advantageous for democratic theory that is loath to demand unattainable virtues from citizens while seeking to preserve a democratic relationship between a people and their politics. Further, in modern mass society, such a model may be more feasible.[70] By understanding politics in their average, everyday sense, it becomes clear that politics are not often or primarily about reason, deliberation, and consensus. Instead, politics are often unreasonable or impassioned, watched and not spoken, and gathered around dissensus.[71]

I propose taking spectatorship seriously and recognizing that what people watch is important. Whether it is a candid political spectacle, as Green suggests, or a spectacle like a baseball game, when citizens gather en masse, it matters. It matters, because such spectatorship informs and spills over into other areas of political and social life. As I will suggest, athletics have an added level of significance because they are highly visible, candid, communal events. To be sure, spectatorship may not be the primary means of democratic engagement, but it can be helpful for understanding social mores and how citizens experience politics on an everyday level. By focusing on one arena of spectatorship—sports and baseball in America—I argue it is possible to see how politics at the ballpark impacts democracy in America.

BASEBALL AS A POLITICAL VENUE

While few would deny that baseball and other modern sports are popular, one may object and wonder if they are politically relevant. There is, after all, a tradition of putting sports among trivial things as opposed to the serious business of politics. This oversimplification is fortunately crumbling under increasing evidence that sport often represents important political values and penetrates the political as a metaphor.[72] Further, sports, and baseball especially, have been linked to a type of civil religion in America.[73] Baseball has also been used by political elites to make rhetorical appeals to the public, particularly in the post-9/11 era.[74] To claim that baseball is an apolitical realm of human affairs is to be naïve regarding its importance in society. As this project will show, baseball can reveal much about existing power dynamics, and, at times, become a platform for challenging these politics.

Baseball also has the longest history as a major sport in America, and therefore has a larger history from which to draw. There is another temporal element that makes baseball especially important as well: baseball games, during the season, occur every day. This makes it more of a routine and less of a festival atmosphere like one sees at weekly football games. This consistency provides a clear view of both the codification of norms and the moments of challenging those norms. For example, Sherri Grasmuck writes about this character of baseball games as it pertains to the Little Leagues. She writes, "The slow pace of baseball, punctuated as it is by moments of such intensity and drama—that long plateau with its occasional upsurges—matters. It allows parents of different backgrounds to come together on the bleachers and feel comfortable, without the need to do much, and yet to share the passion, the disappointments, and the triumphs."[75] This slow and routine character of the game applies at all levels and makes it possible for spectators to interact more than they might watching another sport. This character makes baseball a good canvas for politics, whether they are local or national.

Baseball also has a special place as an American institution because of its history as "America's pastime." This history gives baseball added rhetorical importance. Presidents in particular interact with the game and bring it into the political lexicon. They seek to do so because the game has roots and a connection to the American identity. Walt Whitman notably claimed that baseball "belongs as much to our institutions, fits into them as significantly, as our constitutions, laws: is just as important in the sum total of our historic life."[76] Whitman thus claims that baseball is a defining feature of what it means to be American. Similarly, Jacques Barzun claimed nearly three-quarters of a century later, "Whoever wants to know the heart and mind of America had better learn baseball, the rules and realities of the game—and do it by watching first some high school or small-town teams."[77] Note that Barzun includes both the heart and mind. Baseball shapes how Americans both think and feel. To learn how Americans think and feel, Barzun proscribes spectatorship of local, community games. His suggestion mirrors one of the core arguments of this book: through watching baseball one can learn about America.

Finally, I do not argue that we should examine baseball to the exclusion of other sports. Looking at soccer, basketball, tennis, gymnastics, swimming, and other sports would likely be worthwhile in furthering our understanding of politics. In fact, there are clearly important things happening around racial politics in sports all around the world in the wake of protests in the summer of 2020, but examining politics in other sports is beyond the scope of this project.

In addition to the games themselves, baseball spectatorship is rising with new media and increased coverage of athletes, coaches, and others on and off the field. People watch these interviews, and the content can often launch a dialogue about pertinent political issues. A congressperson giving a speech about race will not garner the audience an athlete will when declining to stand for the national anthem. When an athlete makes a comment about having a gay teammate, for example, it becomes a catalyst for conversations people have in their everyday lives.[78] Similarly, conversations about the decline of participation by black Americans in baseball become a way for fans to be exposed to larger issues around race in America.

A crucial feature for democratic theory is that sport presents an arena for watching politics. It is clear looking at baseball that sport fulfills Green's desire for candor much more than watching elites. While candor is certainly an ideal for elite spectatorship, it is rarely realized. As Green himself claims, leadership debates, public inquiries, and press conferences as they stand presently fall "well short of the type of candor a plebiscitarian would ideally like to see realized."[79] Sports, however, are by their very nature meant to be unscripted and sincere. This is one of the reasons why writers like Plato and Aristotle thought that athletics are exceptionally good at revealing character.[80] Baseball players and the spectacles at games of course differ from elites and political spectacles. Baseball players are not political elites, and therefore are not accountable in the same manner as elected officials. However, they are accountable for their actions: crowds boo and cheer, or choose simply not to show up. Steroid users have long been held accountable before crowds for their perceived moral failures, for example. The history of racial incorporation is full of this type of response—the cheers or boos of the crowd illuminate with candor exactly how the crowd stands regarding issues of race. Because of the candor surrounding sport and spectators of sport, it is possible to understand how everyday folks experience politics.

Finally, baseball reveals that spectatorship is a communal experience and event. Spectatorship of sport is not an isolated or individualistic experience. Instead, sport has an innate ability to transform isolated individuals into a collective "we." Political theorists tend to focus on the formation of a "we" in relation to war, but sports are another realm that creates a "we."[81] This assertion is evident in language used to discuss sports events and teams. Fans and spectators routinely and naturally use this language, saying things like, "we lost yesterday, but we played well" or "it was a big win for us." In baseball, we hear of the "Red Sox Nation," and the claim by Cardinals fans that they are the "best fans in baseball." Each team has a unique community of fans that form around the team. Sports cause people to identify with the team and other fans, and this identification is powerful and revealing.[82] Sport becomes a venue for creating affiliations that transcend typical political divides.

It is important to note that this analysis of politics in baseball proceeds primarily from the vantage point of fans and spectators. This is not the sole angle of the project, but the primary angle. As Al Filreis notes, this perspective is often missing: most baseball writing is from the perspective of the players. This is a problematic oversight, as baseball at the highest level is primarily about spectatorship rather than direct participation.[83] Indeed, the meaning behind games and their importance largely comes from spectators, and this is not a new phenomenon. As Donald Kyle writes, "Most people, ancient and modern, disliking physical discomfort and fearing embarrassing failure, are inclined to be spectators who win their athletic victories vicariously."[84]

This spectatorship influences our political and social lives. Watching baseball is an active form of participation. People pay to watch the game, and in so doing support the game itself. They also give their tacit consent, if not approval, to the event they go to watch. This allows fans to shape the game: they can exit if the game is not to their liking. What they view at the ballpark in turn shapes their understanding and views on politics. Baseball is both representative of politics and a potential site of change.

Indeed, spectatorship is what gives baseball its gathering potential and its political significance. The following chapter will examine how we can begin to think about a community of spectatorship. I will lay out how spectatorship can be harnessed to form healthy, democratic communities, and examine how viewing sport through economic and business terms instead of through the lens of empowered spectatorship can undermine this community.

CHAPTER 2

COMMUNITIES OF SPECTATORSHIP AND FANDOM

A rich reality is needed to sponsor a sense of community. A thoughtful and graceful ballpark tunes people to the same harmonies. It inspires common pride and pleasure, a shared sense of season and place, a joint anticipation of drama. Given such attunement, banter and laughter flow naturally across strangers and unite them into a community.

—Albert Borgmann[1]

How is it that a sport like baseball forms community? Why, in the wake of a defeat, will fans routinely say things like "we lost last night"? Sport has a unique ability to expand and transform the category "we," and this capacity extends beyond just those who root for the same team. Sport can bring people together by serving as a common interest, an easy entry point into conversations, and a reminder of something enjoyable during hard times. Unlike politics, people are comfortable talking about and engaging with sport. How are we to understand this profound community-building potential?

In this chapter, I will show how baseball forms meaningful communities through spectatorship. Being at the ballpark forms the basis for communal fandom. While the fullest mode of spectatorship is being at the ballpark, there are other modes of spectatorship as well, including following the sport on the radio, television, or other media. Although baseball gathers people together based on a common interest, it is also a venue for other local community concerns. These communities can be normatively good for democratic life. However, baseball is not always a positive force for community, and more detached views of the game as a business can undermine community, as the example of stadium funding illustrates. I conclude by theorizing the importance of these types of communities built on interest. While it is natural to focus on political communities, baseball shows how a different type of everyday community based on a common interest is an important component of democratic life as well.

THEORIES OF COMMUNITY

Community is a recurring topic of importance in the history of political thought. Who and what constitutes community was a guiding question in such classic works of political philosophy as Plato's *Laws* and Aristotle's *Politics*. The question of community is relevant all over academia: sociology and anthropology, for example, often debate the value of "communitas," the Latin root of community.[2]

The first feature that emerges when discussing community is the issue of borders pertaining to a community. Only recently, in the form of cosmopolitan thought, has it been advanced that such borders could be transcended, creating new problems for understanding community and belonging in a globalized world.[3] Still, for political purposes, boundaries define communities. There are local, regional, state, and federal borders that delineate different communities.

Communities are also delineated based on interests, passions, or some commonalities. We speak often of the LGBTQ community, or the Boy Scouts, local PTAs, the gaming community, and book clubs, among others. This chapter focuses on a community based on interest and fandom—while geography plays a significant role in how these communities form, at heart, these communities are based around spectatorship and fandom. Fandom itself is about interest and enjoyment. This community, like all communities, has those who are inside the community and those who are outside.

The inside/outside of the community establishes another core feature of community life: communities are about identities. Carl Schmitt puts forth the most extreme version of this dynamic. For Schmitt, politics is the distinction between us and them, a distinction that comes with the possibility of real physical violence.[4] The dynamic requires inequality and certain people and groups who exist outside of the community. As

Schmitt writes, "An absolute human equality, then, would be an equality understood only in terms of itself and without risk; it would be an equality without the necessary correlate of inequality, and as a result conceptually and practically meaningless, an indifferent equality."[5] In this vision, meaningful citizenship requires borders, exclusion, and violence.[6] The idea is that extreme moments, particularly war, illustrate the truth of the community—who is in it and who is not. The political community, to be meaningful, must be existential.

However, these extreme and highly political identities are beyond most everyday ways of identifying with a cause, group, or interest. One of the foundations of American politics is the belief that disagreements need not be lethal; Republicans and Democrats do not have to kill each other and can respect broader processes. Beyond partisan politics, people also identify as citizens of localities, members of associations, genders, races, ethnicities, age groups, and many other identifications that do not demand such heightened stakes.

People frequently identify as fans of sports and teams. From high school football in Texas, to Red Sox Nation on the East Coast, or various teams and colleges involved in March Madness, the propensity for people to identify with teams is ubiquitous.[7] As Daniel Nathan writes, "Rooting for local athletes and home teams often symbolizes a community's preferred understanding of itself, and that doing so is an expression of connectedness. It's an expression of public pride and pleasure, a source of group and personal identity. It's about sharing something, about belonging."[8] In other words, communities of sports fans also involve identity politics and belonging and do so in a manner more consistent with democratic politics than extreme moments of political difference.

When we invoke the term "community," it usually comes pre-loaded with positive connotations. Who does not want to be community oriented or a part of a community? Communitarianism is a strain of political theory born out of a distaste for universalist theories of politics, such as those espoused by John Rawls in his *Theory of Justice*. Communitarian theory holds that citizens are creations of their political and social environments, and government is not simply about securing rights for individuals.[9] These thinkers defend traditional concepts like virtue and the importance of local communities against an increasingly universal understanding of politics.[10] There are horizons on identities, horizons provided by the communities in which people live. The making of identity is thus dialogical or relational between people and their communities.[11] Consequently, community is essential not only for understanding politics, but constitutive even of how citizens see themselves. This theory provides a return to local concerns and a move away from the abstract concept of humanity divorced from particular circumstances of time and place.

This return to community is not without critics. After all, the universalist, cosmopolitan theories emerged post–World War II in reaction to the destruction caused by rampant nationalism and ethnocentric visions of citizenship. A hallmark of postcolonial theory is to reject the conservatism and exclusionary nature of many so-called communities. Agonistic theorists like Chantal Mouffe argue that any community must be inherently unstable and contested. Democracy is about contestation. As Mouffe writes, "to negate the ineradicable character of antagonism and to aim at a universal rational consensus—this is the real threat to democracy."[12] Others highlight the problems with the romance of community and its complicity with capitalism.[13]

Whether we find the idea of community desirable or not, communities are a fundamental part of politics. By their very nature, communities are political and involve power relations. Still, the phrase "community of spectatorship" may strike many as odd. Spectatorship, as it has been understood in democratic theory, is an action in reference to political elites and not a community among other people. How can we begin to theorize a community based in spectatorship?

SPECTATORSHIP AND COMMUNITY

The critiques about spectatorship and its value to democratic life were covered at length in chapter 1, but the communal aspect of spectatorship requires more examination. Rancière provides valuable insight into how spectatorship—and the judgment that comes with spectatorship—can be a communal activity. For Rancière, the theater and any group of spectators is not communal simply by virtue of gathering people in one time and place; instead it is communal because it allows different people to actively interpret together. He writes,

> The collective power shared by spectators does not stem from
> the fact that they are members of a collective body or from
> some specific form of interactivity. It is the power each of them
> has to translate what she perceives in her own way, to link it to

the unique intellectual adventure that makes her similar to all the rest in as much as this adventure is not like any other. This shared power of the equality of intelligence links individuals, makes them exchange their intellectual adventures, in so far as it keeps them separate from one another, equally capable of using the power everyone has to plot her own path.[14]

Spectators are actually linked through difference and their ability to interpret what we see differently. If spectators all understood what they saw in the same way, there would be little to discuss and little reason to connect. By interpreting differently, spectators create the essence of a true aesthetic community that arises only around debate and disagreement.

Sport and baseball can be just such a venue for communal spectatorship. Further, baseball communities are built on an interest in something fun, it creates a leisurely community that connects people in a way that formal politics often cannot, making these everyday communities desirable in democratic life. While we may prefer citizens united by something "deeper," it is hard to argue that sport does not fulfill the role of connecting communities.

As Daniel Nathan writes, "For better or worse, probably worse, many Americans care about sports more deeply than they care about any other aspect of public life. In some instances, sports appear to be (or are constructed as) a kind of social glue that holds together heterogeneous and contentious communities."[15] Sport provides a common bond often lacking in civic life that binds together communities.

One reason for this connection may be the relationship between sport and sacred realms. This happens not only with sport, but with leisure in general. This leisurely way of connecting with others provides a common source of meaning. Josef Pieper, for example, connects true leisure with the divine. He writes, "What is true of celebration is true of Leisure: its possibility, its ultimate justification derive from its roots in divine worship."[16] Leisure has its roots in religion and the sacred. Pieper writes, "Leisure, it must be remembered, is not a Sunday afternoon idyll, but the preserve of freedom of education and culture, and of that undiminished humanity which views the world as a whole."[17] For Pieper, leisure and its sacred roots is connected to the wholeness of human beings. It is antithetical both to modern conceptions of work as well as the idea of leisure as merely a bit of rest from the daily slog. Instead, leisure is about celebration, festival, and coming together in a community. This conception of leisure clearly reinforces the sacred nature of the community of those at leisure or those at play in the form of sports.

This idea has antecedents. Jean-Jacques Rousseau too is concerned with how entertainments affect community morals. Pleasures and tastes born out of entertainment can have real political and social effects on citizens. For Rousseau, there are good entertainments and bad entertainments. The proper kind of entertainment builds community in a republic. It is no coincidence that Rousseau's vision of the proper entertainment hails back to Ancient Greek athletic competitions with their simplicity and connection to religion. Rather than the theater that isolates spectators, this form of entertainment incorporates the spectators and cultivates their moral sense as well. Rousseau writes, "Do better yet; let the spectators become an entertainment to themselves; make them actors themselves; do it so that each sees and loves himself in the others so that all will be united."[18] For Rousseau, the better way to organize our community is around simple and wholesome entertainments. These are contests between citizens that the community can come watch. Like Sparta of old, such entertainments provide the background for a strong community by bringing that community together in the open air.

Rousseau's work shows how these communities of spectatorship are based in freedom and liberty, especially positive liberty. Isiah Berlin's famous essay "Two Concepts of Liberty" demonstrates this point. Negative liberty is the absence of obstacles or impediments, whereas positive liberty is more about one's agency in part of a broader collective.[19] Often, republican thinkers such as Rousseau emphasize positive liberty because it focuses on the control individuals can exert over their own self-government. In like manner, sport spectatorship empowers spectators as they become an active part of the event. This offers important and empowering lessons on individual autonomy and liberty.

In addition to cultivating community morality, sport provides an outlet for communal transcendence in modern life. Sport removes citizens from isolating individualism. This transcendence is possible for regular people in their everyday lives through sport if they connect to the meaning and community provided in modern sport. As Dreyfus and Kelly write,

> Sports may be the place in contemporary life where Americans find sacred community most easily. We saw already in our opening chapter that a great athlete can shine like a Greek god, and that in the presence of such an athlete the sense of

greatness is palpable. It has even become popular to argue that in recent years sport has come to form a kind of folk religion in American society, standing in for more traditional kinds of religious practice and belief. Whether or not it is true is a matter of historical and sociological fact that sport now plays this kind of religious role in America, a related phenomenological claim seems hard to dispute. There is no essential difference, really, in how it feels to rise as one in joy to sing the praises of the Lord, or to rise as one in joy to sing the praises of the Hail Mary pass, the Immaculate receptions, the Angels, the Saints, the Friars, or the Demon Deacons. In part this association between sport and religion derives from the importance of community in each . . . Whether it is in the church or in the baseball stadium, the awesomeness of the moment is reinforced when it is shared by others. When it is also shared *that it is shared*—when you all recognize together that you are sharing in the celebration of this great thing—then the awesomeness of the moment itself bursts forth and shines.[20]

This transcendence beyond the routine of normal life is an important cornerstone for any meaningful community. Dreyfus and Kelly show how, phenomenologically, this transcendence is possible in modern life through sport. This possibility of communal transcendence is what makes sport the gathering point of much community in contemporary life.

Sport also penetrates into the most communal element humans share: language. Richard Lipsky, for example, shows how sport language infects the political sphere. He writes, "The communal bonds that are created in the festivity of sports drama are sustained in language."[21] Lipsky claims that, most often, sports language in politics is used as a conservative device that stifles thinking about new policies and directions.[22] This connection implies a shared world between sport and politics, a relationship that persists. For example, President Obama's presidency was defined in key ways by sports language and metaphor, using sport as a political tool. The persistence of sports language in politics ultimately shows the value of such language for uniting people. As one writer noted regarding Obama's use of sports language, "When Obama talks sports, he shows his American birth certificate."[23] The use of sports language indicates a belonging to the larger American community that is constituted, in part, by a shared interest in sport.

Because of its everyday nature, baseball is especially good at cultivating community. Baseball lacks the Bacchic character of football games but provides a meaningful platform for community as a result. As Albert Borgmann writes,

> A rich reality is needed to sponsor a sense of community. A thoughtful and graceful ballpark tunes people to the same harmonies. It inspires common pride and pleasure, a shared sense of season and place, a joint anticipation of drama. Given such attunement, banter and laughter flow naturally across strangers and unite them into a community. When reality and community conspire in this way, divinity descends on the game, divinity of an impersonal and yet potent kind.[24]

Borgmann points toward how sporting communities can be meaningful for politics. Sport does the same thing as associations: it brings people together and unites them. Borgmann points toward an almost divine community born out of sport.

To undertake this analysis of community and its importance in baseball, it must be asked, what is the experience of going to the ballpark, of watching the game, of participating, of following the sport? What is the breadth of meaningful spectatorship associated with sport and baseball? How does this experience of spectatorship form a community or communities? How does this sport interact with concrete local policy? How can this community be harnessed as a democratic good? What policies undermine the important communal power of sport? These are the guiding questions for the rest of this chapter.

BEING AT THE BALLPARK AND THE NATURE OF SPORTS SPECTATORSHIP

If we are to take spectators seriously as a part of the politics of baseball, we must examine what they watch. At the major league level, the spectacle varies, but there are similarities. In New York, one gets off a subway in the Bronx and looks at the towering new Yankees Stadium. In Milwaukee, one drives to the outskirts of town to find a makeshift community of people grilling, drinking beer, and playing lawn games. In Chicago, one either goes north to Wrigleyville to see the stadium built in 1914, recently made over, or drives south to the more isolated Guaranteed Rate Field—the old gum sponsor sounds quaint compared to this recent venture in naming rights. In Detroit, one enters the heart of the city and sees Comerica Park amidst a district full of exile, regrowth, and change. One grasps the importance of the attempt to rejuvenate the struggling city by once more focusing the attention of the community downtown through sport.

Inside, ballparks are often treated as hallowed ground. The religious element in sport is noted by many and hinted at above.[25] Early Greek sport was inseparable from religious ritual and practice; this relationship remains intact. Ballparks are often treated as a kind of temple. This religious reverence for a space typically depends on time, or how long the stadium has been there. Fenway Park in Boston and Wrigley Field in Chicago, built in 1912 and 1914 respectively, are revered as the longest standing parks. Even when parks are destroyed, their previous locations remain meaningful. Michigan and Trumbull remains an important location for Tigers fans, for example.[26] Against this tendency to revere place, there is a recent trend in stadium building that treats ballparks as disposable. I will discuss this trend and its policy implications later in the chapter.

Inside, stadiums are different as well. Some outfields are symmetrical; others feature nooks and crannies, and Houston had a hill in centerfield. Fenway features the Green Monster, a wall in left field that drastically changes the game that happens below. Place is thus of the utmost importance in determining the events of the game—what is a home run in Chicago is a line drive in Boston and a fly ball out in San Francisco. Each ballpark is unique. With the exception of Tampa Bay, each opens up into the sky (at least some of the time). People mix with others, watching ballplayers on the field under the sky. The fourfold of earth, sky, humans, and the sacred are united at the ballpark.[27]

Inside of every park there is an energy in the concourse. There is generally a joyful mood at baseball games. The game is the primary event that brings people together. As Borgmann writes, "At the beginning of a real game, there is no way of predicting or controlling what will happen. No one can produce or guarantee the flow of a game. It unfolds and reveals itself in playing. It inspires grace and despair, it provokes heroics and failure, it infuses enthusiasm and inflicts misery. It is always greater than the individuals it unites."[28] This undetermined nature of the game gives it the character of an event, and the unfolding of the event is the common theme that connects the spectators. This character of sport—its undetermined nature and unlimited possibilities—gives sport its drama and makes it of interest. Anything could happen, and the crowd is united qua their status as witnesses together.

The game is an event, and by no means is the action on the field always decisive for the event itself. Baseball games are places to interact. Some people talk baseball, others talk about their jobs, and some look at their phones. Some keep score, spending their time absorbed within the happenings of the game. Hardcore fans lament the philistinism of those who come not primarily to watch the game—an anti-egalitarian pastime among the American pastime's elitists.

The role of technology and the transformation of sport will be discussed at length later, but it must be acknowledged that there are varying degrees of interaction with the game itself, and there may even be a community-forming potential in baseball for those who view the game as incidental to their experience of the event. As Richard Skolnik writes, "Baseball is rarely in a hurry. Accordingly, spectators need not always be paying attention; other activities may intrude. Fans seem to feel exceptionally comfortable and playful out at the ballpark. Where else will thousands of spectators join together by rising to their feet in proper sequence to produce a human wave rippling across the stadium?"[29] The ballpark and the event bring people together, even those who are not especially interested in the game.

At the ballpark, fans, spectators, citizens, are all brought together to form a crowd. The political potential of crowds has long been noted, including the dangers that can arise with "the law of the mental unity of crowds."[30] While Le Bon's psychological analysis about the potential dangers of crowd thinking may be correct, at the ballpark the crowd is generally tame. There is, however, a type of togetherness at the ballpark that is not routine in the everyday lives of Americans who fashion themselves as individuals. Elias Canetti shows how crowds can eliminate difference and institute a type of equality regardless of distinctions of rank, status, wealth, and other factors. This type of equality of being in the crowd exists at the ballpark. However, it is fleeting, as Canetti also notes that "the people who suddenly feel equal have not really become equal; nor will they *feel* equal forever."[31] The unity of others that the ballpark presents is a fleeting, if valuable, experience. Spectators become equals as they unite around the same game. The stringent individualism of everyday life makes way for a brief moment of being together. Although crowds and this togetherness is fleeting, fandom, following a team, and being part of that community can last generations.

The game itself unfolds in a unique, cyclical, and open-ended manner. Baseball, alone among major spectator sports in America, has no clock.[32] The game unfolds with nearly unlimited possibility. It is played on an open field of grass with a diamond of dirt. The pastoral connections are obvious and may account for why baseball was from the start considered America's pastime. Teams have competitive cycles. The game begins in spring when everything is in bloom and ends in the autumn with the death of much of the natural world. Baseball operates in accord with the leaves on the trees. Though never precisely the same, baseball exists in cycles.

The players themselves often look democratic to the viewer. In baseball, one can be fat, skinny, short, tall, athletic, or any array of physical characteristics and be a successful baseball player. Basketball demands height; football strength, speed, and size; baseball demands nothing in particular, and the players diversify accordingly. The most notorious and mythic figure in the game is an overweight outfielder from Pigtown, Maryland. The modern game features players of a more diverse background than any other sport as well. There are many Latino players, black players, and Asian players mixing with the white players for whom the game was once exclusively reserved.[33] At the ballpark, seeing this diverse batch of people, spectators see a democratic sport.

When we think of spectatorship, we typically think of the eyes and vision. Spectatorship, watching events, games, speeches, and so on, is about serving as a witness to something. Simply attaching spectatorship to vision we will see is not enough. Beyond the ocular, the ballpark elicits many senses. Spectatorship at times, and especially inside the ballpark, is about more than just seeing and invokes to varying degrees all of the senses, though chiefly this spectatorship is about vision and hearing.

The sounds of children, crowds, and the crack of the bat are all hallmarks of the ballpark experience. Cheering, conversing, yelling, booing—sound comes from all over. Baseball is not like the theater: it is a participatory event. The spectators are themselves active, especially sonically. Rousseau, for example, noted the good of this type of spectatorship compared to watching theater, or for our times, going to the movies or plays. Rather than this passive watching, the person at a sporting event helps create the event itself, mostly through the creation of sound. The crowd and the noise of the crowd changes the dynamic of the game. Were baseball played in a basement watched by no one, it would not be baseball.

The smell of hotdogs, popcorn, and other consumables hangs heavy in the air. The scent of cut grass and dirt are synonymous with the game as well. Olfactory associations have changed over the years—the once thick aroma of cigarettes and cigars, for instance, has vanished into the air—but part of the sensory-rich experience of being at the ballpark has always included a variety of evocative scents.

The taste of food is also a key part of the experience. Offerings such as hotdogs, peanuts, beer, lemonade, and crackerjack are traditionally part of what it means to be at the ballpark. In addition to the classic fare, some minor league stadiums now offer such absurd culinary creations as fried desserts, burgers with calories enough to sustain life for a week, hot dogs wrapped in pizza, and the uniquely Wisconsin cheeseburger—a meat patty topped with cheese curds and doused in nacho cheese—among countless other confections too daring to describe.[34] Food is often an attraction in itself. Games are usually played during either lunch or dinner time, and spectatorship frequently involves eating and drinking. This gives the games a distinctly festive aura: in many ways, games are a time for feasting.

The feel of sitting in the crowd, the hard-plastic green seats, surrounded by other people, all of this constitutes what it is like being at the ballpark. Sometimes fans catch fly balls or homeruns and feel the seams and leather of the ball. There is even danger in watching the games, and the physicality of the activity applies to spectators as well. There has been a recent push to extend safety nets to reduce injuries to fans, but preventing the physical impingement of the game into the stadium is impossible. Being at the ballpark is an embodied experience. Arguably the game's most exciting play, the homerun, highlights the excitement of physically breaking the fourth wall. The ball soars and exits the field of play, and fans become participants, trying to catch the ball for themselves.

In addition to the stadiums of the major leagues, baseball is played and watched in small venues all over the United States. There are minor league affiliates and non-league teams. There are Little League games. Analyzing the politics of these smaller, local spaces is difficult unless one participates in them—in which case the politics is self-evident. Sociological work has shown how these leagues are helpful for understanding their local communities.[35] Much of local politics occurs on cold metal bleachers overlooking baseball diamonds with a distance of forty-five feet between home plate and the pitcher's mound.

SPECTATORSHIP BEYOND THE BALLPARK

Beyond the corporeal being-together at the ballpark, there is a spectatorship outside of the ballpark. The oldest form of baseball spectatorship outside of the park does not involve eyes at all—it appeals to the ear. The radio has long been the way that most people have followed the sport. Baseball lends itself to being heard. Outcomes are concrete and easy to explain. The time between pitches gives announcers room to tell stories. Broadcasters such as Vin Scully, Ernie Harwell, Red Barber, Bob Uecker, and Harry Caray are woven into the fabric of baseball and Americana. The radio provides a way to follow the game, and the listener hears not only what has happened through the broadcaster—they hear the call of the crowd, the crack of the bat, the pop of the glove.

This represents a less participatory way of following the sport. This type of spectatorship is different not only because it does not involve sight, but the spectator can be far removed from the event. The corporeality of the spectator does not interact with the event in the same way. Still, it is an essential mode of spectatorship for understanding the relationship between politics and baseball. Many of the political moments in the sport—integration, labor strikes, steroid scandals—are experienced by most people through means other than physically watching the game. Some of these key events do not occur within ballparks at all.

Another realm for spectatorship is television. Like radio, television makes what is happening in the ballpark more accessible. Television drastically changed all of American sport and is part of the revolution toward centering sport on spectatorship. As Benjamin Rader writes, "With the advent of television the fans at home rather than those in the stadium or the arena came to be the ultimate arbiters of American sport. Before the 1950's, newspapers, magazines, and radio had stimulated interest in sport, but television permitted millions who had never seen a major league baseball game, a pro football game, or the Olympic Games to hear and see the spectacles in the comfort of their own home."[36] The reach of sport in the age of television multiplied exponentially. Games became tailored for television broadcasts, and being at the ballpark physically lost its role as the primary mode of spectatorship. The nuance of being at the ballpark is lost, as are the subtler points of the game with the advent of close-up camera angles. However, this mode of spectatorship magnifies the gathering potential for sport as an arena for politics. From the lens of politics, this technological innovation is exceedingly democratic: the world of spectatorship opens up to millions more.

MLB-TV now allows anyone in the country to watch virtually any game they choose (perversely, unless the game involves your hometown, in-market team). Television adds the visual element such that spectators can actually see what is happening. There are still broadcasters who act as intermediaries, a holdover from the radio era. Televised games allow the spectator more freedom for interpretation. No longer must we take the words of the broadcaster as gospel—we can interpret for ourselves. This interpretation applies to watching the game itself (the spectator can judge pitch location, effective movement, strength of swings, etc.), as well as to the things happening at the ballpark. Spectators can see players of different races and ethnicities, they can see patriotic symbols, they can see the size and makeup of the crowd. In short, television expands the reach of the sport and frees spectator judgment more than the radio and brings not only the game, but the politics of the ballpark, to viewers in their homes.

New media also more broadly provides a way for people to engage with the sport and follow the events at the ballpark. Social media gives people up-to-date information on stories and narratives within the sport as well as game updates. The internet, in addition to the television and radio, informs fans about not only what happens on the field, but why. Reporters interview players, which creates a new platform for fans to see baseball's politics. Some of this is aired on television, and much of it sent out on social media. These platforms provide athletes another way of engaging in politics or with spectators and fans.

What we see, then, when looking at baseball fans is a large community of followers. There are people at the park, people listening on the radio, people watching on television, and people following through social media. There are different levels of the game—from MLB, to minor leagues, independent leagues, and Little League. Most of the analysis in this book focuses on MLB because it has the widest audience and the most spectators. Looking at MLB, the community is quite large; millions of fans attend major league parks, and many more watch on television and listen on the radio. The claim that there are millions of baseball fans is not controversial. Whether this community matters or not may be up for debate.

To be sure, this community, unlike democracy as a whole, is optional. One can participate or not; one can follow baseball or not. The same is true of associations, and yet we often view associational life as co-essential for democracy itself. Baseball fans also have certain demographic factors that are problematic. Namely, baseball fans tend to be older, whiter, and richer than most of America.[37] These demographics are lamentable and must be kept in mind when we are looking at political phenomena in the game. They also arguably make issues of race and class that do emerge more important. When looking at democracy at the ballpark, as when we look at democracy in general, we must keep in mind the makeup of those who participate and those who do not.

Why do people become baseball fans? Why do they engage with baseball and invest meaning into the sport? Theories abound. Sport is thought of as a diversion, a means of entertainment, a pastime, a form of leisure, even a means of war by other means. Ultimately, baseball—and I argue, most sport—provides a way for people to engage with things they care about without the seriousness sometimes involved in politics. It involves a type of serious nonseriousness. Donald Hall makes a similar argument, writing, "Like other sports, baseball provides harmless dissipation for those of us who need on occasion to be less serious or ambitious—or depressed—than we usually are."[38] This blend of the serious with the playful makes it a unique venue for democratic politics.

Spectators engage not because they want to participate in the serious affairs of politics with its cavalcade of experts and often high bar required for participation. Many people are familiar with sport and baseball from childhood; it is something they know. This comfort level allows people to engage more freely and to follow the sport more easily than they can the intricacies of politics. Further, in an era of increasing political polarization, it is not the content of the politics that matter, but one's predetermined political prejudice. Baseball's partisanship applies to teams but stops there. In other words, when confronting politics at the ballpark, spectators are not predisposed to blindly accept or reject what is before them.

This analysis reveals the layers of spectatorship. Being at the ballpark, with all of the engagement and embodied experience that it entails, differs from listening on the radio. In between there is television, and now, under it all, sports discourse on social media. Baseball reveals all of the ways that one can be a spectator. All of these varying ways of serving as witnesses, of being fans, connect people through baseball. Baseball provides a common language, a gathering point, and an arena of concern for people. While physically being at the ballpark is the fullest experience of spectatorship that forms community, the other modes of spectatorship are useful supplements for building community. Watching baseball on television is like reading the Bible at home; going to the stadium is like going to church. This periodic renewal lies at the center of the experience and, based on attendance figures, the community takes this duty seriously.

THE BUSINESS OF BASEBALL AND COMMUNITY

When we talk about baseball teams and community there is always another objection—are not baseball teams first and foremost businesses? So far our focus has been on fans—and fans are the primary unit of analysis for understanding politics and baseball—but teams are clearly both part of the community and they are businesses. Why not talk about a community of people who shop at K-Mart? Aside from the dwindling K-Mart community, there are reasons to treat baseball differently: baseball fans identify with the team, the team is a local institution, the teams do not operate strictly as businesses, teams often reflect their communities, and finally, baseball orients people toward a different type of time consciousness.

First, teams operate differently from most businesses. For example, in 2015, the Dodgers operated with an operating income of $-73.2 million, the Phillies $-8.9 million, and the Rangers $-4.7.[39] The Detroit Tigers routinely operated with a budget much larger than their market in an attempt to win a World Series between 2006 and 2016. Baseball teams are not geared solely toward turning a profit (although this does ignore the soaring values of franchises that outpace any spending deficit). Further, communities and local governments do not treat them like any other business: they often provide teams funding beyond what would make sense from a business perspective. Suffice it to say, the ethereal and communal bonds to teams make governments behave differently toward sports teams than they do toward other moneymaking enterprises.

More importantly, baseball fans identify with the team. This claim is largely noncontroversial. Fans wear hats with their team's logo, jerseys of their favorite players, and all sorts of team-related gear. Sports, and baseball in particular, cultivate a communal language: fans speak in terms of "we." If the team struggles, a fan might say, "we just can't get anything going" or simply retell events: "we won," "we lost," and so on. We do not identify ourselves and our interest with business, we do not see fellow customers as one of our own, and yet, fans do exactly this—they identify with not just the team but with other fans. This identification again points toward a robust and participatory kind of spectatorship.

These communities for the most part begin local or regional. There are thirty major league teams, so affiliations are not always tied to one's immediate locality, but their broader region. People tend to root for the team they grew up supporting. One's favorite team usually reveals where they spent their childhood. People support their local teams, and often continue to do so even if they move elsewhere. A Kansas City Royals fan in Maine sees another person wearing a KC hat and knows they are kindred spirits. The community begins locally but extends beyond simple boundary lines. This community is not wholly constituted by geography: it is more akin to a fellowship.

Teams also tend to reflect the community they represent, either intentionally or otherwise. The Brooklyn Dodgers were famously named after their fans dodging trolley cars on the way to games. As Dorris Kearns Goodwin suggests in Ken Burns's documentary *Baseball*, Brooklyn's character was defined by the Dodgers.[40] The closeness between the fans, team, and Brooklyn community is similarly emphasized by Roger Kahn.[41] The modern-day Los Angeles Dodgers, meanwhile, have made a concerted effort to include Mexican players on their major league rosters to reflect their community.[42] Kansas City has recently instituted a Sunday dress-up event to cater to the desires of their community as a salute to Negro League traditions.[43]

There is also a broader baseball community. People with different allegiances can still converse and unite over a common love and enjoyment of the game of baseball. In the mountains of Western Canada, I ran into someone with a Red Sox hat, and we walked for two hours together—about baseball. The game provides a common bond, a shared language among people who otherwise would not have such a commonality. These types of touchstones are the foundation of much everyday interaction. The language and structure of the game provides a commonality for people to connect around, something less polarizing than politics or religion.

Further, baseball cultivates a different type of time consciousness. Most business ventures are fleeting, whereas meaningful community associations are lasting. Baseball is paradoxical when it comes to time: the game itself does not keep track of time, but the history of baseball and the succession of the game is one of its constitutive parts. Baseball fans keep detailed statistics and compare numbers through the years. Parents pass down stories of their favorite teams and players to their children. The cycle of the game mirrors the life cycle of the seasons. Teams rebuild, pennants are remembered (flags fly forever), and the history of one's team is as important as the team's present state. Baseball trains the democratic mind to think long term. It is not a sport built on instant gratification, and the community of fandom is not one you can enter and leave quickly.

However, the economics and business aspect of teams are important to recognize. It is often when teams understand themselves as a business that they undermine their core reason for being and undermine community. Michael Sandel makes this point well. Speaking on the community value of sport, he writes, "But professional sports is not only a source of civic identity. It is a business. And these days the money in sports is driving out the community."[44] Sandel is concerned about how teams fund and build stadiums, franchises moving out of communities, and advocates public ownership as a possible solution to make sure sport remains more about community than business. These points will be discussed below, but they point toward the corrosive nature of thinking of baseball teams simply as businesses. Doing so actually undermines both the community and the value of the franchise itself. This makes sports teams a sometimes precarious part of the community: they can be a rallying point, but they can also betray their local communities if they are understood solely in business and economic terms.

The players themselves are the members of the community of baseball yet to be discussed. In many ways, players are the least important part of the community for understanding politics in baseball, but they nevertheless have a prominent role. Players fulfill a primary function of attracting fans. Good teams have more fans, and good players attract more attention. From a political standpoint, players and their views often attract attention, giving fans a chance to interact with these politics. As community members, most participate in some type of charity. Players thus often serve as the focus of attention, but how the fans and spectators receive their actions, views, and behaviors is more important for understanding politics and baseball.

The three constitutive parts of the baseball community are the fans, the teams, and the players. The primary unit, the most important part of this community, are the spectators, the community of fans. "Fan" is short for "fanatic," though it may also be related to the terms "fancy" or "fanciful," as it applies to followers of certain hobbies and sports. The term originated in its common usage from early baseball fanatics, making baseball the mother of modern fandom as we understand it.[45] People join this group of fans because of an interest in or admiration for the sport. The sport, in this case, brings people together into this community through a common bond. Others who are not fans are still affected by the community, whether that means casually attending a game or hearing about events at a ballpark after the fact. It would be impossible to live for very long in America and avoid interacting in some way or another with sport, and with its quotidian character and long season, this is especially true for baseball.

This community, made up of fans, teams, and players, is a meaningful political community full of potential. Sports create community, but community itself is value neutral, despite the positive connotations of the term. There can be a community of Klansman as easily as there can be a community of people on their local PTA board. In what follows I will examine how this potential can be translated for both good and ill. In particular, I will focus on how positive community can emerge from the politics at the ballpark before looking at how this space can be manipulated to deteriorate local communities through stadium funding.

COMMUNITY CONCERNS AT THE BALLPARK

So far, I have shown how baseball spectatorship itself can be an important source of community in democratic times. In what follows, I will show how this community is normatively desirable and advances other concerns, many political, that pertain to the broader community within which the baseball community resides. We see throughout baseball's highest organized level a consistent effort to embody local communities and become a gathering point for local concerns. Teams hold events, run charities, and assert their role in their local communities.

One of the most obvious visual community events comes on Mother's Day when players all wear pink to raise breast cancer awareness. Items used on the field are sold to raise money as well. This is part of a league-wide "Going to Bat Against Cancer" initiative. Beyond raising funds for cancer research, MLB-wide initiatives include autism awareness, ALS fundraising, an MLB greening program (which celebrates earth day with carbon-neutral games and seeks to raise awareness about the environment and energy efficiency), programs for veterans, a partnership with the Boys and Girls Clubs of America, Jackie Robinson Day, Roberto Clemente Day, and many others.[46]

This type of marketing is important because scholars have recently shown that many people participate in "cause marketing," which has more of an impact than previously assumed. Patricia Strach, for example, looks at the influence of cause marketing on breast cancer awareness in her work *Hiding Politics in Plain Sight*. She concludes that cause marketing indeed shapes how citizens view issues and, in the case of breast cancer awareness, she writes, "Far from the picture of society that is disconnected in which individuals 'bowl alone,' breast cancer organizations bring people together in communities across the country. Organizations give individuals an emotional connection with the disease and with each other and the hope that we will better address breast cancer."[47] The problem, for Strach, is that putting these issues in the social realms at times obscures their political and contentious character. The importance and influence of these mechanisms for change, she shows, is powerful. Her work illustrates that watching politics and issues in places like the ballpark does have clear political outcomes.

Many parks also have dedicated "nights" or "days" to celebrate various cultures and causes. The Fiesta Tigres and Polish American night are notable examples in Detroit. Many places have Pride night as well, including San Diego, the site of a recent controversy. Miami has a Jewish Heritage Day, a Columbian Heritage Night, and a Senior Free Ticket Thursday. The Yankees have a Military Appreciation Day, as do many other teams. The Dodgers have a Firefighter Appreciation Night, and the Pirates have a Faith Night. Other, more lighthearted, events at ballparks include Star Wars night, Pups at the Park, fireworks, movie night, Kids Run the Bases Days, and Singles Nights, among many others. What emerges is a giant venue to celebrate all sorts of communities that exist within the bigger baseball community. It provides a space for recognition of these sub-communities and an opportunity to express oneself in a public space.

We may think that giving the space to Star Wars fans to express themselves is not especially *politically* important (and maybe it is not), but events like Pride Night are important, as a recent incident at Petco Park in San Diego proves. The Padres invited the San Diego Gay Men's Chorus to sing the national anthem. There was a mix-up: the stadium played a woman singing the anthem over the loudspeakers as the Gay Men's Chorus stood on the field. Some people in the crowd yelled insults at the choir. The incident was obviously embarrassing and generated much outrage as well as a detailed investigation into the matter by Major League Baseball.[48] This incident shows both the power of the space and the potential for things to go wrong. Ideally, the ballpark can be a place for affirmation, but the arena of spectatorship is contested, as the chapter on equality will show. While ideally ballparks are a place for community recognition and mobilization, this unfortunate incident shows that is not always the case.

Every single major league team has a charity as well aimed at specifically local initiatives. The Arizona Diamondbacks, for example, have an education initiative aimed at supporting STEM programs in local elementary and middle schools. They also have military initiatives, multiple youth sports programs, and their own Arizona Diamondbacks Foundation whose goal is to, "support three main areas of need: homelessness, indigent healthcare and children's programs of all types, including education and youth baseball field development."[49] The Diamondbacks are not unique in their community outreach.

I will not detail what each of the thirty major league teams does for their communities, but simply provide a few more examples. The Atlanta Braves have a foundation, youth education programs, youth baseball and softball programs, and a plethora of community nights aimed at health initiatives, military appreciation, and ending hunger by providing food to the Atlanta food bank.[50] The Seattle Mariners have anti-bullying programs, a Refuse to Abuse campaign spreading awareness and support for victims of domestic abuse, and a DREAM education initiative spreading their "DREAM Team principles: staying Drug-free, Respect for yourself and others, Education through reading, Attitude, and Motivation."[51] Again, these are but a few examples—each team has a large apparatus of resources devoted to precisely the kinds of local charity that community leaders have long been obliged to provide.

Players are also often active leaders in their communities, thanks in no small part to the now tremendous amount of wealth garnered by playing the sport. A few examples should suffice to make this point. One of the most famous examples of the ballplayer as community builder was Roberto Clemente, who won the Presidential Citizens Medal, the Presidential Medal of Freedom, and the Roberto Clemente Walker Congressional Gold Medal for his work. He died while on a relief mission to Nicaragua. Andrew McCutchen, as another example, tried to carry on that legacy and was involved with the Make-a-Wish foundation and active in the Pittsburgh community.[52]

Other athletes create charity organizations. Justin Verlander created a donor-advised fund when he established his "Wins for Warriors" campaign specific to Detroit and his native Virginia, aiding programs for veterans' mental health.[53] Alex Rodriguez and the Yankees, locked in a battle regarding bonuses the slugger was due for historic home run milestones, ended up agreeing to donate $3.5 million to charity, including the Boys and Girls Club of Tampa, the Special Warriors Foundation, and the MLB Urban Youth Foundation.[54]

All of this makes charity, awareness, and involvement accessible on an everyday level. The ballpark is a community space that brings people together and advances charitable initiatives. In the case of local concerns at the ballpark, being an active participant in this community endeavor represents meaningful civic engagement. Gathering people together makes something more of the experience. Games are not solely about baseball; they are about civic life. The game gathers people to realize this potential.

PRACTICAL POLITICS AND STADIUMS

One of the more obvious interactions between teams and local communities is the creation of the ballpark itself. Stadium funding is at the heart of much politics around local sports teams. The funding of new stadiums is often resented, and rightfully so. Economists in general are against subsidies for sports stadiums. One exception, however, is minor league stadiums and teams. Economists have found that minor league teams have a positive effect on local per capita income.[55] Nor is there an effect on increasing rents, suggesting that a minor league team is indeed a valuable urban commodity, improving local quality of life.[56] At the major league level, however, stadium financing is problematic.[57]

One of the major reasons for the anxiety around creating new stadiums is that these stadiums lack the democratic character of old stadiums: they create premium boxes and exclude the common fan. In the words of Bob Herbert, stadiums become playgrounds for the rich.[58] Indeed, Sean Dinces has collected data that show that the overall number of accessible seats has declined.[59] He shows that while this trend began in the 1950s, it is still growing, creating gentrified stadiums that exclude the working class. This is a trend not specific to baseball, but present in the National Football League and National Basketball Association as well. However, as Dinces notes, "Particularly in the case of MLB teams, this story repeated itself in cities throughout the United States. Ballparks got bigger in terms of square footage, but overall seating capacities shrank while premium seating capacities rose."[60] In other words, public funding for stadiums grows even as these stadiums become more and more exclusive, barring said public from entry.

Sandel finds a similar trend. He writes, "Today, the allure of greater profit is leading team owners to transform their games in ways that destroy the class-mixing habits and sense of place on which sports and democracy thrive. The proliferation of luxury skyboxes segregates the upper crust from the common folks in the stands below."[61] This practice is a clear example of the business and economics of baseball undermining the community and democratic potential of the sport. A cursory view at a few of the newly constructed stadiums shows the problem with these types of stadiums and the effect they have on community by looking at how they were built, where, and why.

Marlins Park is a hallmark of the problems regarding present-day stadium-funding politics. The park itself is aggressively modern, full of vibrant colors and garish statues. It is in many ways a departure from the trend of building retro-feeling stadiums.[62] After threats from the team to leave, local city and county governments eventually gave in and funded over $500 million of the $634 million stadium costs.[63] However, Miami-Dade County was rushed into funding the stadium without the funds available, so they borrowed money by selling bonds, and it is suggested that the price for taxpayers will be in excess of $2 billion when the bill comes due.[64] All of this financial burden on taxpayers hit doubly hard during the middle of the Great Recession. The political fallout included the recall of Mayor Carlos Alvarez and an investigation on the part of the SEC.

Jeffrey Loria, the owner of the Marlins, was the face of this scandal and the mastermind of the deal. To make matters worse, not only did the Marlins not invest in their team once they relocated, they slashed their payroll, traded away their best players, and treated the fans to consistently disastrous baseball, all while the team brought profits for its negligent owner. The Marlins Stadium saga is quintessential of stadium funding gone wrong. Love of a team and the sport was used to marshal local governments to act against the financial interests of their constituents, and the owner of the team profited while tearing down the team itself.

The Atlanta Braves' new stadium has similar issues. The Braves had been playing at Turner Field, first used in 1997. After fewer than twenty years playing in the stadium, funded by taxpayers for the Olympics, the Braves declared they needed a new stadium, also to be funded by the public. The Braves organization uses this strategy in the minor leagues as well. As Ira Boudway and Kate Smith report:

> Over the last 15 years, the Braves have extracted nearly half a billion in public funds for four new homes, each bigger and more expensive than the last. The crown jewel, backed by $392 million in public funding, is a $722 million, 41,500-seat stadium for the major league club set to open next year in Cobb County, northwest of Atlanta. Before Cobb, the Braves built three minor league parks, working their way up the ladder from Single A to Triple A. In every case, they switched cities, pitting their new host against the old during negotiations. They

showered attention on local officials unaccustomed to dealing with a big-league franchise and, in the end, left most of the cost on the public ledger. Says Joel Maxcy, a sports economist at Drexel University: "If there's one thing the Braves know how to do, it's how to get money out of taxpayers."[65]

This model invariably leaves the team and owners with the profits, while the fees given to local governments rarely cover the debt incurred during the project.

To make matters worse, Atlanta's new stadium is even further in the suburbs, likely catering to wealthy people in the area and isolating the team from the inner city. The new stadium is located in the midst of suburban sprawl and forced the county to pay for a pedestrian bridge over Interstate 285 that costs $9 million.[66] The cost to citizens, the location of the park, and the viability of their former facility makes the Braves' decision to move and the elected officials' decision to fund their extravagance all the more baffling. The end result is likely more highway traffic, a team further from its city, and a heavy burden on the citizens of Atlanta and Cobb County.[67]

The Rangers, taking a page out of the Braves' playbook, recently decided that their stadium, Globe Life Park in Arlington, built in 1994, is in need of replacement. The primary reason cited for a new ballpark is that they need air conditioning. No one disputes that Texas is hot in the summer, but paying for half of a billion-dollar stadium project is a steep price. Of course, in order to get air conditioning in an effort to boost attendance (despite having good attendance numbers already), the Rangers threatened to re-locate to Dallas. The mayor of Arlington was leading the charge to fund the stadium, saying in regard to Dallas' interest in the team, "We can't lose the Rangers. We need to this put to bed."[68]

If the general consensus is that public funding of new stadiums is bad policy, why does it continue to happen? In short, these threats are effective. Sandel writes, "Owners are constantly relocating teams, or threatening to do so, if the home town is unwilling or unable to shell out huge public subsidies for stadiums."[69] Looking at the cases and the threat used by teams to leave their areas, it is clear that there is rhetorical power in having a team. As Joanna Cagan and Neil deMause demonstrate, "The explanation from local officials for these subsidies has invariably been that a new stadium is needed if the team is to stay in town, and that indeed a team in town is needed if the city hopes to make a great urban comeback, or remain a 'major-league city.' "[70] Communities want sports teams. Teams give communities something to gather around. Sports in general are an extra-rational phenomenon, and it should not be a surprise that decisions on teams and stadiums are not rational. No politician wants their legacy to be "the mayor who lost the Dodgers." What should be a symbiotic relationship devolves into an abusive relationship because of owners' greed.

The tragedy is that this positive aspect of community—a binding point in the form of a baseball team—is often used against that community's better interest. The rhetoric of this community gathering point allows a few already rich owners to profit while taxpayers foot the bill, even those who are not baseball fans. This trend of creating ballparks that are hostile to their communities is not new, either. The most notable example is the construction of the Dodgers' stadium in Los Angeles and the displacement of the Latino residents from the Chavez Ravine. Residents boycotted and refused to leave their homes, but eventually the homes were razed and the stadium built. Political scientist Chris Zepeda-Millan captures what this meant for the Latino community, saying "The Dodgers symbolized the white male power structure literally displacing us."[71]

Of course, some stadiums are not as painful for local citizens and can foster community. Beyond problems with how stadiums are funded, place is a crucial element for cultivating community. Comerica Park, Camden Yards, and AT&T Park are all examples of better modern stadium projects. They are all within old downtowns and used limited tax payer funding. In general, the practice of public funding is more in line with what some call "corporate welfare," nefariously using the rhetoric of the community strengthening bond a team provides while owners profit and taxpayers foot the bill. The ethereal bond of the community and the very real public good that it provides is manipulated in the area of big stadiums and mass spectatorship.

Albert Borgmann makes this point—that baseball can be an important community institution—focusing on the example of the Baltimore Orioles:

> Recently, a thirst for reality and a sense of community have asserted themselves in Baltimore. When the Baltimore Orioles decided to build a new baseball stadium, they did not pick an open space outside of the city as a landing site for an enclosed, air-conditioned, and astroturfed spacecraft that could have descended just as plausibly on Frankfurt to contain soccer or on Tokyo to accommodate sumo wrestling. Rather,

they cooperated with city and state authorities and decided to build at the edge of downtown on the site of an abandoned rail yard, replacing public utility with public pleasure. The site is bounded on one side by a huge and venerable brick warehouse. Rather than tearing it down, the architects incorporated it as a backdrop for right field and as a space for offices. The stadium itself will respond to the masonry of the warehouse with its brick arches. It will recall the character of the old beloved city stadiums in Chicago, Detroit, and Boston. It will be open to the sights of downtown Baltimore as well as the wind, rain, and sun. Games will be played on grass. When you sit in the stands, you cannot doubt that here is Baltimore, this is summer, and a game of venerable traditions is being played.[72]

Note the conditions that Borgmann views as essential for creating a ballpark that unites the community—place, local governments cooperating with businesses in the community, a concern for the past, and an authenticity that roots baseball to the fourfold of earth, sky, divinities, and mortals. This union of the local with the original elements is important for cultivating a stadium and team that can be a positive part of the local community.

The policy takeaway from all of this is complex. On the one hand, it is clear that teams can be a positive force within the community. Beyond serving as a gathering place for important causes and charitable initiatives, teams give a community a stronger sense of identity and a space for people to gather. This positive contribution is often used to undermine community interest in the form of stadium funding. This is consistent with a more agnostic view of community life. Are communities important and often very positive things for citizens? Of course, but they can also be perverted and dangerous. Baseball communities are like other communities: they require attention and maintenance from citizens, fans, and local governments to maintain their value to democratic life.

Writers like Sandel are helpful in thinking of moving away from a strictly economic or business perspective on sporting franchises and toward a more community-oriented view. He even suggests moving toward community ownership models such as that employed by the Green Bay Packers.[73] Rather than subsidize wealthy owners building new stadiums as they threaten to rip away a pillar of the community, why not work toward giving these teams back to the communities that love them? Such a model would do much toward eliminating greed in the sport and making baseball more community oriented and democratic.

FLEETING COMMUNITY: BASEBALL THEN AND NOW

The community around baseball changes all of the time, not simply because of stadium construction and economics. The baseball community is always changing. The sport was born during the Civil War, and the only way to watch was to go to the ballpark. Radio increased the reach of the sport and broadened the spectators, and television did the same. The rise of digital media and streaming platforms has made the sport as popular as ever and seen by even more people than before, despite losing its place as America's only or even biggest major sport. The community of spectators following baseball is likewise in flux. There are dramatic political shifts like desegregation and other less noticeable shifts caused by the birth of new fans and the death of old. There are more ways to gather around the sport than ever, and this change in spectatorship has changed the types of communities that form, creating online communities and displacing others with changing technology.

Sheldon Wolin argues that we should think of democracy not as a system of government, but as a fleeting and fugitive moment. Wolin wants democracy to be thought of "as a mode of being which is conditioned by bitter experience, doomed to succeed only temporarily, but that is a recurrent possibility as long as the memory of the political survives."[74] This emphasis on instability leads Wolin to accept a different type of democracy that embraces the anarchic element of democracy and shirks consensus.[75] There is no everlasting community, and community itself is only formed and realized in emergent moments.

For the most part, fandom and spectatorship are akin to this kind of fleeting community Wolin describes. By and large, being at the ballpark is a moment of communion and togetherness that vanishes with the final out. Dreyfus and Kelly, describing the community that arises around sport, make recourse to the analogy of the wave. This is a persistent metaphor in the Western canon, and they use it to describe the experience of fleeting community through sport. The game can carry people together momentarily as though washed away. Further, it can gather everyone together in a moment. At games, spectators are all focused on the same thing or the sacred event, and Dreyfus and Kelly refer to Homer in saying that this idea of *physis*, what they call whooshing, illuminates what really *is* and makes it shine. This understanding of being is opposed to a scientific understanding of being. This whooshing moment is in fact the height of reality, and this reality has the character of communal being-together.

This event is about being together. As they write, "And the moment of exultation in a ballgame can be like that as well: one wishes it would last forever while knowing that it can't. That sort of moment offers what autonomy cannot: a sense that you are participating in something that transcends what you can contribute to it."[76] Very rarely do we transcend daily life. We are absorbed in the concerns before us. These events offer us a different mode of being for a while. There is a danger in this mode of being together, the madness of the crowds, the loss of oneself to something bigger, but danger is usually associated with meaning. And citizens need to learn to use our judgment and exercise judgment regarding transcendent moments.

However, against this fleeting community in sport and baseball, there is a counterbalance. In baseball, past and present are also united in a particular way. Most of the time, fandom is passed on from one generation to the next as a means of connecting people through time. The game itself is passed down, as some have suggested, from father to son as a way of connecting youth and adulthood.[77] In America there are very few old, revered institutions and, for many, baseball clubs represent just that—a gathering point handed down from generation to generation. This is why many viewed the departure of the Brooklyn Dodgers as such a betrayal: it broke the link between generations. This lasting bond of course is also what gives team owners power when trying to get funding for new stadiums. The teams become ingrained in the lives and histories of many people. People want the teams to stay to preserve their relationship to the team, their past, their family who came before, and the generation that comes next.

Baseball in particular has a sentimentality involved in fandom that gives fans and members of the community a different relationship to the past. Fans of baseball tend not to think only of players or teams from the last ten years—they think of teams and games that happened over 100 years ago. Stadiums are filled with statues of these legends, and children learn about the history of their favorite clubs. Borgmann notes the capacity for baseball to tie citizens to the past and combat what he calls hypermodernism. He says that baseball is a "community of celebration" that "radiates festivity and coherence into society. It is focal by nature; it radiates as well as it collects. It gathers the past as it does for the middle-aged softball player who, poised at the plate, recollects and impersonates Ernie Banks; it opens up the future to the young catcher who imitates Carlton Fisk."[78] There is a communion with the history that came before that teaches the next generation of the past even as they go forward to shape the future.

This type of long-term thinking offsets the mostly fugitive character of communities built around sporting spectatorship. To be a fan for a day, a week, a month, or a year is to not truly be a fan at all. It takes learning the history of the club, the rules of the game, the nature of the league, and much more to be fluent in conversing with others among the community of fanatics. It is still possible to join the community and the fun of being together at the ballpark without this in-depth knowledge, but the level of participation in that community is lesser.

Beyond the large communities of spectatorship, there are more local communities formed around playing the game at different levels. At the lower levels, baseball and softball participation is on the rise and, combined, was the most participated in sport of 2016.[79] One would expect increased participation given MLB's "Play Ball" initiative, and this means even more communities are being built around the sport at the local level. Bill Clinton noted this community-building effect in his radio address on October 21, 1995:

> If you watch one of the 178,000 Little League teams in this country, you also will see real community in America. Two and a half million of our children get together to play this sport, boys and girls. And that's not counting everyone who supports the teams and shows up for the games and practices and bake sales. Communities large and small grow up around baseball: kids playing a pick-up game until it's too dark to see, folks getting together for softball after work, families walking together to see a home game at their local ball park.[80]

The largest and most visible manifestation of communities of spectatorship around baseball are at the major league level, but a communal being-together can be learned at local games as well. In a political landscape that often divides people, community-forming institutions such as baseball are increasingly important.

This examination of baseball has important implications for our understanding of community and democratic politics. First, this is indeed a meaningful and important way to bring people together. Baseball plays a role in identity formation, spreading awareness, promoting charitable causes, and providing visibility and space for local community concerns. The fugitive nature of being together at an event is balanced by the long-term demands that being a fan entails. All of this shows how there are meaningful communities that emerge around sport. Given the centrality of community life to our understandings of politics, these communities clearly merit serious consideration. Their everyday nature is not a reason to ignore them in favor of elite politics; it may even be a strength.

Second, the sport and its community can be harnessed as a positive part of local life or can be used to abuse local interests. The community is what its members make it. As a result, political theorists and scientists need to be more attentive to sport and its place in democratic life. Sport's gathering potential is an important asset in a world of individualism, but only if this potential is realized for good. Divides within the community, and policies that further separate cities from residents, need to be fought because they do not advance what sport is all about. They do not help facilitate an experience with sport that furthers the needs of their local communities.

Finally, this transforms how we view spectatorship and the political value of spectatorship. If watching a game can be the basis of forming meaningful community and shining light on communal concerns, we cannot view spectatorship as a passive activity or antithetical to democratic life. This example shows that spectatorship can actually help form healthy democratic communities. Further, the experience of spectatorship is not as passive as usually portrayed and is not solely about vision. There is an embodied element to being together at the ballpark that illuminates how all-encompassing a spectator experience can be. Spectatorship, then, far from being antithetical to liberal democracy, can play an important role in facilitating flourishing democratic societies.

Who a community includes and excludes is an essential question when talking about community and being together. How do most people confront the problems of inclusion and exclusion? And, of course, as with any community, baseball does not always bring people together but can divide people as well. As Daniel Nathan writes, "Yet sport has not and does not *just* bring us together, *e pluribus unum*-like. Rather, the history of American sports is also one of exclusion, of segregation, that has forced some people—African Americans and women, most obviously, but many others, too—to play apart. My sense is that Americans tend to avoid dwelling on this. When not ignoring this fact, people have found ways to spin it to good effect."[81] Nathan highlights a discomfort: in the midst of a community that feels so positive and refreshing compared to other everyday politics highlighted with incivility and polarization, there is also a dark side. People are left out. The next chapter deals with exactly this problem and the politics of equality that exist around baseball and baseball spectatorship. A community is defined by borders and identity, and we cannot truly understand a community without understanding who is left out. Looking at baseball, I argue that who is left out, how, and why, also illuminates and brings a depth to our understanding of American politics around inequalities regarding race, gender, and sexuality.

CHAPTER 3

THE POLITICS OF EQUALITY
AND EXCLUSION AT THE BALLPARK

I'm grateful for all the breaks and honors and opportunities I've had, but I always believe I won't have it made until the humblest black kid in the most remote backwoods of America has it made.

—Jackie Robinson[1]

When I tell people that I am writing a book on baseball and politics, they inevitably ask about Jackie Robinson. The story of Jackie Robinson strikes people as obviously and importantly political. The preceding chapters illustrated how sport could be such a venue for one of the more important figures in American race politics. However, politics around inequality did not emerge with Jackie Robinson and integration; nor did these politics go away as some willfully obtuse retellings of his story imply.

Baseball has always been about inequality: who can participate and who cannot; who can speak with authority and who must keep quiet; who is equal and who is lesser. Segregation and inequalities exist not only by law, but through social constructs. Before Robinson, a game featuring eighteen white players was *also* a political statement. A game with no women in prominent coaching or front-office roles *is* political; it does not become so only once a woman breaks this barrier. That there are no openly gay players in Major League Baseball *is* political, and always has been, long before the first openly gay player inevitably receives much praise and criticism.

Instead of focusing only on individuals and moments where something changes and barriers are broken, I propose thinking seriously about the everyday manner in which politics of inequality play out at the ballpark. What do people see when they watch the sport, and how does that shape our understanding of inequality? To extend the metaphor, who can play and who cannot?

Looking at baseball, I show how inequalities are both revealed and challenged. There are concrete examples in baseball, most notably desegregation, in which the sport is a venue for influencing politics and attitudes that can shape policy. While most popular media focus on the positive impact baseball has on racial inequalities in America, I argue this is not always the case. Rather, baseball is primarily a realm for watching inequalities. This means that the spectacle is not always positive and heartwarming—those emergent moments are rare. Indeed, as I will show, much rhetoric post–World War II enforces a Protestant vision of work ethic and whiteness. Similarly, looking at baseball often reveals societal inequalities around gender and sexuality. As a result, looking at baseball spectatorship we see not only the rare moments of empowerment, but the common experience of enforcing existing inequalities.

EQUALITY FROM POLITICAL THEORY
TO BASEBALL PRAXIS

How has the world of political theory grappled with issues of inequality, and how does that relate to the experience of inequality at the ballpark? A core tenet of liberal political thought is that equality is essential to any functioning democracy. Much has been written in the American context about the democratic problems created around race, class, gender, and sexuality.[2] While this work is vital to our understanding of inequality and how it affects the American political system, it has less to say about how inequality is felt in our everyday lives. Complex policy, a legacy of systemic inequality, and the persistence of mores that perpetuate inequality can sometimes elude the average citizen. How do average citizens encounter and experience the types of inequalities that political scientists spend so much time exploring?

Democratic theory exhibits a similar tendency toward espousing the need for equality without detailing how citizens encounter inequality. John Rawls, for example, highlights the importance of reason to democratic life, claiming that rational politics and reasonable doctrines lead to consensus and an egalitarian society.[3] Deliberative democrats have followed in Rawls's footsteps by highlighting the importance of rational discourse for facilitating an egalitarian order.[4] This literature is highly sophisticated, and much of it recognizes problems with reason-based politics presented by culture and passionate politics.[5] Still, a fundamental desire to bind reason and politics with a commitment to deliberation as the primary mode of political expression and empowerment remain a hallmark of deliberative thought. For these thinkers, consensus is the goal of deliberation.[6]

This assumes, of course, that egalitarian politics can create consensus—a tenuous claim. Further, rational consensus does little to highlight inequalities or challenge them. The universal standard of reason is supposed to preclude any inequalities around racial, gender, and other lines, but in practice consensus obscures inequality and does little to advance true equality. Sheldon Wolin, for example, argues that Rawls omits contentious issues and dissent by accepting only what is "rational."[7] On Wolin's reading, Rawls is certainly liberal, but not democratic. Wolin positions himself as a harsh critic of those who shirk difference and espouse liberal principles while ignoring political realities.[8] These realities ought to include everyday understandings of politics. As Wolin writes, "The demos signifies not only citizenry in general but the carriers of everyday cultural traditions, a role that was never captured in the narrowly political conception of democracy held by Athenians."[9] Thus, instead of accepting rational and elite politics, Wolin pushes toward a broader conception of politics and a more unstable form of democracy.

Consensus is often contrary to democracy. Rancière argues that not only is consensus not a desirable political goal, but that it is not even political, writing "Consensus is the 'end of politics.'"[10] Rancière argues that rather than politics, such consensus is a feature of police. The essence of police "lies in a certain way of dividing up the sensible."[11] This division of the sensible certainly recalls liberal democratic obsessions with "the reasonable." This insight of Rancière's is a good one: such consensus around what is reasonable is not political. Rather, the reasonable itself becomes decisive and excludes competing political visions. A similar critique is made more explicit by agonistic democrats.

Agonistic democrats who argue that consensus is not desirable have their roots in the thought of Carl Schmitt, who argues that politics are about disagreement and contestation. Chantal Mouffe adopts this Schmittian insight, but rather than conclude that liberal democracies are untenable, she embraces the paradox of democracy. The paradox of democracy rests in an uneasy relationship between liberalism and democracy. Namely, although one may want to defend liberal democratic institutions, it is not assured that democratic procedures will satisfy liberal concerns for matters such as human rights.[12] Due to the paradoxical nature of liberal democracy, a tension persists between liberalism and democracy that cannot be resolved, but must be accepted. Thus those who try to resolve this tension, as Habermas does privileging democracy, and Rawls does privileging liberalism, are misguided.[13] Mouffe argues "that the belief in the possibility of a universal rational consensus has put democratic thinking on the wrong track."[14] Instead, inequalities and differences ought to be displayed and different visions allowed to compete with one another.

The problem with those who seek to find rational consensus is that they ignore the power dynamic of the political.[15] In other words, by attempting to avoid exclusion by adhering to rational principles, one is in fact wielding power and excluding those one deems "not rational." This attempt to find a rational consensus actually disguises political power. No rational consensus is to be found, simply a political power that deems all dissent unreasonable.[16] The attempt to organize consensus around what is rational reaches its peak when applied to the globe by cosmopolitan writers.[17]

Mouffe argues for an agonistic model in which political visions and citizens are allowed to compete freely, not as friends and enemies, but as friends and adversaries.[18] Thus, in contrast to Schmitt, those with different political views need not be existential enemies. For Mouffe, "the aim of democratic politics is to transform *antagonism* into *agonism*."[19] One aim of democracy should be to instruct citizens how to be adversaries and how to compete, rather than pretend that they reach a rational consensus on political matters. As a result, Mouffe preserves the agonistic nature of politics—and the fact that politics involve competition, winning and losing, is an obvious truth of political life—and seeks to make this competition fit within liberal norms.

Sport and baseball fit nicely into this agonistic vein of competition. In sport, one can see different visions of the good compete, and one can see how inequalities are fought and other times reinforced. Baseball is a place where different visions of what is right and wrong compete within the public sphere. In particular, regarding equality, baseball presents an opportunity for citizens to watch politics around equality unfold and express their views on these politics. Importantly, this opportunity is not only for elites and for those concerned with that type of politics. Rather, this provides a venue for everyday people to confront these important issues facing democratic politics through a shared interest in sport.

The traditional way of understanding how inequalities are contested or seen through sport is through the playing of sport itself. Jackie Robinson breaking the color barrier is a visual challenge to prevailing inequalities that works because Robinson is on the field playing the game. The idea is that this representation of diverse athletes, like representation elsewhere, matters. For example, take Hanna Pitkin's idea of descriptive representation. In descriptive representation what matters most is the resemblance between the citizen and their representative. Pitkin writes,

> For these writers, representing is not acting with authority, or acting before being held to account, or any kind of acting at all. Rather, it depends on the representative's characteristics, on what he *is* or is *like*, on being something rather than doing something. The representative does not act for others; he "stands" for them, by virtue of a correspondence or connection between them, a resemblance or reflection.[20]

Applying this conception of descriptive or mirror representation, then, the takeaway is that the sight of diverse people playing the game matters and, in fact, represents spectators in an important way. Indeed, scholars have found that representation of diversity, even if difficult in a heterogeneous population, is important.[21] For example, it has been shown that women are better at representing women.[22] Further, black women are better at representing other black women.[23] This idea is fairly intuitive: it makes sense that seeing someone of your race, gender, or sexual orientation playing a sport would reinforce that playing this sport is a possibility for you as well.

Beyond simply watching the game and those who play it, the realm of sport spectatorship is rising with new media and increased coverage of athletes, coaches, and others on and off the field. People are watching these interviews, and often the content can launch a dialogue about pertinent political issues. While formal politics may not spur a conversation about issues of gender, when an athlete misses a game to watch the birth of their child, it becomes fodder for public consumption and debate.[24] When an athlete makes a comment about having a gay teammate, it becomes a catalyst for conversations people have in their everyday lives about issues around gay politics.[25] Similarly, conversations about the decline of participation by black Americans in baseball expose fans to larger issues around race in America.

Announcers and other intermediaries also play a large role in this process. Having a diverse cast of announcers is especially helpful. But all announcers can be open to expanding who is allowed at the table. Announcers often filter the experience of spectatorship, and the way they talk about athletes impacts how people view those athletes. As a result, the experience of watching inequalities is not solely about watching what happens on the field; it is about what happens in the broader baseball world and the apparatuses that surround the game.

Baseball is a type of agonistic politics that can illuminate the political world for average, everyday people. Turning to baseball and the examples of race, gender, and sexuality shows how spectatorship of the sport reveals the history of these politics and presents political issues. A significant criticism of vocal models is that they misunderstand exclusion and power dynamics: sports present a realm of extreme visibility in which one can see these exclusions and power dynamics unfold. Looking at baseball, the value and potential of the spectator model reveals itself as a means of understanding politics around equality and inequality.

BRIEF HISTORY OF BASEBALL
AND RACIAL EXCLUSION

One cannot properly understand baseball without considering how baseball interacts with race politics. Many with modest knowledge of the sport readily acknowledge the role that race has played in baseball history and vice versa. Baseball is a vehicle for reflecting racial inequalities and, in rare moments, challenging those inequalities. Indeed, looking at baseball's history, it is clear that the game has often been at the center of competing visions of race, ethnicity, equality, and citizenship in America.

Before integration, early baseball maintained an inflexible if informal "whites only" policy. However, as scholars like David Roediger have pointed out, the concept of "whiteness" is not stable and has evolved over time. In the early twentieth century, many immigrant groups previously not considered "white" became "white."[26] This process of immigrant assimilation can be seen clearly in baseball as the early game had a strong immigrant presence. Many of the nicknames used emphasized one's status as an immigrant and were used in both a degrading and playful manner. Such nicknames included Dutch, Swede, Red, Parisian Bob, the Golden Greek, the Old Roman, Potato, Frenchy, Irish, the Flying Dutchman, Pickles, the Hebrew Hammer, Swedish Wonder, Indian Bob, Chief, and the Pride of Havana.[27] These nicknames serve to highlight one's ethnicity and heritage, and these players were assimilated into the team structured "we" of their clubs and fan bases beginning in the dead-ball era.

Immigrants eventually dominated early baseball and provided Americans with a more diverse group of players to watch (and cheer for) than many had previously encountered in their everyday lives. That immigrants were incorporated so easily foreshadows the process of assimilation that Roediger describes. However, baseball's color line was described in *The Sporting News* in 1923 as follows:

> In a democratic, catholic, real American game like baseball, there has been no distinction raised except tacit understanding that a player of Ethiopian descent is ineligible . . . No player of any other "race" has been barred . . . The Mick, the Sheeny, the Wop, The Dutch and the Chink, The Cuban, The Indian, the Jap or the so-called Anglo-Saxon—his nationality is never a matter of moment if he can pitch, hit or field.[28]

The writer's stance reveals with much candor the most problematic exclusion in American democracy. The writer portrays baseball as democratic and inclusive with one major exception: the black and white color line. He manipulates the sport to articulate a particular vision of the political world in which democracy and exclusion of black Americans are coterminous.

That the black and white line was the decisive one is evident in the example of Latino baseball players. Early inclusion of Latino players illustrates the extent to which baseball was a means for having dialogues about citizenship, acceptability, and race. To incorporate Cuban players in the major leagues, managers and scouts had to make a case for their family heritage to verify that these players were not black. For example, the Reds justified signing Rafael Almeida and Armando Marsans in 1910 by making appeals to their racial superiority. Adrian Burgos writes that supporters of the signings stressed that the pair "came from the island's elite and that their ethno-racial ancestry placed them well above typical Cubans. Their parents reportedly had descended from the elite of Portugal and Spain."[29] The crucial deciding factor around their eventual inclusion was this appeal to their European heritage, that is, their "whiteness."

Early baseball reveals these varying levels of ethnic inequality and exclusion. Mostly white spectators grew accustomed to watching and rooting for people from various ethnic backgrounds. The game was an arena in which ability could sometimes trump ethnicity; it has been suggested, for example, that Jewish and Italian players were not fully integrated into the game until Hank Greenberg and Joe DiMaggio became national icons.[30] Baseball of the early to mid–twentieth century tells the story of American racial intolerance of the same period: the political horizons of the spectators were limited, and the lesson learned from watching the spectacle was that although many racial and ethnic differences could be overcome, crossing the black and white line was unthinkable.

The refusal to incorporate black players into Major League Baseball and society in general led to the creation of Negro League Baseball, which itself became a powerful force in the black community. Games were popular and drew large crowds. The quality of play in the league was high, probably on par or above MLB. While the Negro Leagues were great for community, entertainment, and advancing baseball to those systematically excluded from MLB, the fact that the league had to exist represented the political horizon of the un-crossable color line. The Negro leagues saw the rise of many of their own stars, notably Josh Gibson, Satchel Paige and Cool Papa Bell. While there was little crossover between MLB and the Negro Leagues, after the official MLB schedule ended, there were incidents of white major league players augmenting their salaries by "barnstorming" and playing in unofficial All-Star games versus players from the Negro Leagues. It is commonly held that the Negro League All-Star teams dominated these competitions. Nevertheless, these competitions were on the periphery and most Negro League players were unknown to the typical white fan.[31] In short, the leagues were separate and unequal.

JACKIE ROBINSON AND CHANGING POLITICS

This context is meant to give a brief idea of how spectators had grown accustomed to watching the black/white racial divide enforced at the ballpark even as other ethnic groups were brought into the fold. Jackie Robinson and desegregation ushered in an emergent moment because the divide the public was accustomed to watching was obliterated. Robinson first played major league baseball in 1947, seventeen years before the Civil Rights Act. In the context of a society that observed rigid separation between black and white citizens, the spectacle of a black man playing with white men and excelling was politically transformative. Many fans taunted Robinson with abuse, but others found themselves rooting for a player previously thought of as "other" as a part of their team. Accounts verify that this is exactly what happened: people came ·to change their minds about race because of Jackie Robinson and, later, other black players. Baseball players have testified that playing alongside black players changed their horizons.[32] Fans similarly have noted the effect that watching Robinson and other black players had on their attitudes around race.[33] Further, many other black players followed Robinson, and every team was integrated after the holdout Boston Red Sox finally signed a black player in 1959.[34]

However, integrating baseball did not institute equality among players, fans, or in society. The story of early baseball immigration, if anything, shows the extent and intensity of racism in America. Robinson faced hostile crowds constantly and endured much abuse from fans and opposing players. Notably, in 1947, the Phillies' dugout spewed racial taunts for the entirety of the game. The string of abuse was so bad that fans even wrote the commissioner.[35] Clearly, Robinson did not take his place on the baseball field and end discrimination in America. Yet, if we want to understand racial inequalities, these politics at the park are illuminating, and baseball provides an extended history that allows us to see the evolution of race politics. Robinson represents the beginning of progress in a forum that exhibited on a large stage before crowds the very real racial abuse many suffered in society. Robinson and the advent of desegregation forever changed the politics around race in America.

Robinson was not the lone black player in MLB for long. By 1959, 17 percent of all players were black, demonstrating that segregation was outdated in one of America's most popular public institutions. Fans of every team were showing up at games and rooting for players once thought radically different from themselves. While this sight was a shock for some fans, it represents an important expansion in the political horizons of citizens, particularly young people attending games. Athletes are often role models for young people, and the importance of a diverse team on the field made the thought of integration thinkable. Post–civil rights movement baseball continued to exhibit diversity while contesting racial identities. The 1970s Pirates are notable for fielding the first team in which none of the starting nine players were white. Their pitcher Dock Ellis famously challenged racial discrimination when he claimed he would not be chosen to start the All Star game because he was black (he eventually did start the game in 1971).[36] Later, waves of immigration saw increased incorporation of Latinos and Asians, creating a league that has, on the whole, become diverse.

The memory of integration and Jackie Robinson is a moment that MLB seeks to keep alive. On the fiftieth anniversary of Robinson breaking the color barrier in 1997, MLB retired his number 42 across the entire league.[37] On that day, President Clinton remarked of integration in baseball that, "It was a milestone for sports, but also a milestone in the 50-year effort that really began at the end of World War II to change America's attitudes on the question of race."[38] Beginning in 2004, April 15 has been "Jackie Robinson Day" at every ballpark in the country. For those games, players from all thirty teams wear number 42 to honor Robinson and keep his memory alive, creating a spectacle that demands reflection on Robinson specifically and American racial politics generally. The event serves as a reaffirmation of the political moment that integration represents. By staging such an event throughout the league, MLB highlights issues of race in American life. Baseball is a platform that reinforces a vision of race in America in which many would like to believe.

President Obama, visiting Cuba to watch a baseball game, recently claimed of the sport, "It can change attitudes sometimes in ways that a politician can never change, that a speech can't change. . . . All of those kids who started growing up watching the Brooklyn Dodgers, suddenly they're rooting for a black man on the field and how that affects their attitudes laying the groundwork for the civil rights movement that's a legacy that all of us have benefited from, black and white and Latino and Asian."[39] In other words, the President recognized that this type of remembrance of racial politics past, their successes and the racism that made them necessary, can transform the attitudes of the spectator. Watching these events is far from a diversion: it immerses citizens in important racial politics, and does so in their average everyday lives.

However, against this optimistic (and sometimes propagandistic) view of the power of sport, it must be noted that these comfortable stories about race overlook a bleaker reality. Jackie Robinson is often held up as a trailblazer, but how did he view baseball? Robinson actually viewed race relations with increasing pessimism after his playing days.[40] He decried the tactic of allowing one prominent black person to "make it" in a field, for white folks to point to as evidence of progress, covering over the mistreatment and humiliation involved in that "progress."[41] Robinson's own example was often manipulated in just that fashion. As a historical figure and trailblazer, he is of utmost importance, but this should not provide observers with an overly rosy picture of race relations. As Robinson writes, "There is one irrefutable fact of my life which has determined much of what happened to me: I was a black man in a white world. *I never had it made.*"[42]

"SCRAPPY WHITE PLAYERS" AND OTHER RACIAL NORMS

The everyday spectacle at the ballpark often does more to reinforce racial divisions than to challenge them. Much of the dialogue around race and ethnicity reveals the extent to which racial inequalities persist. Whether it is racist logos, coded language, an empty stadium, or waning participation, it is clear that one can see political inequalities around race emerge when watching baseball. These everyday inequalities that regular citizens encounter are pernicious because they are not highlighted on a grand stage like the Jackie Robinson story; instead, they pass by unremarked upon, accepted as normal.

One lingering and very visual sign of this inequality is the logo and name of the Cleveland Indians. While the name is not as offensive as the National Football League's Washington Redskins moniker (finally given up in 2020), the logo is plainly racist. "Chief Wahoo," as it is called, is a face painted red with a garish smile. Native American groups have protested the logo, but to little avail.[43] Protestors unite under the slogan "People not Mascots" at the ironically named Progressive Field. The logo is clearly dehumanizing and offensive, and some fans have even begun removing it from their hats in protest.[44] The Indians have begun using an alternate "C" for some games, but keep "Chief Wahoo," although clearly if the team were created today it would never dream of using such a logo (or team name for that matter). They keep the logo because some fans love it. It is a large part of their identity as fans, and it is not hard to find op-eds defending the logo.[45] This case demonstrates that ballparks have hardly been made into hotbeds of progressive politics regarding race. As of this writing, the Indians have indicated they will change their team name and logo in the wake of protests against racial injustice. The fact that it took nationwide protests in the year 2020 for Washington and Cleveland to realize that they amplified racist messages with their names and logos is staggering.

More informally, casual, everyday racism persists as well. Baseball is a game of unwritten rules, secret signals, and strict codes of conduct.[46] While that may often be helpful within the game, the interpretation of these old codes as it persists into the media is almost infallibly conservative and racially biased. Looking at the dog-whistle terms used in baseball over the last few decades, one can eerily see foreshadowing of now mainstream political xenophobia and policing of white norms. The casual watcher of baseball analysis will be struck by how often white players are referred to as gritty or scrappy, embodying a type of protestant work ethic that people so long for in their athletes. Indeed, work has shown the effect that Calvinism and capitalism has had on American sport.[47] On the flip side, one will see black and Latino players described as lazy, without hustle, fiery, or any other number of racial stereotypes and xenophobic tropes. Overall, the tendency is to praise the physicality of black and Latino players while emphasizing the mental virtues of white players.

Research bears out the presence of this type of coded language. Some, for example, have shown that media representation of Japanese baseball players has furthered Asian stereotypes.[48] An analysis of baseball announcers has shown that they exhibit racial bias toward black and foreign players, and work looking at magazine coverage of baseball players has produced similar findings.[49] Anecdotal evidence of this type of language abounds. For example, when Justin Upton, a black player, was traded, teammates and executives used such language in a piece written by Ken Rosenthal, on the condition that they would remain anonymous. As one executive said, "he is not a leader, not an all-out hustle type."[50] It is not hard to read between the lines and find the meaning behind the coded language or understand why these comments were given anonymously. Further, "celebrations" by Latin players have come under scrutiny, as some suggest that these players are not playing the game "the right way."[51] This type of racist language is not unique to baseball but remains a feature of the sport.[52]

One last instance serves to show baseball's role in illuminating issues of race. Recently, protests in Baltimore created an odd spectacle hitherto unseen in the history of baseball. When protests that began in response to Freddy Gray being killed by police turned violent, the Orioles played a home game in a completely empty stadium. Nationally televised, the game and its empty stadium severed the typical relationship between sport and spectator, community and team. After a routine out to first base, Chris Davis routinely tossed the ball into the stands and no one was there to catch it. This game highlighted very real and pertinent political issues around race in Baltimore, specifically, and America generally. The empty stadium and the spectacle around it caused baseball fans to reflect on why they were presented with such a strange sight. For example, Buck Showalter, the Orioles manager, made comments on race that highlight a perspective some casual fans may not have otherwise heard:

> You hear people try to weigh in on things that they really don't know anything about . . . I've never been black, OK? So I don't know, I can't put myself there. I've never faced the challenges that they face, so I understand the emotion, but I can't . . . It's a pet peeve of mine when somebody says, "Well, I know what they're feeling. Why don't they do this? Why doesn't somebody do that?" You have never been black, OK, so just slow down a little bit. I try not to get involved in something that I don't know about, but I do know that it's something that's very passionate, something that I am, with my upbringing, that it bothers me, and it bothers everybody else. We've made quite a statement as a city, some good and some bad. Now, let's get on with taking the statements we've made and create a positive. We talk to players, and I want to be a rallying force for our city. It doesn't mean necessarily playing good baseball. It just means [doing] everything we can do. There are some things I don't want to be normal [in Baltimore again]. You know what I mean? I don't. I want us to learn from some stuff that's gone on on both sides of it. I could talk about it for hours, but that's how I feel about it.[53]

Showalter's comments highlight the relationship between team and community and the extent to which politics infect sport. Further, his attempt to build around his team shows how sport can in turn mingle with politics. The empty-stadium game became a moment for reflection and an occasion to ponder what exactly should no longer be normal.

Baltimore's General Manager John Angelos took the opportunity to speak about broader political issues as well, highlighting the struggles faced by poor Americans. Angelos wrote that "the innocent working families of all backgrounds whose lives and dreams have been cut short by excessive violence, surveillance and other abuses of the bill of rights by government pay the true price, and ultimate price, and one that far exceeds the importance of any kid's game played tonight, or ever, at Camden Yards."[54] Baseball in Baltimore became a platform for discussing real political issues and assessing the status and strength of the community and how we view race and policing in America. The game was a place for people to talk about the actual problems their community faced, and the empty stadium stood as a symbol of the breakdown of normal everyday politics. Racial divides tore apart the city, and this political inequality was seen by the world through the televised spectacle of an empty stadium.

This event presaged events in the summer of 2020 when empty stadiums became the norm as a result of the COVID-19 pandemic, and racial injustice once again came to the front of conversations in the wake of multiple instances of police violence and murder of black Americans. Baseball and players took action and cancelled games. Players protested, a far cry from when Carlos Delgado was the only player kneeling for the national anthem (discussed in the next chapter). As one player put it, "This might be the first year where players can express how they feel. And you still have in the back of your mind that maybe there's some backlash, but we are speaking. This is the most that I've ever seen anyone speak, especially Blacks and African-Americans, in baseball."[55] It is too early to guess what long-term impact this will have, but it is promising that these protests are finally taking hold in baseball, a sport that has been much more conservative and hostile to issues of racial justice than an organization like the NBA.

Finally, even though MLB is more international than ever, there are reasons to worry about its cultural representation, particularly among black citizens. The number of black players has decreased, in part because of the growing cost it takes to excel in the game at the earliest levels and the corresponding inability of underprivileged groups to keep up with paying for advanced equipment and travel expenses.[56] This disparity reflects continued divides along racial and socioeconomic lines. MLB has taken measures to mitigate this decline of participation among black youth, but there is cause for concern. Ogden writes that baseball "has become international, as exemplified by the growing number of Hispanic and Asian players. At the same time baseball, with its thinning ranks of African-American players, is becoming culturally impoverished in repre-senting the demographic panorama of the United States."[57] Once a staple in the black community, baseball's influence is waning.

Just as the history of baseball and racial inclusion shows that the sport reflected the incorporation of different ethnicities and races in soci-ety, the sport remains a realm where race is pertinent and issues of race come to the fore. Baseball both shows the potential for overcoming racial inequalities and the reality of existing racial divides. While the public prefers to focus on the positive effects that those like Jackie Robinson represents, more often spectators live with the everyday reality of coded language and racist symbols at the ballpark. Instances like the one in Baltimore cause these bigger political issues to obtrude. Ideally, everyday interaction with these types of events causes citizens to reflect on race in America, but that is not always the case.

PLAYING AN INVISIBLE GAME: WOMEN AND BASEBALL

The relationship between sport and gender is something many feminist thinkers have examined.[58] Much work has been done especially on gender and college athletics.[59] However, baseball presents a slightly different case for studying gender inequality in sport. Women in baseball represent an extreme case of exclusion in American culture. For most sports, women have a separate professional league, but there is no separate baseball league for women; instead, society ushers girls and women toward a separate sport entirely: softball. While there is a tradition of women playing baseball in America, the decision to enforce a separate game for each gender is problematic. This complete segregation is cause for worry and symbolic of outdated views on gender, though recent events have challenged this entrenched separation.

Baseball was not always a realm exclusively reserved for men. In the early days of baseball many women played, dating back to the 1860s. Women had their own leagues and also had prominent roles in men's leagues. Jennifer Ring describes the origins of baseball rooted in English games like Rounders and highlights the extensive participation of women and girls from informal games to women's collegiate baseball.[60] She also shows how early baseball enjoyed a large contingent of female fans and their sometimes riotous behavior.[61] For Ring, the current prejudice that baseball is a manly game has its origins in A.G. Spalding's interpretation of the origins of baseball. His interpretation was ahistorical and based on a very personal need. However, his interpretation won the day and became the dominant way that baseball was seen because it resonated with his early twentieth-century contemporaries. As Ring writes, "Part of Spalding's nationalistic baseball crusade involved making it profitable and professional. This development was consistent with a trend in American culture in the late nineteenth century. Routinization, specialization, and professionalization were intended to create 'order' out of a complicated social and economic system."[62] This imposition of "order" changed the role of women in baseball.

As Ring notes, "Baseball was declared both manly and American at the same time it was becoming professionalized."[63] Spalding succeeded in crafting the sport as strictly masculine, and the sport remains a place for seeing politics around masculinity emerge.[64] This understanding that baseball is masculine, along with the later creation of softball as a women's game, mostly removed women from the world of baseball. Still, even after professionalization, women participated in the sport. For example, in the early 1900s, Lizzie Arlington, Alta Weiss, Lizzie Murphy, and Jose Caruso played semi-pro baseball alongside men, Amanda Clement was an umpire, and Helene Britton owned the St. Louis Cardinals.[65] While these examples are notable, it is important to recognize that women in baseball were certainly not viewed as equals: the players were viewed as marketing gimmicks, other owners resented that Britton owned a major league team, and Clement was treated differently from her male counterparts.[66] Despite general prejudice against women in baseball, it remains of note that women adapted to and succeeded in the hyper-masculine environment; it is surprising to find that, in many ways, women in baseball were more common a century ago than today.

The 1940s saw many major league players and would-be players exported to fight in World War II, creating a hole in the market for a populace intent on watching baseball. To fill this hole, a women's professional league was created. The women of the league faced a difficult task: they had to perform "a man's game" at a high level while maintaining standards of femininity set by the league.[67] Beginning in 1943, the league (called the All American Girl's Baseball League, or AAGBL) was initially a blend of baseball and softball, but transitioned to regulation Major League Baseball rules by its demise in 1954.[68] Many baseball fans are at least semi-aware of this league due to the popularity of the film *A League of Their Own*, which is based on the AAGBL. At the time, the AAGBL was popular and, at its peak, out-drew men's semi-professional teams, recording an attendance of around one million spectators among the ten teams in 1948.[69] The league eventually folded under market demands and social pressures regarding the role of women in society, and women were subsequently excluded from playing baseball.[70]

The AAGBL was an exception, and women in baseball became a rarer sight not because of top-down discrimination, but because of changes at the bottom of the baseball ladder in the Little Leagues. In the

1920s, girls playing Little League baseball became a topic of controversy, and eventually led to the rise of softball as an alternative in the 1930s. Softball quickly became "a vehicle for the most strident sex segregation in American sports."[71] By 1939, Little League Baseball was established as a male-only arena of participation.[72] Girls were excluded from Little League Baseball until a 1974 Supreme Court decision ruled that girls could participate.[73] The end of legal segregation of the sexes and the advent of Title IX certainly did much to advance women participating in sport generally, but baseball remains a male-dominated arena.

The history of excluding women in baseball remains problematic particularly from the vantage point of representative spectatorship. While changes in attitudes on race in America can be seen in the reaction to integration, women in baseball have to a large extent been invisible. Incentives have pushed women toward softball. Girls do not have baseball leagues in most areas, and there is no collegiate baseball for women, while softball offers an opportunity for scholarships. The result is to push talented girls and women away from baseball and toward softball.

This invisibility is distressing when one considers the state of women's baseball through a comparative lens. In other countries, women's baseball thrives. In Japan, for example, the Japanese Women's Baseball League (JWBL) is a professional league for women. Women's international baseball is also largely ignored in the United States. The United States does field an international team that is successful despite paltry funding and support. Ring writes, "In contrast to their invisibility at home, when Americans (female baseball players) enter the international arena they are treated as celebrities, and regarded as the team to beat."[74] In contrast to countries like Venezuela, Cuba, Korea, and Japan, women's baseball in the United States has a very low profile. This disparity indicates a broader problem of gendered bifurcation in the country at large and has limited the political horizons of citizens.[75] Women in baseball in the United States are, to a large extent, an afterthought. The gendered differences between baseball and softball have held; Americans are accustomed to seeing the two genders separate, with women excluded from America's pastime.

CHALLENGING GENDER INEQUALITY IN BASEBALL

An obvious question arises: given the invisibility of women in baseball, how can gender inequality be challenged or even seen in a sport that presents so few outlets and opportunities for female participation? From the youngest ages, girls are siphoned off to play softball; there are very few resources for girls and women to play baseball. Still, examples of girls and women playing baseball in Little League, as well as higher leagues, challenge the dominant gender paradigm in the sport. In addition to females actually playing the game, gender representation among broadcasters, writers, and executives is a way to begin to challenge the inequality and provide visibility.

Tellingly, the exclusion of women in baseball is being challenged where it began: in the Little Leagues. Mo'ne Davis recently attracted national attention for her dominance in the Little League World Series. Davis, with her seventy-mph fastball, has defied stereotypes of "throwing like a girl," and demonstrated in the most watched Little League World Series game in history that a girl can not only compete with boys in baseball, but dominate them.[76] Davis has continued to shine in the national spotlight, playing in celebrity basketball games and attracting many admirers.

In addition to Little League participation, women have also made headlines playing baseball with men at more advanced levels. For example, the Sonoma Stompers, a professional team in Independent League baseball, recently signed two female players. They became the first team to have two women on the field of a professional baseball team since Toni Stone and Constance Morgan played in the 1950s in the Negro Leagues.[77] They were preceded in Independent League baseball by Eri Yoshida, nicknamed the "Knuckleball Princess" after her signature pitch. Yoshida played for the Chico Outlaws in 2010.[78] There is much debate about what counts as professional baseball. According to John Thorn, MLB's official historian, professional teams like the Stompers are separate from major league teams and their minor league affiliates, and if that is the standard, women have not played "true" professional baseball in over a hundred years.[79] Regardless of whether the Stompers count as "real" professional baseball or not, Kelsie Whitmore and Stacy Piagno playing against other professional male baseball players is an important event from the angle of spectatorship. They received ample news coverage, which changes how people view the role of women in baseball. As Whitmore explained: "Growing up, I never really had a female baseball player that was at a high level that I [could] look up to. To think that, 'Hey, everything's gonna be okay because they're doing it, so I can do it.' I never had that growing up. I want to be that for younger girls."[80]

Whether women playing baseball with men is ultimately how we think of equality within baseball or not is an open question. Given the history of the sport and gender inequality, it is an enormous task to imagine what an alternative organization within the sport would look like without the existing gender divisions. Women playing in baseball will thankfully push these boundaries. For example, Melissa Mayeux, a French shortstop, was added to MLB's pool of international registration list at the age of sixteen. She was the first woman to be added to that list, which makes it possible for a major league team to sign her.[81] Much like the issue of race, a woman playing baseball with men will not end gender discrimination, but it will expand the political horizons of citizens and may be one way to move forward toward organizing sport beyond its gendered roots.

Beyond creating new leagues—and challenging the baseball/softball division for those who wish to play baseball—a way to contest gender inequality in the sport is to recognize and support the women's teams that do exist. This entails supporting and fostering programs on multiple levels. Some work is being done on this front at the Little League level. Marilyn Cohen describes a few such examples. One is the Chicago Pioneers Girls Baseball league, formed in 2006, which provides an avenue to play baseball for approximately eighty girls in the area.[82] The Pioneers successfully petitioned to play a boys' baseball league in order to have an opportunity to play baseball against other teams, though they face funding issues that are not offset by an organization such as Little League International.[83] Cohen also mentions the Carolina Minders Girls Baseball League, which supports girls playing baseball at a young age.[84] Groups such as these provide ways of opening up baseball and returning it to its original status before it was declared a masculine game with doors barred to females.

At a higher level, the women's national baseball team should be given more support and attention. There have been recent battles in international sport around women's hockey and women's soccer, but women's baseball has flown under the radar.[85] As Dorothy Seymour Mills points out, "Looking for financial and promotional sport is a perennial problem for American women baseball players, but as long as men believe baseball is theirs alone, women will be blocked from the kind of support that the National Basketball Association gives to women's basketball."[86] Funding could advance the profile of the national team, which might change the perception that baseball is only for men, particularly in the international context. Events like the World Cup and World Baseball Classic have helped to introduce fans to the sport, given the passionate fans and international character of these events.

Another way to expand participation in baseball for women is to bring them into other aspects of the sport, beyond simply playing the sport themselves. One of the most obvious and important ways to do so is by hiring women broadcasters. In 2016, ESPN did exactly that, hiring Jessica Mendoza to share the broadcast booth on Sunday Night Baseball games. Of course, being the first woman in this position has not been easy. As Betsey Morais writes:

> Mendoza's visibility makes her an easy target, yet the abuse hurled at her is routine for female sports journalists—a cohort that has grown in number, if not in favor. Baseball, the only form of amusement still called a pastime, is particularly conservative. Women were allowed inside MLB clubhouses starting in 1978, only after a female reporter for *Sports Illustrated*, Melissa Ludtke, fought for admission in court. Even today, a woman's arrival in the booth is momentous.[87]

There was initial blowback, especially on the internet, but among talk radio hosts as well. However, Mendoza continues in her role and remains a beacon for re-thinking where women fit within the game.

Hiring more women writers is another way to provide a role for women within the game. As the passage above indicates, only recently have women reporters had the access that their male counterparts have had for years. This provides a way for different voices and changes the boys club to a more open environment. Similarly, diversifying genders in upper management is a way to re-think how open baseball is to contributions from women within the game. There is no reason to believe, for example, that a woman could not be an excellent general manager or scout. Indeed, 2021 will be the first season with a woman working as general manager with the Miami Marlins hiring Kim Ng.

Finally, there is representation that can challenge the inequality that exists beyond the reach of baseball itself. Representation within the media matters as well. For example, scholars have shown how representation of gay characters on the TV sit-com "Will and Grace" can change how people think about homosexuality.[88] Baseball had its own groundbreaking show, although unfortunately it lasted only one season. "Pitch" features a woman who becomes a professional pitcher for the San Diego Padres. Meg Rowley notes the show's impact on her: "The decision to put Bunbury, a young black woman, at the center of this world was meaningful for all the women it purposely included who are so often neglected in baseball's telling. The show seemed to know and embrace what and who it was representing."[89] This representation outside and beyond any official organization within the game itself can shape how people see baseball and the role of women within the sport.

The question remains: what would an alternative organization in sport look like without these divisions? This is a question only now being tackled in earnest within and without the sport of baseball. Spalding's declaration that baseball is a man's game was never actually true, and people are finally beginning to doubt his assertion. The game has a long way to go to be considered egalitarian in regards to gender, but it is advancing, and this advance shows the reality of gender inequalities generally in society and the shifting ground upon which these inequalities rest. There are more and more women in the world of baseball, shaping what people think of the game and who can participate within the world of baseball.

LOOKING FORWARD:
BASEBALL AND SEXUALITY POLITICS

Regarding gay rights, baseball is arguably well behind U.S society at large. This is the opposite of integration in the 1940s. That it has taken so long for baseball to have an openly gay active player reveals that discrimination against gay citizens remains a very real issue. More often than not, baseball has revealed the divisions between gay and straight athletes rather than challenge them. However, by looking at the recognition of gay ex-players and the role baseball has tried to assume on the issue, one can see that even in baseball attitudes on sexual orientation are shifting.

Glenn Burke, the first openly gay ex-baseball player, played in 225 games from 1976 to 1979 for the Dodgers and Athletics. Burke's homosexuality was widely known throughout the clubhouse, but was not made public until his playing career ended. While he was well liked by teammates, his sexuality is thought to be why he was traded from the Dodgers to the Athletics, where manager Billy Martin reportedly attacked him with homophobic slurs in front of teammates.[90] Ultimately, Burke's sexuality likely caused an early end to his career.[91] His trajectory indicates that he played at a time when exclusion of gay athletes was clearly de rigeur. Still, his career also does much to push back against homophobic conceptions of gay males and athletics. He himself claimed, "They can't ever say now that a gay man can't play in the majors, because I'm a gay man and I made it."[92]

Indeed, Burke's legacy has been a source of inspiration and indicates how views on homosexuality have changed. When Burke retired he was essentially ignored by baseball for twenty years (although the A's helped pay for his medical expenses), but recently his contribution is being more widely recognized, as his family was asked to be involved in the 2014 All-Star game. According to the *New York Times*, "As part of a concerted effort to demonstrate an atmosphere of tolerance and inclusion, the league invited Burke's family to Tuesday's All-Star Game in Minneapolis—its first official recognition of Burke's early role in a movement just now gaining traction across the sports landscape."[93] The memory of Burke's accomplishment is being used in a positive way to create a spectacle that reminds people both of Burke's accomplishments and what it means to unwarrantedly exclude gay players in baseball.

Billy Bean, the second openly gay ex-baseball player, played in 272 games from 1987 to 1995 for the Tigers, Dodgers, and Padres. Bean kept his sexuality a secret from both the public and his teammates, and this double life ultimately led to his early retirement. Much of his story was recently told in a documentary aired on MLB Network. Bean is also notable because he was recently hired as the league's ambassador for inclusion. Bean's hiring and the work he will do consulting with teams to make the game more inclusive, addressing issues of race, gender, and sexuality, indicate that baseball takes its role in American political life seriously.[94]

Indeed, on July 16, 2013, MLB and then Commissioner Bud Selig released a statement on policies made to prevent discrimination based on sexual orientation.[95] It is clear from this statement that MLB has responded to calls for more inclusivity and, as a result, they are raising the issue of inequality based on sexual orientation. Selig himself acknowledged that furthering equality is the responsibility of MLB because of the role it has in American political life:

> I expect all those who represent Major League Baseball, as a
> social institution that has important social responsibilities, to
> act with the kind of respect and sensitivity that our game's
> diverse players, employees and fans deserve. We welcome all
> individuals regardless of sexual orientation into our ballparks,
> along with those of different races, religions, genders and
> national origins. Both on the field and away from it, Major

League Baseball has a zero-tolerance policy for harassment and discrimination based on sexual orientation.[96]

These actions demonstrate the change that has taken place over the last few decades. Exclusion of gay athletes, once a non-issue, has risen to the place of national spectacle, drawing attention to pertinent issues of exclusion around sexual orientation. Baseball itself recognizes that as a social institution it has a responsibility to prevent discrimination.

Further, these discussions spill from the clubhouse into public knowledge through player interviews with the media. One notable instance of a player sparking wide public discussion of sexuality and sport is Mike Piazza and his reaction to reports that he was gay in 2002. Piazza denied the rumors, but the mass amount of media attention indicates the salience of the issue. In his autobiography, Piazza explains that he resented not that his sexuality was questioned, but that his honestly was held in doubt.[97] In any case, the instance is memorable in that it presented the issue of sport and sexuality to a wide audience due to the spectacle created around Piazza and baseball.

More recently, then Detroit Tigers' players Justin Verlander and Torii Hunter were asked their opinion about gay players. Torii Hunter admitted he would have difficulty accepting a gay teammate, saying, "For me, as a Christian . . . I will be uncomfortable because in all my teachings and all my learning, biblically, it's not right."[98] In contrast, Hunter's teammate Justin Verlander said that he would absolutely accept a gay teammate, saying in an interview with CNN, "I feel like we have that atmosphere here. I don't think one of our players would be scared to come out. . . . We've got 25 guys, it's a family and our goal is to win a World Series. What your sexual orientation is, I don't see how that affects the ultimate goal of our family."[99] While Verlander's comments do not strike a resounding blow for political and social equality, they do indicate a more progressive, inclusive vision of the baseball clubhouse than in the past. Further, his comments were given in the wake of Hunter's comments and provided an alternative perspective for the public to see and hear. The crucial point is that both Hunter and Verlander provided a candid response. Because of their status as athletes, they garnered attention and gave press to an important political issue. Their comments brought attention to a present inequality, and Verlander at least showed openness to change. Both sides reflect a realistic view of how the average, everyday public views gay rights issues.

Still, like many other American sports leagues, MLB has never had an openly gay player. Inevitably, this will change and baseball will again be a testing ground for social change. A reporter recently spoke to seven baseball executives, all of whom expressed willingness to sign a gay player.[100] In fact, 2015 saw baseball's first openly gay umpire in action. Dale Scott has been an umpire since 1986, and his sexuality has been known by his peers and coworkers since the late '90s, but it was not made public until the October 2014 issue of *Referee* magazine, a subscription-only magazine with little circulation.[101] However, Scott has given interviews and expressed hope that his example will open the door to others:

> If this story or the *Referee* picture motivates somebody some-where who's an amateur umpire or is trying to go to umpire school and is trying to get a job in the Major Leagues but maybe has doubts because of their sexuality and sees this and it gives them some confidence, that's great. I understand the smallest story or piece of information can motivate someone somewhere. I think that's great.[102]

Scott retired after 31 years as an umpire, and there is certainly little doubt about his professional capabilities; now his example as the first openly gay official in professional sports represents a meaningful change in baseball and American society.

While there has yet to be an openly gay MLB player, Devon Davis, playing in the Brewers' minor league system, recently came out, and the reaction shows the importance of taking baseball's role as a social and political phenomenon seriously.[103] Baseball, although hardly ahead of the curve on gay rights issues, has provided a venue for airing issues about exclusion of homosexuality in the American public. The examples of former gay players and the dialogues in the clubhouse provide a way of making issues of gay rights present themselves to the broader public. It is likely that baseball will soon have an openly gay player excel on the field and set an important standard regarding the irrelevancy of one's sexual orientation when it comes to inclusion in sport and society.

CONCLUSION: ADAM JONES IN BOSTON

One story that unfolded in the spring of 2017 clearly highlights how politics of equality are seen and experienced at the ballpark. This story serves as a coda to this chapter and shows anecdotally how these politics unfold. While playing in Boston at Fenway Park, Adam Jones, a black outfielder for the Baltimore Orioles, was harassed by fans. Fans shouted racial slurs and threw peanuts at him. These fans were escorted from the game. The conversation that ensued illustrated the process I have been describing: that baseball reflects inequalities while also providing space to contest them.

Jones spoke out in the immediate aftermath. Following the game, he mentioned that up to sixty people were ejected, saying, "It's unfortunate. The best thing about myself is that I continue to move on, and still play the game hard. Let people be who they are. Let them show their true colors."[104] Jones bore the indignity of the affair with a grace he should not be expected to show, but he also highlighted something important: these racist feelings and viewpoints are real and must be confronted. Fenway Park in particular is a hotbed for this type of abuse. For example, CC Sabathia has claimed that over his seventeen-year career he has been subject to racial slurs only in Boston.[105] That said, it is important to recognize that racism is not a Boston problem, but an American problem.

The conversation quickly went beyond Jones when other players spoke up. Along with Sabathia, Matt Kemp, then an Atlanta Brave, spoke out, saying "It's nothing new to any of us. He let it be known that's what we go through. I mean, it's pretty much normal, especially in some of these different cities."[106] The players detailing their experiences helps shed light on the continuing existence of open racial abuse. Dusty Baker, one of the few black managers in baseball, said he was not shocked by what happened to Jones and that "It shows how much further we got to go."[107] Officials from the Red Sox, the governor of Massachusetts, and the commissioner of baseball all chimed in to denounce what occurred at Fenway and affirm that the events that unfolded were unacceptable.[108] None of these official statements should come as a surprise.

The following day, the crowd at Fenway Park took their responsibility and power as spectators to show that the fans taunting Jones did not represent all of them. Chris Sale took a walk around the mound, giving Jones time in the batter's box, and the crowd responded by cheering and giving Jones, an opposition player, a standing ovation. The ballpark consequently became a space to speak out against the racism that took place the day before. What emerged was an opportunity for education. As Jones said: "Hopefully the awareness comes. People around in the stands will hold other fans accountable."[109] Ultimately, this incident and its aftermath reveal the power of spectatorship and the unique opportunity that mass spectator sports give to understanding issues of inequality. The same venue that gave a space to show how racist views linger provided a place for the crowd to speak out against that element that exists within the body politic of the crowd and society in general. Further, Jones and his agent are seeking out policies to police parks where abuse of this nature takes place, which could create structural changes within the sport.

This incident embodies the duality of sport: sport can enforce inequality and at the same time present a venue to challenge these reigning inequalities. Baseball is a valuable space for understanding everyday politics and how citizens experience inequality. Of course, citizens experience inequality every day in a myriad of ways that are not seen, but sport provides a spotlight to these issues. Regular political discourse would likely not present the opportunity that this sporting event did to discuss racial politics. The governor commented on race politics because of baseball. This otherwise would not have happened. The fact that baseball is sometimes good for race relations and other times itself exclusionary is not an argument against its value, but an essential insight that demands further thought.

Examining the case of race, gender, and sexuality, it is evident that baseball is probably most useful for challenging inequalities around race. This is due to the history of the game, the existence of different races and ethnicities playing the game together, and the current dialogue around racial issues within the sport. Still, the example of gender in the sport is illuminating, and challenging baseball as an all-male space is a significant step toward thinking about sport beyond the traditional sexual and gendered lines. Similarly, while there have been no openly gay baseball players, it is hard to imagine this will last much longer. One day soon, MLB will include an openly gay player, and what has come before indicates what will likely happen: that player will face intense scrutiny and criticism from some, but will be a hero for many others, as well as becoming a lasting icon of the sport. This is how the agonistic realm of baseball arbitrates issues of inequality, a process that highlights political inequities that need to be seen and does so precisely in front of those who may otherwise ignore them. It has been noted that baseball may be particularly conservative, which makes challenging inequalities within baseball all the more important.

Lingering inequalities exist within the game that reflect inequalities present in the broader society. In many ways, these inequalities are more open in baseball and more important given the game's conservatism. This provides the unfortunate platform for reaffirming inequalities, but it also presents the opportunity to challenge these inequalities on a large stage. From these cases, it is evident that if MLB as an organization wanted to continue its role as a progressive institution, something it celebrates and reaffirms in the case of Jackie Robinson, there are some steps it could take. I will briefly discuss a few normative conclusions before looking at big-picture takeaways.

First, it is clear that more can be done in equal hiring. A report put out by the Associated Press graded MLB's racial and gender hiring practices a C+.[110] This was down from the year before in terms of both race and gender. What stands out in the report is certain areas that remain a problem. Jackie Robinson in his autobiography spoke about the need for black managers, and that sadly remains an area of concern. MLB managers are still overwhelmingly white. They scored better at the central office professional staff, with 28.1 percent people of color and 29.3 percent women. Obviously, these numbers could improve, and hiring more diverse people would create an atmosphere of inclusion and equality. Another part of this equation is focusing on recruiting a diverse group of players. As mentioned, MLB is especially lagging behind in regards to black players. Programs are in place to address the situation, as diversity in terms of descriptive and mirror representation is important.

Outside of the game, people who discuss baseball have a responsibility to do so in a way that does not perpetuate stereotypes. The issue of coded language makes this point clear; regardless of what an organization or MLB tries to do, if the people describing the game do so with dog whistle terms, they perpetuate inequalities. This puts responsibility on the media that cover the sport. They mediate, to a large extent, how the game is consumed, and their role reinforces or mitigates what occurs on the field.

Finally, spectators also have a responsibility, as highlighted by the Jones incident just described. A stadium that is complicit with racial slurs requires spectators unwilling or undesiring to confront their fellow citizens. Fans themselves must take some responsibility for the atmosphere they create; there is a reason that players report Boston as a hotbed of racism compared to other cities, and all fans must strive for a more egalitarian sport. Beyond this physical space, fans also need to think about how they discuss the sport. The issue of locker room talk has re-entered the lexicon, and it is important to take responsibility for how we speak about sports with others and what vision of sport this language enforces.

Issues of equality at the ballpark again demonstrate that meaningful political empowerment flows from and into the sport. Existing inequalities manifest themselves in baseball, and those inequalities are sometimes challenged through the sport. An everyday form of entertainment—in this case baseball—can actually help form a more inclusive community through the appeal to the "we" represented by the team. Rooting for players who are different from ourselves, or seeing players like ourselves break previously stringent lines, expands the political horizons of the spectator and fan. Further, unlike deliberative models, the audience for this spectacle is not composed of those predetermined to embrace egalitarian norms. As a result, baseball presents an actual realm of contestation around these issues in everyday political life, where they actually matter. This shows the importance of social institutions like baseball to democratic life. While democratic theory demands debates about inclusivity and equality, more average realms of life such as at the ballpark are where people watch "the other" become "one of us," or where they see racist norms enforced. If we want to understand the breadth of democratic life and these important political dynamics, it is important to go beyond the halls treaded by elites and to look at what goes on at the ballpark as well.

In part, baseball can fulfill this role because baseball is the site of competing visions of the good and dialogues around heroes and villains, virtue and vice. Inequality is bound up with understandings of good and bad in popular public and social morality—in other words, inextricably entwined with ideas of the good and what it means to be excellent and virtuous. This is especially true of sport because of its connection to excellence and virtue. This chapter has examined how various inequalities demonstrate the potential of baseball to promote conversation; the next chapter details how other visions of the good life and virtue can be advanced through the sport as well.

CHAPTER 4

FROM LITTLE LEAGUE VIRTUES TO BIG LEAGUE SPECTACLES

Whoever wants to know the heart and mind of America had better learn baseball, the rules and realities of the game—and do it by watching first some high school or small-town teams.

—Jacques Barzun[1]

Why is sport tied to education? What do we learn by playing sport? Why do we so often equate sporting success with moral virtue? Part of the answer is that sport is a test of character, a test that provides a direct connection between virtue and sport. Conceptions of virtue, the good life, and what is good and bad are part and parcel of any attempt at political theory. Further, as the ancient Greek example demonstrates, virtue and standards of good and bad are often codified in sport. Sport and athletics can educate citizens in qualities deemed desirable, such as grit and perseverance.[2] It is therefore unsurprising that athletics were the realm of displaying *arête*, virtue, and excellence in ancient Greece. What is surprising is that contemporary political theory often neglects sport as just such a realm for displaying and cultivating virtue. The reticence to talk about virtue within democratic life has certainly contributed to this oversight, but the result is that theory struggles to grasp how everyday citizens cultivate and display virtue. Simply because democratic theorists are often loath to focus on virtue does not mean that everyday citizens are immune to the politics of virtue in their lives, and sport is often where these politics unfold.

The task of this chapter is to understand how virtue arises in baseball and what this means for our politics. Virtue, as used here, refers to excellence of both moral character and physical skill. We see in the history of baseball especially that the obsession with virtue in sport that began in ancient Greece lives on today. How does this process work? First, this project highlights a difference in technology that changes how virtue is now seen in sport. Communities of spectatorship, as detailed in chapter 2, are bigger, and there are more ways to watch the event than ever. The primacy of being at the ballpark remains important, but one can watch virtue politics in the comfort of one's own home as well. While this chapter deals with Little League education and actually playing sport, I also argue that watching displays of virtue is important for cultivating virtue.

To show how visions of virtue emerge in baseball, I will focus on a few concrete examples that reveal this relationship. The chapter begins with an overview of the place of virtue within political theory, beginning with the ancient Greek connection between virtue and athletic competition and then moving to modern debates about the role of virtue in political life. The third section deals with what I call Little League education and how people learn virtues from playing the game. The fourth section examines eras of morality in baseball to show how baseball can reflect the values of society. This section also looks at the politics of heroes and villains to understand the connection between physical and moral virtues. The fifth section takes a current and disputed virtue—patriotism or nationalism—and looks at how these politics unfold in baseball. The chapter's conclusion brings the parts together to argue that baseball and other realms of everyday society like sport are essential for understanding what virtues society views as valuable and how they are both learned and watched.

ARÊTE IN THE ANCIENT WORLD

Virtue and visions of what is virtuous are rampant in the world of political theory and have been since the rise of philosophic thought in the Western world. Virtue, or *arête* in Greek, was central to the ancient Greek world. *Arête* in Greek translates closer to something like excellence, rather than the Christian sense of the term "virtue," although present-day use of virtue has similar connotations to its ancient roots.[3] For the Greeks, *arête* was often wedded to competitions, or the *agon*.[4] Competition gives one an opportunity to display one's virtue and excellence. As such, *arête* was intimately linked to the competitive world of athletics. This relationship dates back to Homer and the Olympic tradition. As Donald Kyle notes, "Homer's epic provides the earliest and greatest descriptions of athletic competitions in Western Literature. . . . By task and tradition, he [Homer] upholds an agonistic heroic ethos, a moral order stressing honor and piety, and a hierarchical social order based on elite display and non-elite deference. His patrons wanted to be reassured that they were scions of a tradition of excellence, even as their aristocratic world was being undermined."[5] Kyle recognizes that athletics were not tied simply to physical excellence, but to a moral and social order as well. These stories provided the background for later Greeks to understand virtue, and it was in athletics that virtue and excellence were displayed outside of war.

The connection between athletics and war has often been used to undermine the importance of athletics in the ancient world. One prevailing narrative is that athletics were of secondary importance, used primarily to train citizens for war.[6] As Steven Johnstone notes, however, most athletic events, including activities such as hunting, did not teach the skills required for hoplite warfare.[7] Instead, athletics cultivated *arête* and virtue as an end in and of themselves, outside of utility in war. Kyle writes, "Greek *arête* was primarily public and martial, but, outside of Sparta and beyond ephebic or cadet training in Classical Greece, the actual military value of most athletic training has been overstated."[8] In other words, athletic training was not a practical endeavor undertaken just to create good soldiers—it was a realm for cultivating and displaying virtue.

This relationship is evident in Homer's work. In the funeral games, for example, athletics sanctify the death of Patroclus. Achilles gathers everyone for the funeral games after burning an elaborate pyre for Patroclus. He brings prizes for the contestants, and they engage in a lengthy series of events, including a footrace, boxing, wrestling, a chariot race, shot put, archery, and more.[9] Among other things, the games are a chance for competitors to show their skill and for the divine to commune with the athletes. For example, Athena favors Odysseus in the footrace and trips up Ajax to give Odysseus victory.[10] A common argument is that these games serve as a review of the major characters within the story of *The Iliad*.[11] However, beyond their narrative utility, the games took up a prominent role in Greek society and art, furthering the epic tradition.[12] The games provide a space for recognition and grief, and ultimately, aid in the remembrance of Achilles's fallen compatriot in the moment and the millennia that follow.

Pindar and his odes to heroism also advance the connection between athletics, virtue, and excellence. Hawhee shows how Pindar's poetry represents the quest for *arête* through athletics and offers "a pedagogy of the movements of virtuosity that emerges in the context of agonal festivals."[13] Hawhee claims that, for Pindar, "victory (*nikê*) is not necessarily the sole proof of *arête*, but rather a *symptom* of becoming virtuous."[14] Felson and Parmentier similarly show how Pindar's odes were meant to inspire the reader to desire this type of virtue and excellence. They write: "The result is that when reading any of Pindar's numerous odes celebrating victors, it is not simply the victory that is praised, but the virtue or *arête* of the athlete involved. They can strive to emulate the activities of exemplary figures, both mythological and contemporary, whose efforts transcend the limits of the human condition through the practice of *aretê* 'excellence' or 'virtue.' "[15] For Pindar, remembering and preserving excellence and its value is the point because arête is central to any good life. He writes, "Excellence soars upward like a tree fed on fresh dews, lifted among the wise and just towards the liquid upper air."[16]

For Plato, the boundaries between physical and moral excellence are even further blurred. Plato famously connects virtue to his idea of the *Agathon* (good) and posits that knowledge is essential for being virtuous. Plato shifts the focus of this *agon* from the world of the body to the world of the mind, but recognizes the importance of athletics to cultivating virtue. For Plato, games and athletics are particularly important in the education of virtuous citizens. In his *Republic*, Plato devotes much of books III and IV to describing the education of the guardians, which is to be half musical and half gymnastic. Athletics are essential for striking the proper balance between body and soul. Plato writes, "Have you ever noticed what happens to a person's mind when he concentrates exclusively on gymnastic and totally neglects music? Or to one who does the contrary? . . . The first kind of behavior results in a temperament of harshness and savagery. The second produces softness and effeminacy."[17] In other words, physical and moral excellence work together to reinforce each other. Without one type of virtue, one cannot have the other. As a result, Plato's athletes will participate in the "toughest contests" as part of their education.[18]

In Plato's *Laws*, games feature prominently. Plato's Athenian, for example, states, "It is for no other ends—if for any—that contests and preparatory contests ought to be waged. For these are useful in peace and war, in the political regime and in private households."[19] Contests perform a valuable social function: they educate citizens in virtue. Not only are games useful for politics, but Plato's Athenian is bold enough to assert that "in all cities, everyone is unaware that the character of the games played is decisive for the establishment of the laws, since it determines whether or not the established laws will persist."[20] Games are the backbone of the political order, and changing games lead to changing politics. Games are decisive because they teach citizens virtue, and teach them how to work hard or toil. If citizens are not made to toil in play, one cannot expect them to toil in the more serious matters of political life.

Xenophon similarly found a connection between virtue and sport. The chief virtue learned from sport in Xenophon's *On Hunting* is *ponos*, translated as either toil, struggle, or suffering.[21] This ability to toil and attain virtue in the correct manner Xenophon shows is learned through an education in sport. As Xenophon writes, "For among the ancients the companions of Cheiron to whom I referred learnt many noble lessons in their youth, beginning with hunting; from these lessons there sprang in them great virtue, for which they are admired even today."[22] Xenophon praises hunting because it teaches virtue, and this virtue is not simply about physical excellence or excellence in the hunt: it translates to the political order as well.

For Aristotle, virtue is synonymous with human excellence and flourishing, in Greek *eudaimonia*, often translated as happiness. The virtuous person is happy and responds to situations appropriately on a spectrum of action in accord with the golden mean. Virtue thus lies between the vices of excess or deficiency.[23] Virtue for Aristotle is both a matter of morality as well as embodied action. As he says, "One should consider a vulgar task, art, or sort of learning to be any that renders the body, the soul, or the mind of free persons useless with a view to the practices and actions of virtue."[24] Thus, for Aristotle too there is a connection between body and mind when it comes to virtue. In addition, Susan Allard-Nelson notes that, for Aristotle, excellent actions are undertaken for their own sake, are pleasurable, and are the result of deliberation and choice.[25] To be virtuous or excellent is to reach the full potential of what it is to be human. Without virtue or excellence, one does not live a complete life.[26]

VIRTUE IN THE MODERN WORLD

The role of virtue in the modern world is quite different. In fact, most strains of contemporary democratic theory tend to reject the need for virtue and excellence in the political sphere. One of the core disagreements between the Federalists and Anti-Federalists, for example, concerned the role of virtue in the political sphere. Anti-Federalists, like Machiavelli, Cicero, and other republican thinkers who preceded them, thought that virtue was a precondition for republican government. Cato expresses this sentiment, writing,

> It is alleged that the opinions and manners of the people of America, are capable to resist and prevent an extension of prerogative or oppression; but you must recollect that opinions and manners are mutable, and may not always be a permanent obstruction against the encroachments of government; that the progress of a commercial society begets luxury, the parent of inequality, the foe to virtue, and the enemy to restraint; and that ambition and voluptuousness aided by flattery, will teach magistrates, where limits are not explicitly fixed, to have separate and distinct interests from the people, besides it will not be denied that government assimilates the manners and opinions of the community to it. Therefore, a general presumption that rulers will govern well is not a sufficient security.[27]

Cato's argument is that morals and opinions change, and citizen virtue is required for any project in self-government. He goes on to say that while some may believe that Americans cannot be tyrants, Americans are like all other people and without cultivating virtue can fall into luxury, flattery, and ambition, ultimately ending in tyranny.

The Anti-Federalists lost the day, as Madisonian arguments about institutions prevailed. This is not to suggest that the Federalists did not think virtue was important, but their faith in institutions ultimately relegates consideration of virtue to a second-class issue. This is most evident in *Federalist No. 10* in which Madison argues that violent passions, compulsions, and interests can be managed due to the size of the republic and the proliferation of factions. The argument is not that citizens must be virtuous for the republic to flourish, but rather that their passions will cancel each other out. There is an argument about human nature that underlies this belief that virtue cannot be essential for democratic life. As Madison writes, "Had every Athenian citizen been a Socrates; every Athenian assembly would still have been a mob."[28]

It should not be surprising given what has been written about contemporary democratic theory in preceding chapters that many contemporary writers also disregard the importance of virtue. John Rawls's focus on reason and procedures precludes concern for virtue within citizens. The argument is instead that if democratic institutions and processes are arranged properly, desirable results will follow. Rawls is not interested in thinking about lofty virtues like courage, wisdom, or justice, but virtues that make cooperation possible. This is evident in *Political Liberalism*, where he writes that "the values of public reason not only include the appropriate use of the fundamental concepts of judgment, inference, and evidence, but also the virtues of reasonableness and fairmindedness as shown in abiding by the criteria and procedures of commonsense knowledge and accepting the methods and conclusions of science when not controversial."[29] Virtue is only used in reference to what facilitates rational debate within procedural norms. In other words, these writers hold an anti-perfectionist stance in regard to virtue.

What is evident from Rawls's description of virtue is that it lacks the inspirational character of the virtue that Pindar is showing to his readers. In the Greek world, *arête* was an aspirational ideal; in the contemporary world, virtue is stripped to preconditions for good civic life. Judith Shklar epitomizes this turn in her work *Ordinary Vices*. Shklar does not undertake a discussion of virtues, but rather the vices that make liberal democratic life impossible, chief among them cruelty. In addition, Shklar wants us to be wary of the ordinary vices of hypocrisy, snobbery, betrayal, and misanthropy.[30] The re-evaluation of these vices and their danger to democratic life relates to what Shklar calls the "liberalism of fear"—the idea that fear is antithetical to political liberty and liberalism as a project.[31] However, this focus on vices rather than inspirational virtues may be a problem. As Sharon Krause points out, in discussing the concept of "liberalism with honor," inspiration is essential.[32]

This turn away from virtue is also problematic for a few reasons. One reason is that much contemporary theory has to assume a need for virtue. As Peter Berkowitz argues, most contemporary strains of political thought, including deliberative democracy, feminism, and postmodernity, assume the need for virtue without wanting to acknowledge this need because virtue now lacks the grounding available to classical liberal thinkers, be it reason, the Sovereign, or the family.[33] The issue is not whether virtue matters or not, but whether we have the language that can successfully invoke a vision of virtue or virtues for the public sphere.

Further, virtue is important in and of itself and deserves to be recognized as part of any political and especially democratic, model of citizenship. William Galston, for example, believes that the modern state should not be agnostic or neutral to different ways of living, values, virtues, or goods in the democratic world. Galston claims that ignoring this issue is a problem and, yet, that is exactly what scholars have done. He writes, "For two generations, scholarly inquiry has been dominated by the belief that the liberal polity does not require individual virtue."[34] There is a need to discuss virtues, but the grounding to do so is lacking. What results is contemporary theorists either returning to the ancients, or making arguments for specific virtues needed in democratic life

Alasdair MacIntyre and Robert George are two of the most prominent authors who return to the ancients and Aristotle in particular. MacIntyre laments the enlightenment's rejection of Aristotelian teleology and the subsequent failure to think properly about virtue. As he writes, "What is lacking however is any clear consensus, either as to the place of virtue concepts relative to other moral concepts, or as to which dispositions are to be included within the catalogue of the virtues or the requirements imposed by particular virtues."[35] MacIntyre argues that Aristotelian tele- ology that centers on human measures and human flourishing is the only response to subjectivism or nihilism most evident in Nietzsche's work. He calls Nietzsche the "ultimate antagonist of the Aristotelian tradition" and advocates for thinking about virtues as Aristotle does: rationally and intelligibly.[36] George draws on Aristotle to argue for moral legislation defending government's role in instilling virtues among the citizenry.[37] This work shows well that Aristotle's method of thinking about virtue is not wholly lost or irrelevant to contemporary attempts to think about virtue.

Beyond reviving ancient concepts of virtue, others have tried to the- orize virtue and its role within contemporary society. One way of thinking about virtue in modern society is to follow Alexis de Tocqueville and call for watered-down virtues that are less demanding but fit for democratic life. Tocqueville, it has been pointed out, does accept that institutions mitigate the need for politically virtuous citizens.[38] For example, Tocqueville claims that "in the constitution of any people whatsoever, one reaches a point at which the lawgiver is bound to rely on the good sense and virtue of the citizens."[39] With the leveling down represented by the spread of democracy and equality, these virtues can include such attributes as self-interest rightly understood. This lacks the heroism of ancient virtues, but it is useful for maintaining liberty in the democratic world.

Authors have followed Tocqueville's insight and also advocated for certain virtues in the public world. Richard Avramenko and Richard Boyd, for example, list seven of what they call "subprime virtues" that are essential for democratic life. These include truth-telling, promise-keeping, frugality, moderation, commitment, foresight, and judgment.[40] Avramenko has also examined the role of courage and its importance in both the ancient and the democratic world.[41] Boyd elsewhere argues that civility is a virtue essential in the modern world, eschewing claims that civility is too conservative or nostalgic to still be relevant.[42] John Lombardini examines laughter in Aristotle's work to show how wittiness can be a virtue and lend itself to good democratic discourse.[43] Galston lists a variety of virtues required for the democratic world, including fidelity, self-restraint, tolerance, civility, reliability, courage, law-abidingness, loyalty, and others.[44] He makes a distinction as well between virtues fit for citizens, general virtues, virtues of leadership, and virtues of liberal politics. All of this work shows how different virtues remain necessary to the political process generally, and that certain virtues are especially necessary in the democratic world.

Finally, communitarians, a group of writers discussed in chapter 2, argue that we need to take seriously virtues that enhance good citizenship and community. Stephen Macedo, for example, discusses a variety of virtues and claims that "the liberal virtues will, nevertheless, distinguish a community flourishing in a distinctively liberal way from a community simply governed by liberal justice.[45] To build a community necessary for democratic life, the rational and hollow concepts of justice and reason are not enough—virtue must be present as well. This stance does not make communitarian thinkers anti-liberal; as Philip Selznick notes, communitarians are liberals in the tradition of John Dewey: they believe that we "should combine a spirit of liberation and question for social justice, with responsible participation in effective communities . . . it is a call for a deep reconstruction of liberal theories and policies."[46] Communitarians share a distaste for politics built on reason and institutions alone and believe that virtue is especially necessary for forming democratic communities.

However, most of the modern thinkers writing about virtue completely neglect the corporeal element that ancients thought were essential to any understanding and especially cultivation of virtue. Modern political theory does not value arête, excellence, civic virtue, and physical toil in the same way that ancients did. This oversight exists despite the persistence of the connection between these things in everyday life. In other words, society still assumes that there is a connection between physical excellence and moral virtue, while political theorists and philosophers ignore this relationship.

What emerges from these debates is a problem: communitarians do not necessarily have a mechanism for promoting the virtues that they value, and writers who do have such a mechanism, such as George, advocate for government to enforce and instill these virtues. Rather than take this route, I propose baseball as a mechanism for learning virtue. Baseball and sport can socialize virtue without requiring mass intervention on behalf of the state. Baseball, because of its everyday nature, does not advance grand or elite virtues like wisdom, but rather smaller, more ordinary virtues.

This work also continues the tradition of ancient writers taking virtue in sport seriously, especially for its impact on social and political life. I argue that athletics remain an important gathering place for visions of virtue and teaching citizens virtues through participation and spectatorship. Ancient writers understood this connection between physical *arête* and moral virtue, but it is largely ignored in contemporary work on virtue. This project addresses this oversight as well.

In the rest of this chapter I will show how baseball in particular is instructive regarding everyday virtue. First, baseball shows how virtues can be inculcated through playing at the Little League level. Second, examining baseball through time shows how morality and visions of virtue are projected into the game. Third, the politics of heroes and villains reveals much about prevailing understandings of virtue and the continuing blend between athletic excellence and moral virtue. Finally, I dive into recent debates around patriotism to show how virtue can be debated because of the sport. In the chapter's conclusion, I examine recent cheating scandals and the implications of MLB deserting any emphasis on virtue. I show how it is necessary to think carefully about sport and the citizenly virtues that can be learned through a proper experience of sport.

LITTLE LEAGUE EDUCATION

Sport and virtue are linked today as ever and the mechanisms for transmitting virtue through sport remain largely unchanged. The training of virtue in sport begins at a young age. Whether on a soccer pitch, a track, or a basketball court with friends, it begins wherever one first plays sport. As Sheryle Drewe writes, "The physical education class provides a unique arena for the practicing of moral behavior."[47] In the case of baseball, the Little League level is the beginning of an education in virtue. Of course, many have suggested the value of this type of education, and it is essentially the reason that physical education is still a large part of primary school curriculum.[48] While this book mostly focuses on spectatorship, it is worth briefly exploring how the experience of playing the game can inform understandings of virtue and later the spectatorship of virtue. Upon examination, it is clear that baseball teaches such virtues as hard work, sportsmanship, respect for rules, perseverance, and teamwork, among others. These virtues, I argue, often reflect the virtues thought to be valuable to democratic society as well.[49]

Hard work is one of the virtues learned in sport. We often think of hard work as opposed to play, and yet this claim is fairly intuitive: most sports are physical activities and thus require exertion and often stamina. In order to excel, one must work and train to improve, and this training inculcates an ability to work hard. The same is true of skill sports like baseball. One must practice throwing, fielding, sliding, and the routines of taking ground balls, fly balls, and playing catch. As Steven Overman notes, "the argot of sport is replete with the terminology of work: teamwork, workout, speed work, weight work. Coaches punctuate practice sessions with persistent admonitions to 'work harder.' Athletes have learned to rationalize their sport experience within the context of work."[50] And, of course, hard work in athletics is in line with the broader American prejudice that esteems the value of hard work. While this virtue exists independently within sport, it supports the virtues of the broader American cultural and social background.

Another virtue one learns is the virtue of good winning and good losing. There is a kind of propriety that one learns through sport. This could be called grace, either in the face of victory or defeat. But people learn early on and quickly that playing against bad winners or poor losers is not much fun. This virtue would be especially beneficial in the political sphere as well, given the rise of polarization and the politics of resentment. Good winning and losing is essential to sport and essential to democracy: a system essentially built on winners and losers.

Relatedly, baseball at youth levels inculcates a respect for the rules. If one does not respect the rules of the game, the game itself dissolves. Further, the rules are persistent and applied equally to everyone: three strikes end an at-bat, four balls allow the batter to advance to first base. Players learn a type of equality of all under the rules. This experience of equality may be valuable to democratic life, but it is something that players experience even if they were to play the game in a totalitarian regime. Franklin D. Roosevelt captured the relationship between sportsmanship, rule abidingness, and the American project, claiming, "Baseball has been called the national pastime and rightly so because it stands for the fair play, clean living and good sportsmanship which are our national heritage. That is why it has such a warm place in our hearts."[51] Baseball is especially felicitous to the language of democracy because of the equality under the rules.

Perseverance is another virtue taught through sport. This virtue is often associated with endurance sports like distance running, but it is present in baseball as well. Baseball is, after all, a sport that largely instructs participants in how to deal with failure. The best hitters are expected to get a hit less than a third of the time, meaning that the most common experience is failure and persevering in the face of this failure. As Richard Lipsky writes, "The popular biographies of players also communicate self-denial and sacrifice. We learn (if we don't already know from our own early attempts at athletic success) how they struggle and the obstacles they overcome in order to reach the privileged pinnacle of their profession."[52] Games and baseball are about struggle and persevering through these struggles. This virtue is of course useful in a democratic society, particularly a capitalistic society.

Finally, teamwork is learned through sport. In the case of baseball, pitchers cannot be successful if they are not able to work with their catcher. Fielding requires communication all across the infield, and balls hit to the outfield require relay throws that might involve an entire team. There must be an awareness of one's teammates in order to succeed. Even hitting, often thought to be one of the more individual showdowns in sport, requires a knowledge of the situation and where one's team stands in order to succeed. These examples, of course, are only from the game itself. Practice and training require myriad team drills and coordinated work that demonstrate the value of working together with one's teammates. Teamwork is a skill essential for democratic and associational life.

This list is not exhaustive of the virtues one can learn through playing baseball or other sport; rather, it is to point toward some virtues that are inherent to baseball to show that while these can be watched as well, those who play baseball from the youth level learn these virtues. The aim is to show how this connection between virtue and baseball is developed from a very young age. This gives participant's ideas about what is appropriate and inappropriate behavior and what is praiseworthy and what is blameworthy. Jacques Barzun, for example, found that baseball teaches other virtues:

> Accuracy and speed, the practiced eye and hefty arm, the mind
> to take in and readjust to the unexpected, the possession of
> more than one talent and willingness to work in harness without
> special orders—these are the American virtues that shine in
> baseball. There has never been a good player who was dumb.
> Beef and bulk and mere endurance count for little, judgment
> and daring for much. . . . Baseball is a kind of collective chess
> with arms and legs in full play under sunlight.[53]

Notice that Barzun pays special attention to the mental virtues cultivated
by the game. While playing is an embodied and physical act, the game is
not solely or even primarily about cultivating physical excellence. Rather,
it tests and encourages mental and, I suggest, moral virtues.

Further, this connection between virtue and the game is part of the
political lexicon. As Bill Clinton noted, "Baseball also teaches us tolerance.
It teaches us to play as hard as we can and still be friends when the game's
over, to respect our differences, and to be able to lose with dignity as well
as win with joy—but real tolerance for differences."[54] His remarks point
to some of the virtues discussed above, as well as tolerance, which will
be discussed later. It is clear that these virtues learned from sport are not
solely about physical prowess but are civic assets as well.

Indeed, it is easy to see how many of the virtues learned through
playing the game are amenable to democratic life in America. For example, Lipsky, writing about baseball, notes how the game was used as both
a refuge and a socializing force for immigrants: "The immigrants were
linked in the native American mind with crime, perversion, and radicalism. Baseball became an excellent way for the newcomer to escape
moral censure. The folk understanding saw the game as a 'builder of
character.' It was felt sports developed the desirable social character traits
that would benefit American society . . . the team was seen to foster the
ideals of honorable struggle and fair play, which, it was felt, translated
into the language of self-government and good citizenship."[55] It should
be clear from this example and those before that virtue learned through
sport is meaningful for democratic politics. However, beyond the virtue
learned through playing sport, I suggest that some virtues can be learned
through spectatorship.

This spectatorship, it should be noted, can also be formative because
it is not only about adults watching games. While children do not often
watch CSPAN, they do watch sports and baseball. Watching the game

reinforces the lessons learned on the Little League diamond. This process works through the cultivated display of virtue in baseball. The political horizons of even young people are influenced by the displays at the ball-park. The process normalizes and socializes dominant virtues and it is thus especially important to take this process seriously.

To make this argument, I will illustrate the process by looking at how different eras of baseball reflect American morality and how the politics of heroes and villains can reinforce visions of what is virtuous and what is not. These virtues both reflect civic virtues, not simply physical excellence, and serve to reinforce these virtues through spectatorship. I will then turn to the contemporary virtue of patriotism and how it is displayed in baseball and watched by spectators. Finally, I show what happens when baseball is mired in scandal and undermines rules of fair play.

ERAS OF MORALITY: HEROES, VILLAINS, AND THE POLITICS OF VIRTUE IN MAJOR LEAGUE BASEBALL

Spectatorship provides insight into how many of the virtues and concerns of the larger society are reflected in baseball. This enduring connection illustrates the power of sport as a center for understanding civic virtue. Others have made similar claims. Notably, Steven Overman has argued that sport in America is an expression of Calvinism and capitalism, cre-ating what he calls "the Protestant Ethic" that dominates American sport. For Overman, these virtues include worldly asceticism, rationalization, goal-directed behavior, achieved status, individualism, work ethic, and time ethic.[56] The relationship works both ways: the social and cultural context influences the games, and the virtues associated with games and playing these games in turn reinforces the virtues. Overman's analysis of this relationship is persuasive, but I want to move away from discussing specific virtues to demonstrate instead how games can reflect social values and therefore reinforce them. To do so, I will look at a few eras of baseball. These "eras" are not meant to be definitive, and while many historians have strict eras into which they divide baseball history, that is not my intention. What I hope to show is how the game can respond to the broader society outside of it and be a place for reinforcing conceptions of civic virtue.

While looking at eras, I will also highlight the heroes and villains of the time to gain traction on understandings of virtue that remain essential to sport and the social context of the time. Recently, Ari Kohen shed light on the importance of heroism in political theory.[57] Kohen traces the shifting vision of heroism offered by Plato and Socrates instead of the Homeric world, but when talking about contemporary heroes he still focuses on war heroes. Indeed, war heroes are great examples for understanding how we view civic virtue, but the moment of war is extreme and outside of everyday life (ideally). Further, the complicated nature of modern warfare obscures war heroics in a way that is alien to the Homeric model of heroism. In sport, however, this type of heroism is alive; especially in baseball, a sport that features the one-on-one battle between pitcher and hitter as its prime action.

Heroes are often used as moral exemplars to reinforce the prevailing understanding of civic virtue. Villains, on the other hand, represent the form of corruption that is predominately viewed as problematic during the time. The politics of heroes and villains also highlights an aspect of virtue often missing from the discourse: the symbolism of the individual for collective understandings of good and bad. Athletes, especially in baseball, come to stand in for something more than the athlete themselves. They become character types and blueprints or warning signs to children and adults alike. These heroes will be discussed within the context of what I am calling their "eras of morality" to show how baseball came to be a locus for understanding American civic virtue beyond simply athletic excellence.

Early baseball had informal beginnings and came from games played in England. Baseball originally spread in urban environments despite its rural appeal. While there were popular spectator events where thousands of fans would watch baseball games before 1860, baseball took off after the Civil War.[58] As Katz writes, "Throughout the nineteenth century, it might be argued, politics remained America's favorite spectator sport. . . . The postwar era marked baseball's first golden age. Laborers could beat gentlemen, mechanics best attorneys, Southerners defeat Northerners, or Baptists battle Methodists on the field with no hard feelings. For a while, blacks would challenge whites."[59] After the Civil War, the game spread throughout the country and, for a time, had a democratic character that would not be entirely restored until much later, and perhaps not yet today.

From the 1870s to 1900, the game began to be professionalized with stadiums, clubs, and more formal organizations. As teams were no longer restricted to gentlemen's clubs, the character of the game changed. Bill James highlights that the first generation of players came from gentlemen's clubs and, as a result, "Respect for umpires was the accepted norm, and prominent citizens often served as volunteer umpires. With the coming of professionalism, and professional umpires, this went out the window, and the game turned rough."[60] When the game turned rough, the game turned violent, with rowdy players hurling abuse at one another and playing aggressively, while fans joined in, abusing players and umpires alike. As Connie Mack, a player, manager, and eventual owner claimed,

> Baseball historians dwell considerably on the "days of violence." These days make exciting reading, but it should be considered in proper perspective, that during the same times there was violence everywhere; it was an age of violence. There was violence in the Wild West when it was being settled. There was violence in the upbuilding of the country. Political campaigns had their riots. Three presidents were assassinated. Labor had its uprisings. Early baseball was characteristic of its times.[61]

Mack's words show clearly the relationship between moral character of the times and games themselves. The violence of the early professional period of baseball was a symptom of the times. In a violent world, America's pastime was a violent game.

Early baseball heroes were more regional and diverse and did not ascend to nationally loved or universal icons. Describing baseball before the 1920s, David Voigt gives voice to this dynamic:

> For rural-minded fans there were farm boy types like Wagner, who learned to throw by tossing rocks with unerring accuracy; for romantics, there was the dashing French gallant, Lajoie; for power-lovers, there was the slugging Sam Crawford; for admirers of primitive virtues, there was Indian Jim Thorpe; for southern rednecks, there was the foul-mouthed, illiterate Joe Jackson, once characterized as "Ty Cobb from the neck down." . . . Had there been no superman like Cobb, the mantle of consensus hero likely would have gone to Walter Johnson, the hard throwing pitcher. A virtuous Kansas farmboy, Johnson went on to win 414 games with the lowly Washington Senators, setting shutout and strikeout marks in twenty years of pitching.[62]

Cobb and Johnson stuck out for two very different reasons. Cobb was almost certainly the best player of the dead-ball era, but he was as well known for his cruelty as he was for his ability, infamously spiking other players, attacking a handicapped fan, and espousing a vitriolic racism not even publicly acceptable at that time.[63] Johnson, on the other hand, was held back by his obscurity, though his character and merit as a heroic figure was not in doubt. President Coolidge said of Johnson, "I am sure that I speak for all when I say that he has been a wholesome influence on clean living and clean sport."[64]

Because of the sport's beginnings, early baseball in the "dead-ball era" attracted its fair share of rough characters. Baseball players were known for drinking and questionable moral standards. In many ways, this side of the game culminated in the Black Sox Scandal of 1918. In the scandal, eight Chicago White Sox players colluded with gamblers to throw the World Series to the Cincinnati Reds. This was perceived as an existential threat to the game, and an effort to purge baseball of this seedy and immoral element took place. The league hired a federal judge, Kennesaw Mountain Landis, as its first commissioner, and he subsequently handed out lifetime bans to all eight players.[65] This was the culmination of calls to restore sobriety and uprightness to the game. Landis was as draconian a commissioner as he was a judge. As Robert Burk writes, "Landis's crackdowns on player conduct, most prominent in the early years of his commissionership, concentrated on four areas of contract violations: (1) game-fixing and similar on-field corruption, (2) off-field moral misconduct, (3) unsanctioned barnstorming or other money-making activities, and (4) contract jumping."[66] Landis's actions, regardless of his own personal faults, helped the game overcome its rough character and align more fully with American values.

It is not a surprise that the true era of baseball heroes as such began after Landis's crackdowns on "immoral behavior." Cleaning up the game brought the game in line with American values and allowed for the elision between physical and moral excellence. As Burk writes, "Tighter regulation of players' moral behaviors, in turn, promised to boost employees' on-field productivity and images as matinee idols in the New Era's increased marketing of stars."[67] The result was a boom in baseball business. The 1920s era of baseball resemble in many ways the era of American exceptionalism. Babe Ruth initiated a change in the game that has had a profound impact ever since. Before Ruth, home runs were not very common. Baseball was a game about making contact and running the bases. Runs were relatively scarce, and the game was more strategic. The home run bypasses that style of play, and Ruth hit more homers than anyone.

Ruth's achievement, however, was more than quantitative. Cassuto and Grant claim that Ruth's greatness was that "he changed his world and the choice of statistics we use to measure it. Viewed in this light, it is the non-quantitative accomplishment of Ruth—the way he changed the measure of success in baseball—that should define him as 'great.' In other words, Ruth's greatness derives not just from his numerical greatness, but also from his 'cultural work.' "[68] The change wrought by Ruth is a cultural one as much as it is a strategic change within the game. This style of play symbolizes an understanding of virtue that is less team based and puts more emphasis on individual excellence and largess.

Babe Ruth remains in many ways among the greatest sports hero in America. Ruth was a sensation and cultural icon at the time. As Amber Roessner writes, "He was so popular that New York Yankees owner Jacob Ruppert had to build a whole new stadium to accommodate his hero-worshippers . . . the venue became known as the 'house that Ruth built.' . . . Sportswriters began portraying Ruth for what he was, a larger-than-life figure."[69] The legendary status of Ruth is not really in question, but what he represented and his embodiment of the times can be lost. Ruth was famous for excess—excess eating, drinking, and hitting home runs—in a time of excess.

What also makes Ruth's case so interesting is that the type of virtue he symbolizes is a kind of defiance to tyranny. Ruth excelled in a time of sobriety not through being sober, but through being excessive. His career spanned the time before and after the prohibition era: both the 18th and 20th amendments were passed while Ruth was in uniform. Ruth's virtue is thus a type of defiance and insistence on liberty and individuality. And yet, as times changed, he evolved. As Cassuto writes, "His outside embodiment of reckless consumption made him an ideal avatar of the Roaring Twenties . . . But Ruth's fame continued to expand even after the Great Depression hit. At that point he became a part of the media-driven dream factory that manufactured hope for a stricken population, even appearing in movies as himself when he wasn't playing baseball."[70] Much has been written about Ruth, and much more could be said, but I want to emphasize his role as a hero in allowing the virtues of his era to be articulated. Ruth represented a shift in the scope of baseball and America, he was voracious as the country expanded, and when the bottom fell out, he became an aspiration and an idea for people lacking hope. He was a figure of national character, a symbol that extended beyond America. As Cassuto points out, when Japanese soldiers charged U.S. troops during

World War II, one of the chants they yelled was "To hell with Babe Ruth!"[71] For many at home and abroad, Ruth and America were synonymous.

The World Wars, particularly World War II, also created an image of the citizen soldier in which the virtues of self-sacrifice and service came to the fore. While many players, including Ty Cobb and Christy Mathewson, fought in World War I, the Second World War gave a bigger stage to the virtues of self-sacrifice and service embodied in the citizen solider. The two most representative players of this model are Hank Greenberg and Ted Williams. These players did not have the outsized absurdity of a Ruth, but a humbler vision of what it meant to be to be a good baseball player and American. During the war, baseball was not set aside, but remained a valuable outlet for American life. When Commissioner Landis asked President Roosevelt if baseball should continue during the war, the president was emphatic that it should:

> I honestly feel that it would be best for the country to keep baseball going. There will be fewer people unemployed and everybody will work longer hours and harder than before. And that means that they ought to have a chance for recreation and for taking their minds of their work even more than before. . . . Here is another way of looking at it—if 300 teams use 5,000 or 6,000 players, these players are a definite recreational asset to at least 20,000,000 of their fellow citizens—and that in my judgment is thoroughly worthwhile.[72]

Roosevelt viewed the institution of baseball as necessary to maintaining the nation's spirits, and the new heroes epitomized a more austere era.

Greenberg is influential in part because he was the first Jewish player to become a true hero and star of the game. The 1930s were an especially difficult time to be a Jewish baseball player or citizen in America. Greenberg's role as a hero to the Jewish community, especially the marginalized Jewish community in Detroit, has been well covered.[73] Greenberg was a standard barrier and consistently described as a self-made player.[74]

While Ted Williams did not have to deal with racial or ethnic discrimination, he was a similar hero, a player dedicated to the game and who played it well without excess flair. Both men fought in the war, and it makes sense that the citizen soldier ideal type of virtue would be more of a team player than someone like Ruth. Williams was famous for avoiding fanfare. Updike describes Williams's final at-bat in Fenway, a home run, after which, Williams, "ran as he always ran out home runs—hurriedly, unsmiling, head down, as if our praise were a storm of rain to get out of. He didn't tip his cap. Though we thumped, wept, and chanted 'We want Ted' for minutes after he hid in the dugout, he did not come back."[75] In the World War II era, the virtues of service and self-sacrifice came to the fore, and did so on a stage larger than ever, reinforcing what were thought to be essential civic virtues that later came to define the "greatest generation."

The period of integration was a period in which baseball became a ground for shifting conceptions of civic virtue, particularly regarding the value of egalitarianism, discussed in chapter 3. It is worth thinking about desegregation as a moment of shifting virtue with Robinson's role at the center of this change. For the first time, baseball began to showcase tolerance as a virtue. In this era, baseball—often considered an especially democratic game—made a great stride toward actually becoming so. Robinson himself reflected a political awareness and conception of equality never before seen in the game. This is seen well in his autobiography *I Never Had It Made*. The concept of "having it made" is a motif in the book, and Robinson explains its meaning, writing, "I'm grateful for all the breaks and honors and opportunities I've had, but I always believe I won't have it made until the humblest black kid in the most remote backwoods of America has it made."[76] Robinson's vision is relational, whereas the virtue embodied by someone like Ruth was individualistic. Robinson's ideal of excellence and virtue involved uplifting others. He wrote, "A life is not important except in the impact it has on other lives . . . I cannot possibly say I have it made while our country drives full speed ahead to deeper rifts between men and women of varying colors, speeds along a course toward more and more racism."[77] For Robinson, his individual achievements are not primarily what his struggle was about; it was about creating a tolerant environment (tolerance is a relational virtue) that offered other black Americans opportunity as well.

The portrayal of this new kind of hero is important for understanding the context of the time. Robinson's book was originally printed in 1972, and he was outspoken about his views in the press long before then. From the vantage of spectatorship, one can begin to realize the impact that such a hero would have. Robinson actively challenged the values of his time and context to promote this particular virtue. Robinson was not as universally beloved as someone like Ruth because of this necessary antagonism, something he recognized. As he put it to a reporter, "If you think of me as the kind of Negro who's come to the conclusion that he isn't going to beg for anything, that he will be reasonable but he damned well is tired of being patient . . . I want to be thought of as [that] kind of Negro and if it makes some people uncomfortable, if it makes me the kind of guy they can't like, that's tough."[78] Robinson's example, detailed in chapter 3, shows how politics of virtue can not only be reflected in the sport, but shaped by the sport as well. Ruth was a symbol of his times; Robinson shaped his context.[79]

After integration, baseball spread westward. Some of the rules changed, with the American League implementing the designated hitter in 1973. The later 1960s and throughout the 1970s was a time of illicit drug use, radical changes, and new styles in baseball. Teams began wearing flamboyant uniforms, players grew out their hair and beards, and the ballpark became an arena for hashing out social issues. This was evident in a player such as Dock Ellis, symbolic of the times for his radicalism and subversion of norms. The broader context was the unfolding of politicizing sport, both on college campuses and elsewhere.[80] There are many notable heroes from this era. Roberto Clemente in many ways embodied the athlete as community builder, as discussed in chapter 2. Other heroes of the age included two far-different players: Pete Rose and Henry Aaron.

Pete Rose was initially thought to be the image of hard work incarnate. His nickname was Charlie Hustle; he broke Ty Cobb's all-time hit record, a feat many thought impossible. Rose, however, committed baseball's one major sin when he gambled on the game. Ever since, he has been exiled and remains a largely seedy character, refusing to reform himself, give up gambling, or stop marketing himself to return to baseball's good graces. While he is still revered in some circles, his lack of moral virtue has prevented his physical excellence from being appreciated and recognized in the way it otherwise would have been. Viewed via a moral paradigm, Rose lacks moderation; his hard work in baseball was overshadowed by his need for instant gratification off the field. Rose is a clear example of how moral virtue, or lack thereof, shapes how a player is remembered and viewed in broader society. It is telling that no amount of excellence on the field could overshadow his off-field behavior; he remains an exile from the baseball world.

Henry Aaron, on the other hand, is a hero held up as a paragon of virtue. Aaron broke Babe Ruth's all-time home run record, and did so with grace. Aaron himself was moderate and modest, and his achievement did much to display tolerance as a virtue. While Robinson broke the color barrier, race was still at the forefront when Aaron played. The prospect of Aaron breaking Ruth's record was fraught with danger, as he received death threats for daring to near the record of someone like the Babe. Yet, when he hit the home run, the crowd in Atlanta cheered. As Vin Scully exulted in his broadcast to millions over the radio, "What a marvelous moment for baseball, what a marvelous moment for Atlanta and Georgia, what a marvelous moment for the country and the world. A black man is getting a standing ovation in the deep south for breaking the record of an all-time baseball idol."[81] Scully noted that Aaron's achievement was an important moment for toleration in baseball, and possible only because of Aaron.

Aaron's moderation was also on display as he aged and remained quiet and in shape: a contrast to the man whose record he broke. Scully himself noted the difference between Ruth and Aaron. As he said, "You could not, I guess, get two more opposite men. The Babe, big and garrulous and oh so sociable, and oh so immense in all of his appetites. And then the quiet lad out of Mobile, Alabama, slender, and stayed slender through his career."[82] Hank Aaron displayed professionalism and moderation, showing the value of a tolerant sport with room for a diverse group of heroes.

The period from the late 1980s to the 1990s ushered in a new era of baseball, in which the home run returned in a big way, a stretch of years generally known as the steroid era. Power was valued, and the nation was transfixed by the chase to surpass Roger Maris's and Babe Ruth's home run records. Many, including then Commissioner Bud Selig, credit this home run chase with rescuing baseball from the dire straits it had entered after the baseball strike of 1994.[83] Eventually, Mark McGwire and Sammy Sosa both broke Maris's record, hitting seventy and sixty-six home runs, respectively, in 1998. Barry Bonds would go on to break Hank Aaron's all-time record. All three of these players were throwbacks to the 1920s model of icon embodying individualism, power, and panache. However, all three were implicated in the steroid scandal, and eventually became heroes no more. McGwire and Sosa had to testify before Congress about their steroid use, with McGwire refusing to speak and Sosa denying his involvement. The shame was complete.

The fallen icon status is most evident in the case of Barry Bonds. Barry Bonds, by most statistical measures, is the greatest baseball player of all time. His achievements on the field were remarkable. Yet Bonds was antagonistic with the media and portrayed as overly self-centered (it is worth noting the role race likely played in this narrative as well). Bonds did not embody the type of baseball player that people wanted, and he frankly did not care (which is, in its own way, admirable). His achievements on the field were Herculean, but since he lacked the moral character and set of virtues that most people value, he was always an anti-hero, even before his steroid use was revealed. Bonds was neither truthful about his steroid use, nor moderate in his abuse of illegal drugs. His moral failing cast a shadow over his physical excellence that remains today.

This stance on the moral character of athletes is different in baseball than other sports, especially regarding steroid use. Baseball has the most stringent programs for steroid users, whereas other sports do not rigorously test athletes and do not ban or even shame athletes who use performance-enhancing drugs. Michael Butterworth offers an explanation as to why this may be the case:

> The disproportionate attention given to baseball was a product of the game's cultural mythology and its connection to American identity. Even though the game is no longer the most popular American sport, it nevertheless maintains its status as a cultural touchstone of American character. More specifically, baseball embodies and evokes mythic ideals of innocence and purity, ideals that were threatened by the emergent crisis over performance enhancing drugs.[84]

Baseball's role in civic life makes it an arbiter of morality, and the moral failings of players like Bonds, McGwire, Roger Clemens, and others was a threat to the ideal of the game, including the ethos of innocence and purity—a place for heroes who not only excel on the field, but provide examples of moral and civic virtue.

Baseball has a way of remembering and memorializing the past and the heroes of the past. This mechanism is the Hall of Fame, which indicates the degree to which physical excellence and moral character are entwined: it also displays the importance of narrative to legend building. This is especially evident in the wake of the steroid scandal. The Hall of Fame has thus far refused to admit known steroid users, or even some players suspected of using steroids, into the Hall despite their merits on the field. The doors are shut now to the heroes of the recent past, and this reflects the game's complicated relationship to the players on the field. The game is not simply about physical excellence; it is about moral virtues as well. Just as Alcibiades thought that his athletic achievement indicated political merit, we believe that athletic virtue should be connected to moral and civic virtue. Our baseball players are supposed to be more than baseball players: they are supposed to be heroes, role models, and reflections of our own values. The Hall is one mechanism of reinforcing this point and reveals that to think about baseball without considering the role virtue plays in our understanding of baseball is to err.

CONTEMPORARY VIRTUE ON DISPLAY: PATRIOTISM AT THE PARK

While there are many contemporary virtues on display at the ballpark, including the virtues that are inherently present in sport such as hard work, teamwork, and sportsmanship, there are also politicized debates about what constitutes a virtue and what is appropriate to display in ballparks. I want to highlight one of these debates among others and focus on how a virtue like patriotism can be debated within the sphere of the ballpark. This case study is meant to highlight the processes I have been describing and show how the ballpark is a venue for watching visions of virtue, and contesting them as well. If baseball can reinforce ideas about virtue, one must ask, what is the sport reinforcing, and are the virtues that it imparts good or bad for democratic life? I argue that while baseball can enforce a positive vision of American patriotism, over-militarization of these spectacles undermines this more positive and leisurely vision.

Patriotism may seem like a strange virtue to examine; it is certainly not an obvious virtue like wisdom, courage, moderation, justice, or piety. Yet, love and dedication to country has often been regarded as a positive attribute. Patriotism, however, is an Aristotelian virtue in that it exists on a continuum, and its extreme form of jingoistic nationalism is clearly a vice.[85] Patriotism as a virtue resides between this extreme and zealous attachment and blind faith in one's country and a detached cosmopolitanism. Alexis de Tocqueville makes this distinction as well between what he calls instinctive patriotism and well-considered patriotism. The former is an ephemeral "unpondered passion," while the latter is more rational, creative, and lasting.[86] Tocqueville praises Americans for striving for this type of well-considered patriotism, which he thinks is essential for democratic liberty.

Moderated patriotism, existing between two extremes, is a democratic good. Bounded patriotism is useful for maintaining liberal institutions and self-government.[87] Rousseau links love of liberty to the civic virtue of patriotism in *The Government of Poland*.[88] Sean Richey has shown that what he calls "constructive patriotism" contra "blind patriotism" can actually increase civic participation.[89] For the purposes of this section, then, patriotism as a virtue means love and devotion to one's country without a blind devotion to country or jingoistic zealotry. This virtue, I suggest, can be learned through baseball if it is appropriately cultivated.

Patriotism is a useful virtue to examine in baseball in part because it has long been associated with the sport. Part of the connection between baseball and American patriotism is that baseball is considered America's pastime. As such, baseball is wrapped up with a vision of what it means to be American. As discussed in chapter 3, part of becoming "American" for many immigrants was playing baseball, and desegregation expanded this beyond the narrow confines of white America. Baseball, as an American game, carried this special importance from the beginning. Walt Whitman said that baseball "belongs as much to our institutions, fits into them as significantly, as our constitutions, laws: is just as important in the sum total of our historic life."[90] So how is it that baseball becomes a realm for spectators watching and expressing patriotism?

Baseball at its highest levels has been used, even early on, by presidents to rally support, show that they belong, and display that they are normal Americans like other average, everyday people. A collection by William Mead and Paul Dickson called *Baseball: The Presidents' Game* compiles evidence from all over showing that every president, with the exception of Rutherford B. Hayes "has had some link with baseball or baseball under one of its earlier names."[91] The cartoons, documents, and photographs within testify to this fact. Their collection covers the years through the presidency of George H.W. Bush, but Bill Clinton, George W. Bush, and Barack Obama have all jumped at the opportunity to associate themselves with the game as well.

The most visible way presidents interact with the sport is through throwing out the first pitch. As Mead and Dickson note, "Throwing out the first ball of the baseball season is an unwritten and valuable fringe benefit that comes with the job of American president. Politically, he wins no matter how weak his arm or how wild his throw. No king or dictator could create such a lofty yet playful role in a joyous setting of innocent springtime celebration."[92] Presidents gain much through this democratic association with the American pastime, and the photo opportunities have continued since the ritual began in 1910. The first pitch is a way of linking baseball to America, and vice versa, and all presidents are offered the opportunity to affirm their role in that ritual. It is not hard to find quotes of presidents praising the role of baseball in American life, and this project has indeed cited many such instances. While these may seem like easy ways for politicians to gain points, they do affirm the need for freedom and leisure in democratic life.

The link between baseball and Americana makes it a fertile ground for debates around patriotism and what it means to be American. Because baseball and America helped shape each other, this should come as no surprise. As Voigt notes, because baseball history parallels American history and offers insight into our national character, to explore this connection is to "gain a better understanding of what being an American has meant, now means, and may come to mean."[93] The fear among critics is that nationalism veers into illiberal places and becomes authoritarian; the hope is that institutions like baseball can be a venue for patriotism that supports liberal nationalism.

There are grave doubts that baseball is an avenue for a normatively desirable type of patriotic display. These concerns are not new. As Voigt pointed out in 1976, "Can a pluralistic society like ours have a national anything? I think that trying to be national in our kind of cultural clime is a millstone about the neck of the game that tries. . . . This might well be the hour for baseball men to abdicate their nationalistic claims before the absurdity of such claims is too far gone."[94] The issue Voigt and others see is the militarism involved in the displays. Games now routinely involve the singing of the national anthem and sometimes feature militaristic displays (more on this below). While singing the national anthem is generally viewed as an overall positive practice, these displays promote overzealous jingoism rather than moderated patriotic sentiment. Indeed, what purpose does flying a bomber over a stadium convey other than to symbolize American ability to destroy another country or its capacity to defend itself? Both of these possibilities indicate a context defined by external threat.

The criticism of these spectacles has grown especially in the wake of 9/11. After the terrorist attack, baseball teams began singing "God Bless America" during the seventh-inning stretch, a ritual that continues in many stadiums today. As Michael Butterworth notes, "September 11 tributes continued in baseball and other sports well past any time during which sport might reasonably have been called strictly diversionary. . . . Moreover, as baseball became a ritualistic performance of American faith and patriotism, it supported George W. Bush's declaration of war against evil and subsequent invasion of Iraq."[95] Butterworth's claim is that these displays served to unite Americans not by something they have in common, but through a fear of the other. Ballparks were thus not spaces fit for democratic life; they did not accept a plurality of opinion but reinforced a particular vision of patriotism and nationalism. Essentially, baseball became a platform for conservative values, particularly a vision of what it means to be American.

Many of the patriotic displays exhibited at sports arenas throughout the country are paid for by the U.S. government. The issue of paid patriotism has come under fire, notably in a report by former Senators John McCain and Jeff Flake. They write: "In all, the military services reported $53 million in spending on marketing and advertising contracts with sports teams between 2012 and 2015. More than $10 million of that total was paid to teams in the National Football League (NFL), Major League Baseball (MLB), National Basketball Association (NBA), National Hockey League (NHL), and Major League Soccer (MLS)."[96] While McCain and Flake detail that much of this money went to the NFL, many teams in MLB also accepted money. Department of defense funds went to teams in the following amounts: Cleveland Indians $12,000, Pittsburgh Pirates $18,000, Houston Astros $25,000, Arizona Diamondbacks $40,000, Texas Rangers $75,000, Philadelphia Phillies $48,085, New York Mets $51,000, Milwaukee Brewers $80,000, Boston Red Sox $100,000, and the Atlanta Braves $450,000.[97] Some of these funds were for items such as signs, tickets, and recruiting tactics, but other funds went toward on-field presentations, sponsoring military appreciation games, paying teams to perform "God Bless America," and other spectacles of patriotic display.

Major League Baseball should think carefully about whether this is the type of virtue it wants to cultivate. This militarized patriotism promotes war and obedience rather than a thoughtful and democratic love of country. Sport in many ways both symbolizes and realizes democratic liberty through its celebration of leisure; these militaristic displays are neither democratic nor leisurely. Further, the existence of this kind of paid patriotism cheapens the genuine displays of patriotism at baseball parks and takes agency away from the spectators. Ideally, the stadium should be a place for expression as well as dissent. It was evident in the community chapter, for example, that baseball teams can give space to many different communities and viewpoints. Why is the issue of nationalism currently treated as a one-sided issue?

Put otherwise, the question could be, why is there no Colin Kaepernick in Major League Baseball?[98] This is an issue that has received some attention. Adam Jones, for example, spoke out in 2016 when asked why there was no protest figure in MLB as there was in the NFL. He answered, "We already have two strikes against us, so you might as well not kick yourself out of the game. In football, you can't kick them out. You need those players. In baseball, they don't need us. Baseball is a white man's sport."[99] Jones's comments highlight current racial disparities between the sports. Since his comments, Kaepernick has been blacklisted from the NFL and no teams will offer him a job, despite inferior players getting contracts. Still, Jones's perspective is important: maybe there is not contestation around nationalistic displays because there is no room for that dissent.

Another reason why there is no Colin Kaepernick is because people do not notice Colin Kaepernicks in baseball. The everyday character of the game makes the protests more subtle, so they do not stand out as they do when Kaepernick takes a knee once a week on Sunday. Well before Kaepernick, in fact, there was Carlos Delgado. In 2004, when many stadiums still played "God Bless America" every seventh inning, Delgado protested the Iraq War by remaining in the dugout. William Rhoden reports that after the United States invaded Iraq, "Delgado, in his own quiet way, said that for him, enough was enough. He had stood for "God Bless America" through the 2003 season but vowed not to do so in 2004. In an act of a simple, mostly unnoticed, protest against the war, Delgado, a thirty-two-year-old first baseman, chose to remain in the dugout while "God Bless America" was played."[100] Delgado sat, and people did not get upset as they did when Kaepernick took a knee. There are many ways to interpret this phenomenon, but it shows that baseball allows more room for genuine dissent than sports such as football. Rhoden goes on to relate that teammates and the team president supported Delgado in his protest.

What do these examples illustrate? They show, first, how baseball is vulnerable to overly embracing a vision of America that politicians and the commissioner want to enforce. However, the nature of the game itself opens the way for expression of patriotism along with dissent. Delgado's dissent was quiet, but it was not banned; nor did he become a focal point for derision and hatred. Fans in the stands can also participate in these activities or not. The constant grind of the game makes the stakes much lower than in other sports and consequently less demanding of people. If you prefer not to stand or remove your cap during the anthem, that's your choice.

As a result of this more relaxed atmosphere, we can begin to theorize baseball as a more appropriate space for embracing a kind of moderated democratic patriotism through the play element in the game with which spectators engage. Rather than sing "God Bless America," it is possible to build a sense of patriotism out of a less polarizing song such as "Take Me Out to the Ballgame." That song is a staple at Wrigley Field, and its lyrics—which oddly prompt a large collection of people at a baseball game to sing about wanting to go to a baseball game—are more whimsical and about the game itself. The lyrics focus not on ways that Americans are divided, but on a very tangible thing, the baseball game, that has brought people together. Baseball games can then be thought of as the source of national pride: the "democratic diversion" without which democracy cannot thrive. There is no need for paid flyovers or militaristic spectacles; there is a way to express and fulfill a civic virtue—patriotism—through sport that is more liberal and democratic than such nationalistic spectacles. The everyday nature of baseball actually provides an opportunity for the game to become a meaningful place for realizing a healthier form of patriotism. On a cold Wednesday in April in Minneapolis, you won't likely see fighter jets flying over the stadium. Instead, people from a similar region come together over something that they have in common, a coming-together that is demonstrative of a healthy civic pride.

CONCLUSION: CHEATING SCANDALS AND THE ABSENCE OF VIRTUE

This chapter is mostly filled with examples of how baseball can inculcate or reflect societal virtues, but it is worth ending by considering what happens when baseball does the opposite. What if, rather than striving to maintain the ancient connection between sport and virtue, baseball, due to business concerns, increased pressure to win, and through a lack of concern for fairness and legacy, instead embraces vices such as cheating? Somewhat recent events such as the Astros cheating scandal lends insight into this breakdown.

First, I should note that this discussion is not intended to be a full, in-depth exploration of the cheating scandal. Such an exploration is a book-length project in itself. I will instead examine the basics of these scandals, who was punished, what this suggests about baseball's role in promoting virtue, and the spectator response (or lack thereof, due to COVID-19).

Cheating is hardly a new phenomenon in baseball, but has long been one of the few cardinal sins in the sport. When the White Sox allegedly threw the 1919 World Series, for example, eight players received lifetime bans from Kenesaw Mountain Landis. Pete Rose also received a lifetime ban from the sport due to gambling on baseball while he was a manager. This does not mean various forms of deception and underhanded practices are not part of the game. Sign-stealing, in fact, is often considered an art that is fair game. The line that has been established is that sign-stealing must be done by players and cannot involve technology. The evolution of video and instant replay obviously provides a tempting opportunity to violate this taboo, and recent cheating scandals have indeed centered on stealing signs with technology.

As of this writing in early 2020, the Houston Astros were at the center of a massive cheating scandal. While there are conflicting accounts, the general charge is that the Houston Astros employed multiple cheating schemes, the most infamous being the project "Codebreaker" and the trashcan scheme.[101] Project Codebreaker implicated many levels of the organization and involved stealing signs with an advanced video system and transmitting those signs to a baserunner to share with the hitter at the plate. This evolved into stealing signs with technology and banging on a trashcan when a pitcher was about to throw a breaking ball. This meant that hitters could expect what was coming, regardless of whether anyone was on base or not. It is possible to watch footage of their games and hear the trashcan indicating what pitch was on the way. Needless to say, this offers hitters a great advantage.

The Astros did not simply use this unfair advantage in close games, but even continued banging on the trash can in blowouts. This did not mean only that the Astros won games they did not deserve to win at the expense of other teams, it also ruined careers for some players. Mike Bolsinger, for example, came on in relief for the Blue Jays against the Astros, and the Astros scored four runs in one-third of an inning off the journeyman pitcher. After the 16-7 Astros win, Bolsinger was sent down to the minors and has not played in the major leagues since. After the revelations of the Astros' sign stealing, Bolsinger retaliated by suing the organization.[102] It is difficult to know how many other careers were affected by the Astros' willingness to break the rules.

In 2017, the Astros managed to win the World Series. Again, it is difficult to tell how much of a role cheating ultimately played in their victory, but the Los Angeles Dodgers team that they defeated were not pleased when details of the Astros' misdeeds came to light. The Boston Red Sox won the 2018 World Series against the Dodgers, only for it to be revealed that they too were implicated in a cheating scandal. Local governments in Los Angeles reacted, and the city council called on MLB to strip both World Series wins and give them to the Dodgers. As councilman Gil Cedillo put it, "This crisis goes beyond the sport and the game, it goes to the very core of being American. This could send an important message to little boys and girls that you need to play hard by the rules, or you can learn that cheating is the new normal. We want it to be clear that this city spoke up for its team."[103] Here is an instance of local government officials doing more than those in charge at MLB to protect the quality and character of the game with an eye toward instilling virtues in young fans. The virtues he notes—playing hard, playing by the rules, and showing young fans that vices like cheating are punished—are important.

Although this scheme implicated nearly all of the Astros players and multiple levels of the organization, subsequent punishments were minimal to nonexistent. In total, the Astros' GM Jeff Luhnow, head coach A.J. Hinch, and bench coach Alex Cora, were the only people punished, each serving one-year bans. At this point, Alex Cora was with the Red Sox as the manager as they were mired in a cheating scandal of their own (where again little accountability has been enforced). All three men were fired by their organizations. The Astros also had to forfeit draft picks and pay $5 million. After the ban elapsed, the Detroit Tigers hired A.J. Hinch as their head coach, and Alex Cora was re-hired by the Red Sox. Luhnow is now suing the Astros for $22 million.

Suffice it to say, this was a massive scandal that poses an existential threat to the sport: if games are not actually fair contests, why watch? Yet no players were punished, no trophies revoked, no careers (outside of possibly Luhnow's) permanently damaged. Baseball's commissioner, Rob Manfred, released sympathetic comments about Astros owner Jim Crane, whom he works for. Manfred, like Selig before him, apparently sees himself as representative of the owners and not baseball writ large, as commissioners like Fay Vincent once did. This is what happens when baseball is viewed more as a business than as a community endeavor. It makes sense that such a viewpoint would not care about baseball's impact on public virtue or value the sport outside of its moneymaking potential. This means the sanctity of the game and the legitimacy of the product is second to what profits the sport brings in. Minimizing this incident may be better for profits, but it degrades the sport.

This lack of concern for the sport is evident in Manfred's comments about the 2017 World Series. He stated, "The idea of an asterisk or asking for a piece of metal back seems like a futile act. People will always know something was different about the 2017 season, and whether we made that decision right or wrong, we undertook a thorough investigation, and had the intestinal fortitude to share the results of the investigation, even when those results were not very pretty."[104] Besides pretending that it took courage not to bury a massive scandal (that probably could not have been buried), the commissioner's words also show how little he values what is ostensibly the holy grail of the sport he represents, calling the championship trophy "a piece of metal." For fans, such a statement is not only disappointing—it's disenchanting. Why invest time and meaning in a sport if the gatekeepers of that sport care so little for its integrity and its competition?

Of course, what makes this case unique is that thus far, because of the COVID-19 pandemic, the fans have yet to have their say. Most games in the abbreviated 2020 season had few if any fans. It makes sense that super-wealthy owners and others representing them would be more than happy to skirt real responsibility and refuse to reckon with what went wrong. We see similar corruption spread in politics when the people do not get a voice. It is impossible to say for sure, but if the Astros had been exposed to fans, it is quite likely they would have been roundly booed all season long by fans of the other twenty-nine teams. Occasions of Rob Manfred being booed in front of the World Series "crowd" in 2020 indicate as much. What this shows is just how valuable spectators are for making democracy work at the ballpark. There has been little accountability here despite the high stakes of the transgression. When fans get to finally speak, one can only assume that might change. This example shows how spectatorship can actually change the sport and how the sport operates. It is one thing for these deeds to go lightly punished when fans are not present. It is quite another to do such things in front of packed stands every day. The power of the spectators to make the sport more democratic is evident in this example.

This cheating scandal is a cautionary tale about how we understand the relationship between virtue and sport. We tie sport to greatness and excellence, and we associate both with virtue. But, again, baseball and democracy at the ballpark is about possibility. It is possible baseball can be a quite useful mechanism for instilling democratic virtues and serving as an agonistic outlet for greatness. It is also possible that these virtues and the sport itself can be undermined by an exclusive and narrow focus on victory and profits. What is needed and can be decisive is a fan base and spectators willing to demand the right kind of virtues at the ballpark and integrity in America's pastime.

What this scandal also shows is the danger technology poses for sport. To be as generous as possible to those who cheated at the game, the presence of screens, tablets, and countless cameras throughout the ballpark and clubhouse is a great temptation. If it were not the Astros, it likely would have been some other team willing to violate the rules for gain (and indeed, the Red Sox did something similar). But this requires a bigger examination of technology. How does technology interact with sport, and how does it shape and change the game of baseball? The next chapter examines this question as we begin to think through how spectatorship mingles with technology and what that means for baseball.

CHAPTER 5

TECHNOLOGY, SABERMETRICS, AND DEMOCRATIC MINDS

But the action of the scientists, since it acts into nature from the standpoint of the universe and not into the web of human relationships, lacks the revelatory character of action as well as the ability to produce stories and become historical, which together form the very source from which meaningfulness springs into and illuminates human existence.

—Hannah Arendt[1]

B aseball is often thought of as a pastoral sport: it unfolds without a clock, under the open sky, and has nearly limitless possibilities. Yet, against these characteristics is the growing trend to reconceptualize the game in technological terms—as something to be measured to truly understand. This trend both mirrors broader shifts in democratic epistemology, or the types of knowledge recognized as valid, and presents a troubling possibility that technological thinking could undermine even democratic leisure and play.

What danger does technological thinking propose to the democratic mind, and by extension, democratic life? Epistemological diversity has often been advocated as a democratic good, and threats to this diversity have often been declared undesirable, particularly in the form of a technological episteme. To examine the relationship between technological thinking and democratic life, I scrutinize sabermetrics in baseball, a phenomenon that is part and parcel of a world that thinks through the lens of technology. Sabermetrics (sometimes SABRmetrics) is the empirical analysis of baseball to measure value of players and various plays within a game, usually with statistics. Sabermetrics is one way that technological thinking spreads to people in their average everyday lives. Because of this everyday nature, the ways in which fans confront technological thinking in baseball are important for political theorists to consider. This analysis provides a way to begin re-theorizing how we view technological thinking in other areas of democratic life. In many ways, sport can serve as an oasis from the spread of technology if understood properly.

Political theory has long been concerned with questions about how citizens think and how the opinions of the masses affect democratic life. The lack of consistency in mass opinion is at the heart of early critiques of democracy.[2] Recent work, however, has argued that, in fact, the scattered nature of the democratic mind is good for democracy.[3] This work on democratic epistemology claims that the diversity of ideas is a central part of democracy's strength: a collection of different ways of thinking is more likely to produce desirable outcomes than a system of government ruled by experts.

However, when examining the ways that people think in democratic life, it is important to look at reigning epistemologies and the potential that a mode of thinking becomes predominant—in other words, that this democratic diversity of the mind is threatened.[4] Political theorists have traditionally been hostile to the epistemological trend in which the political world is increasingly seen through the lens of science or technology. Theorists object to *how* citizens think and conceive of the world with the rise of technology. Various terms have been used to describe this change in the democratic mind, be it a shift from thinking ontologically to ontically, an embrace of scientism, the incorporation of technique into everyday life, or an abstraction away from traditional views of the human condition.[5] Whatever the terms, the concern is the same: technology creates new measures of truth and justification, ultimately dominating how citizens think and behave. This shift is characterized by the rise of abstraction, utilitarian thinking, and the dominance of this thought through its own internal logic, all of which poses a threat to intellectual diversity.[6] This threat becomes all the more imposing when it penetrates into everyday life and everyday politics as it does with the rise of sabermetrics.

This chapter interrogates technological thinking in baseball. Specifically, I will examine the rise of technological thinking epitomized by sabermetrics. I will consider baseball fans and a culture that reflects an increased desire for advanced statistics and new means of analyzing the game. I argue that this trend is part of a broader shift toward technological thinking. Sabermetrics is bound up with such thinking; the two phenomena inform one another, and sabermetrics spreads technological thinking, making it accessible for average citizens. That technological thinking is so influential in baseball is important because it indicates that such thinking has penetrated into democratic consciousness even in its everyday pleasures. The demand for quantitative rigor has been brought into an arena usually believed to be the domain of chance, fate and skill—that is, the realm of the baseball gods. This shift represents a drastic change in sport from its ancient roots in the sacred and holy into the scientific realm of prediction and control. I argue that while the change is striking, ultimately baseball and sabermetrics reveal the limits of technological thinking and provides a way to think about the rise of technological thinking in other areas of everyday political life.

To make this argument, I'll break the chapter into five sections. The first explores the idea of a democratic epistemology to show the value of diversity in thought. The second briefly surveys the literature on technological thinking to show the danger of this type of thinking to democratic life. The third section looks at sabermetrics to show how they are a form of technological thinking and how they spread this thinking into everyday life. In the fourth section I will describe how to challenge this type of thinking in baseball. Finally, in the conclusion, I apply the lessons learned from baseball to other areas of everyday politics and argue that baseball can be a technological oasis of sorts. I argue that while sabermetrics is indicative of the power of technological thinking, those who emphasize meaning beyond the numbers in baseball provide a way to confront technological thinking elsewhere.

UNDERSTANDING DEMOCRATIC EPISTEMOLOGY

Much contemporary work has gone into vindicating democratic decision-making and the "wisdom of the crowds" above the judgment of experts. The term "wisdom of the crowds" comes from James Surowiecki, but he is not alone in extolling this virtue of democratic governance, nor did Surowiecki invent a wholly new idea. That the majority makes good decisions is at the heart of most democratic theory, and most epistemic theory gets its bearings from Condorcet's jury theorem. Earlier work has engaged with epistemic democracy as well; Joshua Cohen, for example, spoke of "epistemic populism," lauding majority decisions long before Surowiecki.[7] Further, Jeremy Waldron traces the "doctrine of the wisdom of the crowds" all the way back to Aristotle.[8] Josiah Ober also uses Aristotle to understand decision-making in epistemic theory contra typical models based on Condorcet's theorem, so clearly not all work on epistemic democracy takes its bearings from Condorcet's theorem.[9] Thus, while Surowiecki's work is arguably the most well-known, it is part of a larger dialogue.

The broader theory of epistemic democracy holds that democracy's desirability and strength lies in this ability to mesh the minds of the many into outcomes and decisions that are superior to those produced by the elite; the literature essentially turns Plato on his head, while maintaining Plato's desire for truth. Advocates for epistemic democracy make three key claims: first, that intellectual diversity must be present in democratic life for optimal governance; second, that democratic processes lead to the wisest, best decisions; and third, that because of these claims, democratic decision-making is to be preferred over elite decision-making.

Diversity of thought is arguably the most essential condition for those in favor of epistemic democracy. A diversity of opinions, values, and perspectives is needed in order for the resulting decisions to be democratically "good."[10] Diverse opinions are valuable when some observers are wrong or even biased.[11] While differences of opinion do make coming to an overarching consensus difficult, it provides the possibility of revising opinions and maintaining diversity.[12] As Surowiecki puts it, relying on social proofs and imitation stagnates group thinking and creates herding: diversity is at the heart of innovation that improves democratic decision-making.[13] The idea is that with diverse opinions and information, the group will pool these varying perspectives and more likely arrive at a correct decision regarding the matter at hand.

One story in particular highlights this argument, and Surowiecki opens his book with it. He describes a fair in 1906 that held a contest to guess the weight of an ox. Francis Galton tallied up the 787 guesses that people made and was surprised at the result. As Surowiecki writes,

> Galton undoubtedly thought that the average guess of the group would be way off the mark. After all, mix a few very smart people with some mediocre people and a lot of dumb

people, and it seems likely you'd end up with a dumb answer. But Galton was wrong. The crowd guessed that the ox, after it had been slaughtered and dressed, would weigh 1,197 pounds. After it had been slaughtered and dressed, the ox weighed 1,198 pounds. In other words, the crowd's judgment was essentially perfect. Perhaps breeding did not mean so much after all. Galton wrote later: "The result seems more creditable to the trustworthiness of a democratic judgment than might have been expected." That was, to say the least, an understanding.[14]

This story is an anecdotal way of describing the core argument behind democratic epistemology. Galton is the elitist of the story, assuming that intelligence is reserved for the select few, only to be humbled that democratic decisions are more correct than elite decisions.

"Correct decision" typically means the best decision, or using the language of collective wisdom, the wisest decision. While it is clearly difficult to create a standard by which to say universally that crowds make the wisest decisions, theorists have defended the use of the term "wisdom."[15] Hélène Landemore, for example, defines collective wisdom as an emergent and distributed phenomenon that includes both decentralized phenomena like information markets and more centralized deliberative exchanges.[16] While this wisdom is usually entwined with some standard of rationality, that need not always be the case.[17] The key argument is that the collective intelligence of the group leads to desirable outcomes and good or wise decisions.

Finally, this theory holds that if diversity of opinion leads to the best outcomes, this process is preferred to decision-making by elites or experts. Elizabeth Anderson, for example, channels Dewey to show how diversity of opinion can be harnessed to create the Diversity Trumps Ability (DTA) theorem, which argues that diversity is "epistemically superior to technocracy, or rule by experts."[18] This last point is the main upshot of this theory: Plato was mistaken in asserting that the masses are unwise and that the judgment of the few—that is, experts—should be preferred to decisions made by the masses. Instead, this theory provides a vindication of democratic decision-making.

Epistemic democracy is not without critics. Some have focused on attacking the bases of the theory, namely that *some* epistemic theory draws heavily on Condorcet's jury theorem.[19] Others have cast doubt as to whether democracy has the epistemic benefits that proponents claim.[20]

Nadia Urbinati levies an even larger critique of this literature, arguing that because epistemic democracy focuses on the outcome of the democratic process—that is, that the crowd is wise and makes good decisions—this theory is at heart opposed to democratic procedures and in this way is unpolitical.[21] In other words, for epistemic theorists, democracy is instrumental to truth rather than a good unto itself. For Urbinati, this character of epistemic democracy is dangerous; it uses a measure unfit for looking at democracy. Rather than asking if something is democratic, these theorists are asking if a decision is good. As Urbinati writes, "despite the differences among ways of employing *episteme* in politics, putting value in the achievable outcomes over or instead of the procedures may prepare the terrain for a sympathetic welcome to technocratic revisions of democracy."[22]

Indeed, epistemic democracy is not the only strain of democratic theory overly concerned with outcomes that consequently values truth over democracy. Deliberative democrats have long put strictures on what politics should look like. Namely, they endorse politics as long as it meets the demands of reason.[23] However, epistemic theorists, their critics, and deliberative democrats would all agree on one thing: that diversity of ideas is essential for democratic life. The danger is when one episteme takes over and dominates the minds of citizens—and there are reasons to believe technology presents such a threat.[24]

PROBLEMS WITH TECHNOLOGICAL THINKING

Since the mid–nineteenth century, political theorists and philosophers have been concerned about a world increasingly seen through the lens of science and technology. The concerns of these various thinkers share three key characteristics: (1) that citizens will see the world only abstractly, (2) that technological thinking will privilege utilitarian concerns, and (3) that this type of thinking has its own internal logic that omits dissent. While such thinking is classified in many ways, I call it "technological thinking" because, at heart, all of these epistemic trends are wrapped up in the spread of technology. The application of empirical methods and the language of economics to human affairs is also a part of this mode of thinking. Drawing on some examples in the literature, I will highlight what is meant by these three criteria before showing how they manifest themselves in advanced metrics in baseball.

That technological thinking involves abstracting oneself from the phenomenal world is a fundamental claim made by these theorists. The problem with abstraction is that the human element becomes disconnected from the political world. Jacques Ellul captures this concern succinctly, writing: "Man becomes a pure appearance, a kaleidoscope of external shapes, an abstraction in a milieu that is frighteningly concrete."[25] In other words, technology, or "technique" as Ellul calls it, abstracts human beings from their lived world and, as a matter of principle, insists on metrics ill-suited for understanding human affairs in the midst of the concrete world. Hannah Arendt fleshes out the inevitable implication of this abstraction in *The Human Condition*. The ultimate result is the alienation of human beings from both themselves and the world, eventually coming to view the earth from an Archimedean viewpoint, above and beyond earth itself.[26] This is obviously not a wholly new phenomenon, dating back to the Greeks, but it is taken to the extreme in the modern world until, ultimately, this alienation creates a fundamental break with how humans have traditionally viewed the earth and their place within it.

Charles Taylor provides a clear example to illustrate why this abstraction can be problematic. He writes, "Runaway extensions of instrumental reason, such as the medical practice that forgets the patient as a person, that takes no account of how the treatment relates to his or her story and thus of the determinants of hope and despair . . . all these have to be resisted."[27] Taylor gets at something fundamentally problematic about this abstraction—it misses the point. Technological advances in medicine have abstracted the caregiver away from the fundamental purpose of their profession, which is to care for others. Instead, abstracting from caregiver and patient, doctors operate as if fixing a vehicle. The essence of what it means to be human bound by an ethic of care is lost.

This abstract view of the world emphasizes utilitarian concerns above all else. The language that has purchase is a language of efficiency that maximizes resources. Ellul points to utility as the ultimate measure, saying that technique "forbids all research which it deems not to be in its own interests and institutes only that which has utility. Everything is subordinated to the idea of service and utility. Ends are known in advance; science only furnishes the means."[28] Utility reigns supreme and questions about why go unexplored; efficiency becomes the measure. Martin Heidegger similarly writes of the rise of a way of thinking he calls enframing. With enframing, the tendency is to see everything in terms of resources and energy and how these can be of utility to humans. He writes, "The earth now reveals itself as a coal mining district, the soil as a mineral deposit. The field that the peasant formerly cultivated and set in order appears differently than it did when to set in order still meant to take care of and to maintain."[29] Instead of looking at one's lived world as something to maintain, it is regarded as an array of resources for human exploitation. The primary concern regarding the earth becomes how much value it has to humans and how to get maximum yield at minimum expense.[30]

For many of these thinkers, using efficiency as the measure of value is problematic because it leaves a void of meaning. Arendt, for example, argues that utilitarianism is unable to distinguish between utility and meaningfulness.[31] Efficiency and maximum utility supplants any meaningful "for the sake of which" something is performed. Citizens care that resources are maximized, but not the end for which they are so optimized. For Arendt, the only escape is to turn away from utility and efficiency as the measure. She writes: "The only way out of the dilemma of meaninglessness in all strictly utilitarian philosophy is to turn away from the objective world of use things and fall back upon the subjectivity of use itself."[32] In other words, the logic of technological thinking cannot be disputed—it must be rejected.

Arendt's answer is a response to the internal logic inherent in technological thinking that does not permit dissent. Eric Voegelin describes the shift in thinking that creates this internal logic: truth and classical reason have been supplanted by rigorous thinking. By looking at the positivist turn, he shows how it omits dissenting truth claims:

> This situation was created through the positivist conceit that only propositions concerning facts of the phenomenal world were "objective," while judgments concerning the right order of soul and society were "subjective." Only propositions of the first type could be considered "scientific" while propositions of the second type expressed personal preferences and decisions, incapable of critical verification and therefore devoid of objective validity.[33]

Voegelin shows how this "objective" way of thinking is ultimately self-reinforcing by classifying any challenge as "subjective." There is no truth outside of the objective world, and appeals to subjective meaning or valuations are irrelevant. Consequently, saying that viewing the world abstractly and in terms of utility is wrong because it does not provide dignity to human beings is itself a meaningless statement: it is imbued with subjectivity and thus irrelevant.

This type of thinking presents numerous problems, but the primary issue is that people and things are thought of in the same way, in abstract terms of efficiency; the special quality that has traditionally been understood as part and parcel of humans and human affairs is pushed to the margins, if not rejected outright. As a result, only technological thinking is viewed as objectively true: dissent is rejected as subjective and therefore invalid. As Heidegger points out, we begin to see such language as "human resources" emerge, as the language of technology and economics comes to dominate everyday life and the way we think and speak of it. With the loss of meaning and the widening propensity for abstractions, technological thinking is a political and social threat with its own internal logic: a threat that seems impossible to stop.

This thinking spread especially during the "behavioral revolution" in the 1930s and later in the United States. This revolution emphasized the importance of quantified and objective ways of understanding political behavior. This revolution in turn shaped the later "Sabermetric revolution," and the language of quantitative social scientists descended upon baseball fans. Baseball was thus a mechanism for spreading this type of thinking to people that otherwise would not think in such a manner. To examine this phenomenon, I turn to sabermetrics in baseball to show the introduction and spread of this technological thinking into everyday life.

THE "SABERMETRIC REVOLUTION"

What is sabermetrics and how does it represent a form of technological thinking? Simply put, sabermetrics is the application of empirical methods and models to understand and analyze the game of baseball. Baseball has traditionally been a game that revolves around statistics and imbuing numbers with meaning. In the baseball world, numbers like .400, 60, 73, 714, 755, 56, and 2,632 are iconic.[34] Statistics such as batting average, home runs, runs batted in, runs scored, strikeouts, earned run average, wins, and saves dominated the sport for nearly a century. These are simple and descriptive statistics, and they perform a vital role within the world of baseball: they preserve the past. They document what happened and allow this information and its facticity to be handed down from one generation to another.

However, with the onset of sabermetrics most of these measures have fallen out of favor. Most of these measures are simple descriptions of events, and viewed as misleading compared to sabermetrics. What emerges instead with the rise of sabermetrics is the use of tools typically reserved for statistical analysis that revolutionizes not only the numbers used to evaluate the game, but ultimately how the game itself is seen. This shift mirrors the rise in technological thinking. Fans are increasingly seeing the game in the quantified and objective way that is the hallmark of technological thinking.

While even early in baseball's history there was dissent about the utility of these prevailing statistics, it was not until the 1980s that the first sustained attack on traditional statistics began.[35] The central figure in this sabermetric revolution is Bill James, an astute writer whose annuals push the bounds of traditional statistics and inspired many fans. James challenged traditional statistics in his works and became a major figure among fans for his quantitative analysis that brought the logic of technological thinking to baseball. Eventually, James's thinking found its way into baseball's front offices, and some of the statistical models he concocted brought to bear on actual Major League Baseball fields. James now works for the Boston Red Sox, and every baseball team has an analytics department, although the degree of reliance on sabermetrics varies from team to team.

However, when looking at the importance of sabermetrics and what it indicates about technological thinking, the use of sabermetrics by front offices of MLB teams is not as relevant. It makes sense that those in charge of a billion-dollar business would be open to many types of input to improve their product, increase revenue, and become more efficient. This claim is crucial: the use of sabermetrics by MLB teams as businesses is not the salient political point. In fact, within baseball, sabermetrics can represent a democratic story of sorts.[36] The important political point when it comes to thinking technologically is the mass popularity of sabermetrics among fans in their everyday lives because its use among fans shows people thinking technologically even when they have nothing tangible to gain.[37]

While James may have ignited the revolution, Michael Lewis's book *Moneyball* and the film that followed spread the idea of thinking about baseball in a more quantitatively rigorous manner to the masses. The book sold over a million copies, and the film grossed over $75 million.[38] That *Moneyball* was such a hit caught some by surprise, as the content is drastically different from much of the previously popular writing on baseball by authors such as Roger Angell and former Yale President and

MLB Commissioner Bartlett Giamatti, who specialized in capturing the game's emotional relevance and place in American culture.[39] *Moneyball* is clearly about characters and their emotions, like most compelling narratives, but the drama in the story is about using and embracing instrumental reason and thinking technologically.

Lewis claims that the heart of his story is about reason and science in human affairs. He writes, "A baseball team, of all things, was at the center of a story about the possibilities—and the limits—of reason in human affairs. Baseball—of all things—was an example of how an unscientific culture responds, or fails to respond, to the scientific method."[40] The book largely casts Billy Beane, General Manager of the Oakland Athletics, as a revolutionary figure. Beane (not to be confused with the player Billy Bean, discussed in chapter 3) embraces advanced metrics and brings them to bear on the real world, consequently taking advantage of all the other general managers too naïve or obtuse to see that there is a new, better way of seeing baseball. As Lewis writes, "Everywhere one turned in competitive markets, technology was offering the people who understood it an edge. What was happening to capitalism should have happened to baseball: the technical man with his analytical magic should have risen to prominence in baseball management, just as he was rising to prominence on, say, Wall Street."[41] That is, technological thinking and the tools of economics should be used to evaluate baseball players and game strategy. For Lewis, the odd thing is that it took so long.

The general thrust of *Moneyball* is that by shifting how Beane and the Athletics view baseball—that is, by ignoring the way things are traditionally viewed and instead looking at things through a cold, calculating lens of analytics—the A's gain an advantage that the other twenty-nine teams lacked. As Lewis claims, Beane "is able to think of players as pieces in a board game. That's why he trades them so well."[42] Beane is portrayed as able to get the better end of deals with rival executives because he embraces an abstract way of viewing players in terms of value rather than as embodied humans. However, Lewis shows that there is a tension between this technological way of viewing baseball players in terms of value and the real embodied existence of the players.[43]

Still, since the early 2000s, statistical analysis has taken off in baseball, and other sports as well, though baseball remains at the head of the charge. Among fans, this type of analysis has become increasingly popular: Baseball Prospectus, Fangraphs, and Brooks Baseball are examples of still-growing sources on the forefront of creating new models, measures, and statistics.

While I will not detail the endless statistics and measures or explain them at length, a common theme among statistics such as Batting Average on Balls in Play (BABIP), Fielding Independent Pitching (FIP), and others is that they seek not to evaluate and document outcomes, but rather to model what *should have* happened. BABIP, for example, is used to show batting averages that may be unsustainable, or those who have gotten particularly lucky or unlucky as to whether the balls they hit in play turn into outs or not. This model allows users to predict regression to the mean either for the better or worse. FIP is an improvement on Earned Run Average (ERA) because it controls for defense by looking at things like home run rates, walk rates, and strikeouts. While ERA documents the runs that a pitcher actually gave up, FIP and xFIP (a more advanced version of FIP) show the number of runs one would typically *expect* a pitcher with those peripherals would give up. They abstract from outcomes to document what would normally be expected. Many of these models, unlike reality, adjust for park factors, so instead of documenting what happened in the place it occurred, they abstract to a park that does not exist and adjust expected performance accordingly to what happens at Nowhere Park.

Further, other metrics seek to scale statistics relative to era to compare players more accurately across time. While many sabermetric models and statistics are aimed at prediction or telling us what should have happened, these stats tell us how our favorite hitters or pitchers would fare in another time. ERA+, OPS+, and others adjust to both the player's ballpark and the league context. The idea is that outliers relative to their peers can be compared to players from other eras to understand who was truly exceptional and who was a product of their time. The consistent aim is to provide a "truer" portrait of how we view and evaluate players both past and present.

Statcast is another relatively recent advancement that shows TV viewers such details as route efficiency by a fielder and speed and trajectory of batted balls. In the words of MLB's website, because of Statcast, "Baseball will never be the same."[44] Instead of watching a good catch, Statcast shows the viewer the efficiency with which an outfielder moved toward the ball. In addition to showing a player run the bases, Statcast shows the runner's peak speed and acceleration rate. Statcast details pitcher release points and perceived velocity from the hitter's perspective, rather than simply documenting a pitcher's velocity on a radar gun. The elements of the game are broken down into their constitutive parts, and the viewer is left to marvel at the minutia of all the new data. These sabermetric broadcasts blend elements of traditional narrative with new analytics to navigate the "tension in any sabermetric treatment of baseball between the cool empiricism of numbers and the gauzy comfort of narrative."[45] The "gauzy comfort of narrative" is increasingly withdrawing as the "cool empiricism of numbers" takes over the game.

These statistics are patently different from statistics of the past. While simple statistics like runs batted in, home runs, and batting average preserve events as they occurred, the new statistics are more about prediction and control. They do not recollect moments of greatness; they interpret what ought to have happened and predict what will happen in the future. This is not in itself a bad way of looking at baseball—it is obviously useful and enlightening—but it is a drastic change in how the game itself is interpreted, understood, and enjoyed. What emerges is a proliferation of new data and a large market for this type of thinking. These quantitative methods and models have found a mass market in the democratic world.

SABERMETRICS AND TECHNOLOGICAL THINKING

It is clear that sabermetrics marks a shift in how the game is viewed and understood. How does this help advance the technological thinking described above? The "sabermetric revolution," like the technological episteme described by Ellul, Arendt, and Heidegger, can be understood through three central characteristics: abstraction, utilitarianism, and internal logic that omits dissent.

The necessity to abstract from the game is one of the first principles of sabermetrics. For example, in *Moneyball*, Lewis delights in pointing out how Beane cannot even watch the games lest he get emotionally invested and fail to abstract himself from the experience. In reference to a baseball scout, Lewis praises the man for his "vast experience to which he had no visceral attachment."[46] Further, as Lewis notes, advancing sabermetrics made abstraction essential. He writes of a system for generated data that "replaced the game seen by the ordinary fan with an abstraction. In AVM's computers the game became a collection of derivatives, a parallel world in which baseball players could be evaluated more accurately than they were evaluated in the real world."[47] Hits, runs, and RBIs are replaced with data points on where balls land and how fast they traveled. The probability that such a ball would be a hit or not is more important, for predictive purposes, than the real-life outcome of the game.

The statistics discussed earlier show the extent of this abstraction: the field is broken into quadrants, and balls hit become data points. The playing field for the models does not exist; it is rather an amalgamation of all fields and environments. Gone are elements like wind, shape of stadium, positioning of fielders, and ability of the defenders in the field. Instead, the models used to come up with these statistics by which we view players exist disconnected from the embodied world of people playing baseball.

Utilitarian concerns are arguably the primary reason that sabermetrics rose to prominence in front offices. Lewis portrays the introduction of analytics into baseball as Beane's attempt to learn the "art of winning an unfair game" due to Oakland's miniscule payroll. Since the Athletics lack the financial might of other teams, the primary goal is to maximize value. As a result, they need to learn how to identify traits in players that are undervalued by the market and offload those skills and traits that are overvalued.[48] Of course, one would expect front offices to value efficiency, but this emphasis on value is dominant in fan consumption of advanced metrics as well.

In fact, the most important statistic from the "sabermetric revolution" hinges wholly on viewing players in terms of utility, namely in "wins." This metric, originally called Value Over Replacement Player (VORP), was designed to answer the following questions: "How many runs did a given player generate over the worst acceptable major leaguer a team could find at his position?"[49] In other words, how much is a player worth to their team relative to the average player who would be replacing them from the lower leagues? The more modern version of this statistic is called Wins Above Replacement (WAR), which has various versions—ESPN, Baseball Reference, and Fangraphs all employ different formulas—but it strives to capture the same thing in terms of wins. WAR is meant to tell us how much value a player added, how many wins he was responsible for, compared to an imaginary placeholder representing a typical replacement level player. Kettman notes that it is controversial for just this reason, saying, "it relies on comparing a given player to the abstraction of some hypothetical median player, the 'replacement.'"[50] Thus when looking at a player's contribution, the idea is that one can say approximately how much of the team's success that player created.

That sabermetrics has an internal logic that omits dissent is clear. For example, the title of Baseball Propsectus' 2006 volume is telling: *Baseball between the Numbers: Why Everything You Know about the Game is Wrong.*[51] Various pundits, including Nate Silver, Jonah Keri, James Click, Keith

Woolner, and others, purport to tell the reader not just about the numbers they have generated, but *why* the numbers are superior to previous, non-technical knowledge about the game. In fact, many of these metrics were made to discredit prevailing beliefs in baseball regarding such phenomena as clutch hitting, defensive ability, and other narratives, such as players at the end of contracts perform better than their counterparts.[52] The new numbers discredit the old beliefs, and their quantitative rigor is evidence of their superiority. Never mind that in the decade since its release, new numbers have shown that much of what those authors themselves thought in 2006 is now wrong. These technological "truths" are true in the way that most ideologies and orthodoxies are thought to be true.

This way of thinking about the sport, it should be no surprise, emerged after the sport was transformed by technology—both the game itself and the spectatorship of the game. Baseball is an especially fertile ground for thinking about the spread of technology because baseball is a pastoral and sentimental game. Baseball's rise was connected to American roots in rural life, and these roots are on display in the shape and makeup of the field itself: the large grass expanse speaks of a time where such things were common. Baseball, as noted in chapter 2, connects the fourfold of earth, sky, divinities, and mortals. The susceptibility of play to weather conditions, for example, indicates this orientation. Baseball games are routinely cancelled if it is raining. There are elements involved that human beings have not mastered that shape the conditions of play. This is of course, not the same in other sports like football and soccer where they play regardless of weather, or basketball, which is played indoors. Baseball and its relationship to its environment does not exhibit the type of human control and mastery that other sports do.

However, some modern stadiums change this orientation through technological innovation. Some stadiums, including the Tampa Bay Ray's current stadium, are domes. The sky is taken out of the equation, as is the earth itself. Artificial turf and the false sky represent a technological desire to master conditions and reshape the spectacle itself. Other stadiums, including those in Miami and Milwaukee, have retractable roofs. The Texas Rangers are building their new stadium in large part so that they can have air conditioning.

Similarly, games at the major league level have been transformed into mass sporting spectacles. Most stadiums sit at least 40,000 spectators, and games are viewed or listened to by millions. With this change comes a corresponding change in environment. Most stadiums have gigantic electronic scoreboards, and some have become virtual theme parks, filled with carnival rides, games, countless shops, and even pools.

As discussed in chapter 2, technology is also shifting how the game is consumed and what it means to be a spectator. Television and the internet have changed how people watch and consume the game and made it more available than ever, even if people do not engage in the full experience of being at the ballpark. With technology shaping the game as well as how it is seen, it comes as no surprise that the game is increasingly seen through the measures of technological thinking.

In the end, sabermetrics exhibits a remarkable similarity to the type of technological thinking that political theorists fear will dominate the public sphere. Sabermetrics and the transformation of the sport reinforce this technological thinking and insert this thinking into our everyday lives. Fans who would not have any reason to see the world in such a fashion begin to look at their favorite pastime through this lens. And baseball has not only been the vehicle for spreading this type of thinking, it also advances such thinking beyond its borders.

In fact, this way of understanding sport has made its way into the political and economic sphere. One prominent figure in this crossover is Nate Silver, who got his start analyzing sabermetrics, and now brings that same type of analysis to politics. His work brings to bear measures and statistics to understand politics that are similar to baseball statistics. For example, Silver's website, Five Thirty Eight, kept track of representatives' "Trump Score" to measure their support of the former president. Silver is not alone in such crossover work from baseball to politics. In 2017, Manuel Teodoro and Jon Bond published an article that uses sabermetrics to understand presidential success. To understand presidential politics, they draw on the Wins Above Expectation stat as well as the Pythagorean Expectations formula. These statistics essentially look at runs scored and runs allowed to determine what an expected win total would be, thereby highlighting teams that over- or underperform. Teodoro and Bond use a similar formula to evaluate presidents and their legislative success against what would be expected.[53] This is as clear an example as one could imagine to illustrate how technological thinking as represented by sabermetrics is not isolated to sport alone. The type of thinking and understanding developed in baseball bleeds into our everyday lives and our politics. Given the rise of such thinking within the sport and beyond, it is natural to ask how it is confronted in this everyday venue.

THE FOG AND MEANING BEYOND NUMBERS

The above discussion of sabermetrics and technological innovation in the sport is to explain how the phenomenon of analytics in baseball and the "sabermetrics revolution" mirrors and spreads the type of technological thinking many theorists regard as inimical to democratic life. The internal logic that rejects dissent further stands as a threat to epistemological diversity: when no other perspective is allowed to make truth claims, sabermetrics will presumably dominate. This sole possession of truth claims is indeed something that *some* of those writing in favor of sabermetrics advance. Sabermetrics is sometimes seen as the only legitimate way to evaluate baseball and baseball players. While it may be true that most of the advanced analytics are better for evaluating player value and predicting future outcomes, others have shown that seeing the game through sabermetrics alone is insufficient: a technological mindset overlooks fundamental features of baseball.

A recent op-ed in the *New York Times* by Steve Kettman explains why a numbers-driven experience of the game is not sufficient. Kettman's thesis is simple. He writes, "Thanks to 'Moneyball' and stats-driven fantasy leagues, advanced statistics have changed how fans think about the game. On the whole that's a positive trend—but not when the numbers begin to eclipse a more nuanced appreciation of baseball."[54] Basically, the numbers are generally useful, but they can obscure the meaning of the game. This, of course, is not the fault of the numbers. Kettman continues: "Like children, the numbers themselves are blameless. It's how we use them—or misuse them. There is a risk that numbers become an end in themselves, and arcane stats proliferate. A good rule of thumb is that the more a stat relies on abstraction, the less likely it's going to be consistently useful to a wide audience."[55] As is typical of anti-technological thinking, Kettman sees in sabermetrics the danger that numbers become an end in themselves. Mere abstraction remains: the real game plays out in front of us and we can no longer see it.

What is it that we are missing? For Kettman, we lack a personalized version of baseball that appreciates the details. He notes the shift in journalism from telling the story of a game to relating statistical information from the game, changing how we see baseball itself. This overlooks what he calls the twists and turns of the game, which is bad "since it's the glimpses of character that emerge during these unlikely sequences that give baseball its essential flavor."[56] Kettman claims that fans should appreciate the slowness of the game and take the opportunity to let the mind wander with the action rather than abstract from the play at hand.

John Sexton, president of New York University, has similarly called for thinking about baseball in a different way:

> We live in the age of science; the wonders of knowledge and the results created by it surround us. Its possibilities give us hope for a better world. In some quarters, however, the promise of science has spawned what might be called "scientism"—a belief that just because something is said (*ipse dixit*, as scholars like to say), science captures or will capture all that there is to know in any sense of that word. I do not believe this.[57]

Sexton sees the problem with viewing the world and baseball through the realm of what he calls scientism: it obliterates truth claims outside of those evinced by quantitative measures.[58] Regarding sabermetrics, he writes, "To some, such data is the key to understanding baseball; to others, myself included, it is reminiscent of medieval theologians debating the number of angels that could dance on the head of a pin."[59] For Sexton, sabermetrics misses the point and obscures the mystery inherent in life and baseball. Through a rigorous analysis of quantitative data, it misses the forest for the trees. Sexton adds: "The difference between sabermetrics and mystery is the difference between the veracity of Poisson distributions and the wonder of Joe Dimaggio's magical hitting streak."[60] The desire to make the magical and mysterious fit into models of probability robs the event of its meaning and significance.

Sexton argues that baseball should preserve space for mystery, because the game, like religion, can "help us develop the capacity to see through to another, sacred space."[61] Outside of the logic of sabermetrics and technological thinking, Sexton calls our attention to another realm of meaning: the difference between viewing the game as a poet or as an economist. The economist misses the mystery; the poet sees a deeper truth. Looking at the game technologically obscures a fundamental feature of baseball and sport: that it brings people together, "creates communities, [and] foster[s] bonds of lasting power based on shared memories and experiences."[62] Further, paying attention to the game and its potential in this manner may change how we view other things as well. Sexton writes, "Baseball calls us to live slow and notice. This alone may be enough—if it causes some to perceive the world differently and more intensely."[63] Sexton here echoes Kettman's call to watch the game slowly. By being open to the game and its experiences, we truly understand its power.[64] Further, experiencing something like a baseball game can teach us how to see the meaning and the value of other activities beyond their quantitative measures. For Sexton, baseball can ultimately be a road to God, and certainly beyond the technological thinking sometimes advanced as the truth of the game.

Even within the game, sabermetrics constantly requires revision. Ben Lindbergh provides an excellent example in the form of catcher framing. Scouts long thought pitch framing was an important part of a catcher's job, but since sabermetric-oriented students of the game could not quantify pitch framing, they disagreed. With the advent of PITCHf/x, it became possible to quantify this skill, and it was revealed that the scouts were right all along: pitch framing is extremely valuable.[65] There is, then, a need for humility when using sabermetrics; an openness to dissent is necessary. Technological thinking and those who use sabermetrics are loathe to recognize Socratic wisdom, but doing so may be the only way to truly learn more about the game, rather than merely having the pretense of knowing. This move toward a more open-ended understanding of baseball was recently echoed by John Henry, owner of the Boston Red Sox, who claimed accountability for over-relying on numbers.[66]

Finally, Bill James himself, father of sabermetrics, has questioned some of the methods of the new analytics. Citing an important difference between transient and persistent phenomena, James shows that randomness may be greater than previously thought. He writes, "We ran astray because we have been assuming that random data is proof of nothingness, when in reality random data proves nothing."[67] In other words, we have assumed that everything we cannot prove does not exist, forgetting the lesson of Shakespeare's Horatio. James explains much of this misunderstanding with an analogy:

> In a sense, it is like this: a sentry is looking through a fog, trying to see if there is an invading army out there, somewhere through the fog. He looks for a long time, and he can't see any invaders, so he goes and gets a really, really bright light to shine into the fog. Still doesn't see anything.
>
> The sentry returns and reports that there is just no army out there—but the problem is, he has underestimated the den-

sity of the fog. It *seems*, intuitively, that if you shine a bright enough light into the fog, if there was an army out there you'd have to be able to see it—but in fact you can't. That's where we are: we're trying to see if there's an army out there, and we have confident reports that the coast is clear—but we may have underestimated the density of the fog. The randomness of the data is the fog. What I am saying in this article is that the fog *may* be many times more dense than we have been allowing for. Let's look again; let's give the fog a little more credit. Let's not be too sure that we haven't been missing something important.[68]

Even within the realm of sabermetrics, James leaves room for doubt. He rejects the third tenet of technological thinking, that it has an internal logic that does not allow itself to be questioned. By questioning this type of thinking and allowing for other possibilities, James reveals the limits of technological thinking.

CONCLUSION: BASEBALL AS AN OASIS

In examining technological thinking in baseball, we can see how average citizens approach these problems. It is one matter to describe the dangers of seeing the world through technological thinking and the comprehensive doctrines it will instill in people; it is another to watch actual people interact with this type of thinking. When we look at average people interacting with sabermetrics and baseball, we see that technological thinking and the methods of economics and their analytic rigor are popular: the market for these analytics is massive and seems to constantly expand in scope. Fans are increasingly eager to understand the metrics used by the front offices in baseball, and those ignorant of the new modes of analysis are maligned. Sabermetrics can become a measure of intelligence, and those who reject its logic fail the test.[69]

By laying out the phenomenon of sabermetrics in baseball, we can begin to think about how we view this way of thinking as it invades other areas of everyday life, and it is clear that this process is already underway. Michael Young, for example, gave a vivid description of what a world dominated by meritocracy would look like, and this meritocracy realized in baseball is making its way elsewhere as well.[70] Regarding education, for example, it is clear that many long to measure educators as we measure baseball players in terms of value. Teachers are evaluated by encompassing quantitative measures, and students are similarly measured by their scores; it has been shown that this system is problematic, and yet it persists.[71] At the college level, an expansive view of liberal education is being replaced in favor of an emphasis on STEM programs that promise a more productive and efficient use of one's time at college.[72] Abstraction, utilitarian concerns, and an internal logic reinforcing this narrow viewpoint now dominate education as well. Other workplaces are similarly trying to value workers in this quantitative fashion, often with dehumanizing effects.[73]

While we may be comfortable thinking of baseball players in terms of value and WAR, thinking about citizens in terms of value is dangerous. Sabermetrics in baseball teaches us a lesson about the need to establish limits on how we view things: the game, the world, players, and fellow citizens. Maybe viewing a baseball player as essentially valueless or below replacement level is not a problem when analyzing the game, but learning to view people in this fashion is problematic when we stop abstracting and encounter the political world and actual human beings. It is especially problematic because this judgment is final. Even if later revisions show that a calculation (the technological basis of judgment), was in error, the initial evaluation is not made with uncertainty. Indeed, this way of looking at people is persuasive. It is tempting to quantify the world around us, but in so doing we miss something important. What we gain in analytic precision, we lose in depth of meaning. The illusion that we can understand the value of someone, a baseball player or a citizen, through any measure or model causes us to miss the complexities of the game or the world in favor of the chimera of knowledge.

Education and the workplace are just a few examples of places where this technological way of thinking has also grown. This analysis of baseball and sabermetrics should serve as a way of thinking about this type of thinking wherever it grows. The game is a less serious realm of everyday life that provides a platform for thinking about serious political matters. In encountering this technological thinking in baseball, citizens can begin to think through the problems and benefits of this thinking, a necessary task for confronting this logic elsewhere in everyday life.

Fortunately, as the baseball example shows, despite the strong influence of technological thinking, there is a consistent call to chastise sabermetrics and to make room for meaning in the game outside of analytics. Fans are hesitant to embrace viewing the game solely through an analytics lens, possibly because doing so is not seeing the game at all. I mentioned a few objectors to the total rise of statistics, but others also emphasize the meaning to sport and baseball outside of fodder for analysis.[74] A persistent call has been sounded to preserve and recognize meaning outside of the numbers.

Indeed, while MLB is concerned with incorporating new technology and appealing to a new generation of fans through technology, I would like to suggest that baseball remains popular precisely because it exists outside of the omnipresent march of technology. Despite these shifts in how the game is played and how it is watched, baseball remains primarily pastoral in nature. Embracing these roots and the disjuncture they represent to contemporary society may be the heart of the popularity of the sport, not a weakness or an anachronism.

There is also an aesthetic value in baseball that people enjoy and that is ruined by technological advancements. As Borgmann writes,

> Baseball with its love of records and statistics, its broadly based and highly tiered organization, has perhaps more focal force than any other single institution in this country. It is a real bastion against the hypermodern hordes. While it too suffers from hyperactive attacks and hyperreal attrition, it remains a realm of real celebration. If we are equal to its commanding presence, we will act sensibly and vigorously to restrain hypermodernism.[75]

Baseball can contest the overwhelming spread of technology and what Borgmann calls "hypermodernism." However, it can do so only if it is viewed correctly and if the statistics and organization of the game is built toward gathering people together. This points toward less abstract and more concrete ways of thinking about and interacting with the game. Indeed, baseball *could* be one means of combatting the tendency in technology to abstract and isolate.[76]

Writers concerned with the influence of technology and the diversity of the democratic mind should take heart from the example of baseball and the interaction between people and technological thinking in everyday life. In everyday life, a new epistemology faces resistance. While sabermetrics and analytics have insular truth claims, fans continue to demand truth outside of the numbers. They recognize that there is more to sport than what empirical data can quantify. The example of baseball and sabermetrics shows us that despite a tempting platform of technological thinking that offers a comprehensive understanding of the sport, citizens still recognize the density of the fog that guards the realm of meaning outside of the technological thinking. The challenge is finding a voice for such dissent.

CONCLUSION

BASEBALL AND EVERYDAY POLITICS

If baseball is a Narrative, it is like others—a work of imagination whose deeper structures and patterns of repetition force a tale, oft-told, to fresh and hitherto-unforeseen meaning.

—Bartlett Giamatti[1]

Most baseball writing is in narrative form: the histories usually try to tell a story and the essays, memoirs, and even scholarly work often contains firsthand experience of memories playing the game, watching the game with family, or lessons passed down through generations thanks to the sport. The game is romantic and often oriented toward a past that is not there and was likely not how we recall it. The sentimentality of baseball lends itself to narrative. The few political scientists who have taken the game seriously also resort to this firsthand narrative account at times.[2] These stories convey meaning and a moral for the reader.

Throughout this project I have (mostly) avoided such types of evidence, but my interest in the game dates back to childhood, and beyond looking at the sport as a social scientist, much can be learned by looking at baseball and baseball narratives. Personally, I recall growing up and learning lessons from the game myself. My family were my coaches, and we spent our summers playing the game. My dad would throw batting practice for me, and I would practice my own pitching while he hit. I remember once pitching to my father at a softball field near our house. I threw a pitch down the middle as hard as I could, and he hit it out of the park into the woods behind the field, well over 300 feet. The very

145

next pitch I threw it again as hard as I could and drilled him in the back, and he laughed. As a shy and timid kid, I was learning to stand up for myself and own the plate. When I remind him of that incident, to this day we still laugh.

On brisk summer nights in Northern Michigan my mother would throw a tennis ball to me in the backyard so that I could practice diving catches as the sun began to fade. I imagined I was Chipper Jones, covered in grass stains and bound for glory. In the end, the game for me was more about relationships and memories. I quit playing in high school, but the memories remain, and the sport can still connect me to my family. These stories are an easy way to recall childhood, overcoming failure, the value of persistence, and my bond with my parents.

When I started pitching, I would also throw to my grandfather in his backyard. He had been a catcher when he was a young man and delighted in calling balls and strikes. At one point, I think I struck out roughly seventy imaginary batters in a row. Along the way, Grandpa had to fudge a few of the calls and gave me some pretty generous strikes. I would throw to him until my arm couldn't throw any more, and then we would play cribbage and drink iced tea in his backyard. I remember the day when I could throw too hard, and he had grown too old for us to continue our game. My grandfather died two years ago, and these memories are what remain. All of life was reflected in a simple back-and-forth game of catch, space for conversation, and a common bond of a sport, bridging the space between a child and an old man. One of so many small moments that meant nothing much at the time but means everything to me now. This book is dedicated to Grandpa in part because he helped me see the beauty in these small, everyday pleasures.

I saw my first baseball game in Detroit at Tiger Stadium. The stadium was huge, with giant corridors and overhangs. The city was bigger than any place I had ever been, and I was in awe. Before the game, I joined the other kids along the third-base line and got Sean Bergman to sign an autograph. I treasured that keepsake from the mediocre journeyman making a profession of the game he grew up loving. During the game I saw Cecil Fielder hit a home run in person. I was about six years old, and the whole experience was eye-opening, so far beyond my normal life in a town of 8,000. Baseball illuminated a world that was larger than I realized.

As a graduate student in Wisconsin, I saw a different type of baseball culture. In truth, it was Wisconsin culture that enveloped the baseball games. Madison Mallard games are distinctly Wisconsin, as are Brewers games. Before my first Brewers game, I asked my friend what bar they went to, and she responded, indignant, "You don't go to bars, you bring beer for the parking lot." Indeed, we arrived in Milwaukee to find a parking lot filled with people drinking beer, grilling brats, playing yard games, and listening to baseball on the radio. Depositories are available for the hot coals after you're done grilling, and many people who come to tailgate don't even go inside the stadium for the game. This story is the easiest way I know to explain Wisconsin to people unfamiliar with the state. These rituals show how people fashion the sport to fit themselves and their culture. Again, fans make the sport.

These are just a few stories about baseball that form meaningful memories for me. I relate them here, knowing many people reading this book also have such stories, another way we can bond through baseball. Many baseball stories seem fanciful or romantic—they are often extremely *nice* stories. Many of them are nostalgic as well. It would be easy to write them off as unimportant, and certainly not political. Yet, if they are not important, why do people continue to write them? Why do these stories continually recur, and what does that tell us about the concept of democracy at the ballpark?

MEANING MAKING AND NARRATIVE

Hannah Arendt offers some insight into why storytelling matters. Storytelling and narrative is a mode of understanding baseball, but it's also the essence of life. We are born, we die, and in between there is a linear narrative. She writes,

> The chief characteristic of this specifically human life, whose appearance and disappearance constitute worldly events, is that it is itself always full of events which can ultimately be told as a story, establish a biography; it is of this life, *bios* as distinguished from mere *zoe*, that Aristotle said that it "somehow is a kind of *praxis*." For action and speech, which, as we saw before, belonged close together in the Greek understanding of politics, are indeed the two activities whose end result will always be a story with enough coherence to be told, no matter how accidental or haphazard the single events and their causation may appear to be.[3]

The essence of life is that it organizes itself in the form of a story. The telling of a story is also part of Arendt's own work—Lisa Disch claims that this storytelling was Arendt's methodological innovation. This way of doing theory is effective, because, as Disch writes, "A well-crafted story shares with the most elegant theories the ability to bring a version of the world to light that transforms the way people see that it seems never to have been otherwise."[4] In other words, telling a story is one effective way to illuminate political and social worlds.

For Arendt, storytelling is linked to politics because of its relationship to action. She writes: "But the reason why each human life tells its story and why history ultimately becomes the storybook of mankind, with many actors and speakers and yet without any tangible authors, is that both are the outcome of action."[5] Action is the essence of politics for Arendt, and the way that humans interact together. "The political realm rises directly out of acting together, the 'sharing of words and deeds,'" she writes. "Thus action not only has the most intimate relationship to the public part of the world common to us all, but is the one activity which constitutes it."[6] Action comprises the political world and the shared public world we live in, and stories preserve action. These stories are the type of speech that tries to capture action in what Arendt calls "the web of relationships and their enacted stories."[7] Storytelling bridges the gap between the private and public realm and fills an existential need that humans have for agency.[8] For Arendt, stories have a revelatory character that is essential for preserving the relevance of action and speech for human life. The telling of a story is no small matter.

However, most stories reveal themselves only later. The story is often not told until the end is clear, making the present especially difficult to understand. Arendt writes: "Action reveals itself fully only to the storyteller, that is, to the backward glance of the historian, who indeed always knows better what it was about than the participants. . . . Even though stories are the inevitable results of action, it is not the actor but the storyteller who perceives and 'makes' the story."[9] Storytelling itself is a form of action, and creating these narratives shapes how subsequent generations view these actions. This makes telling the truth all the more important. As Arendt claims, "The political function of the storyteller—historian or novelist—is to teach acceptance of things as they are. Out of this acceptance, which can also be called truthfulness, arises the faculty of judgment."[10] Only out of telling the truth, which is the political necessity of any story for Arendt, can we authentically judge the world around us. Judgment, understanding, preserving action—these are all necessary for healthy democratic politics and all cultivated through storytelling.

This shines a bit of light on why stories matter and insight into why the omnipresence of baseball stories is revelatory. Storytelling helps us bridge the gap between the social and political, and baseball narratives attempt to do exactly that in their own way. The games themselves can always be told as a story, and it makes sense that people who care about the game would find their voice in stories. While this project seeks to do something different than pure narrative, I come back to the narrative quality of baseball because it reveals another level in which the game has meaning, which is the fundamental insight that I want to highlight: that baseball *matters*—baseball is political because it is a realm of life filled with meaning. People would not tell these stories if there was nothing significant to tell. These stories get at the fundamental insight of this work: baseball is an important vehicle for meaning, a powerful metaphor, and this makes it useful for thinking about politics.

When we, in our everyday lives, are included in the stories around baseball, we are participating in something. Participating in the story and being involved is the essence of political action. Being involved in the everyday stories around baseball is a form of action. Because of its quotidian nature, baseball provides a way for average people to be involved in something and participate in something larger than themselves. These politics are smaller and less grand than heroic politics or the shocking event of a presidential election, but these everyday politics are more accessible. Heroism is not required to participate, and politics at the ballpark unfold slowly. The games are played almost daily, children can participate, and people can engage with the sport on various levels and to various degrees. Although less grand, these politics should not be ignored.

When looking at democracy at the ballpark, I have argued that baseball both reflects the status quo of many political issues and can be a site to challenge politics as they currently exist. Baseball can only be such a venue, it can only be a powerful metaphor, because it is a place filled with meaning. These stories demonstrate how and why people put meaning into something seemingly absurd as a child's game. People invest meaning in the game because it reminds them of childhood; they learned about life through the game; they remember people, places, and things by touchstones in the game's history; they formed relationships through the game; the game taught them to look at the world differently; and far too many other reasons to count. I encourage anyone to read baseball narratives, such as Potok's *The Chosen* or DeLillo's *Underworld*, because when people tell stories about baseball, they are telling stories about much more than baseball.[11]

Looking at how politics emerge in the sport, I have focused on community, equality, virtue, and technology. There are other political topics we could examine as well, but these topics are intended to reveal the relationship between democratic life and sport. I focused primarily on spectatorship, which means telling a different story than usual. Most baseball stories focus on players; I wanted to talk about the fans, why they matter, and how we can think about a community of spectators created through sport. This community, I argued, is not passive, but allows for an active process of judgment formation and collective political learning. What is put on display at the ballpark before thousands of people in the stands and millions of people all over the world, I claimed, *matters*.

Regarding community, I have shown how baseball can illuminate concerns within the community, and how baseball can be abused to the detriment of the community. I have argued that events that give space to groups within a community are important, as are initiatives that raise awareness, and that stadium funding that harms cities should no longer occur. Beyond these normative arguments, I theorized what I call a fleeting community and shown how while being at the ballpark is ultimately a fleeting experience, there is a bond and a long-term aspect to fandom that makes this community more important and valuable than might first be recognized. The connection between people formed out of sport is akin to something like associational life.

In terms of equality, I have shown how baseball reveals existing inequalities and challenges these inequalities around race, gender, and sexuality. Regarding race, Jackie Robinson and integration is obviously the biggest moment in which the game became a site for challenging political inequality around race. I have also shown how dog whistle terms and other types of language and policy within the sport reveal the extent of many persistent political inequalities. Gender is a different case because of the unique exclusion of women in baseball; I have argued that this exclusion is problematic from the angle of spectatorship and shown how baseball has become a way to talk about gender inequality and to challenge these broader issues at the ballpark. Sexuality is similar to gender in that there has never been an openly gay baseball player at the highest levels of the sport, and I have argued that this shows how far we still have to go in terms of creating a more egalitarian world. On this issue, baseball lags behind other areas of social life, and I have suggested that it is important to grapple with why.

As to virtue, I have shown how the game is one way of cultivating useful civic virtues. While these lessons are learned at the Little League level, they are also later enforced through spectatorship. As the examples of heroes and villains shows, spectators do not care solely about physical excellence; rather, one's possession or lack of moral virtues is often decisive for how a play is viewed both during and after their careers. Looking at the specific virtue of patriotism, I showed how baseball could be a form for harnessing a desirable and democratic vision of patriotism as a virtue and how often in practice, baseball encourages a different, less helpful vision of patriotism. I also showed how cheating scandals undermine baseball's role in advancing democratic virtues. These examples show how virtues displayed in sport shape our understanding of civic virtue as well. As a result, if we want to understand virtue and how it is cultivated in public life, political scientists need to focus on sport as well as formal political structures.

Technology in baseball is one of the more difficult stories to tell because it is still evolving. I focused primarily on sabermetrics and thinking technologically because it represents an even bigger change than any of the other specific technological advances I mentioned. Sabermetrics seek not simply to change how the game is played or how players are evaluated, but ultimate to change how the game is *seen*. Sabermetrics try to shape how we view the game and ultimately create a deeper distrust for what we see. These metrics sometimes tell us that the events we have witnessed and told probably should not have happened as they did: there was luck involved, the hitters must have hit the balls at the fielders, and we should expect regression to the mean. While this is a valuable insight, ultimately, I argued that as in the realm of politics, we ought to avoid allowing this technological way of viewing the sport overrun other understandings of the game. I cited authors who used the opposing drives to skepticism and appeals to faith to argue that sabermetrics need to be approached cautiously. In turn, these arguments highlight how we should view the advance of this type of thinking into our social, political, and economic lives. There is meaning beyond the numbers, just as there is value in citizens beyond their quantifiable output.

THINKING ABOUT OTHER SPORTS

This project has focused on baseball for reasons I will not repeat, but it should pave the way for thinking about other sports as well. Primarily, this work theorizing a meaningful sporting community shows how the social realm can be a proxy for political issues, and shows how sport can in turn shape politics. After discussing these transferable understandings, I will highlight ways in which baseball as a case study may be unique and some of the politics at the ballpark may be a feature only of the ballpark.

First, regarding theorizing a community around sport, it is clear that this community of spectatorship is not unique to baseball. Other major sports in America enjoy gigantic crowds and massive followings. These also create meaningful communities that involve identification, devotion, and gathering together. The communities around basketball, football, and soccer in America are all large, and likely quite different from the baseball community, but they also offer a way of gathering people together. This coming-together forms an important type of community that should be taken seriously, especially with the decline of traditional associational life.

Baseball is useful for showing the need to better understand how the social realm of sport can be a proxy for political issues. This happens obviously in events like the Olympics, but it also happens in smaller communities as well. I have mentioned the "Friday Night Lights" phenomenon, and much work in sociology has paved the way for understanding how the social and political issues manifest themselves in sport.[12] This emphasizes the value of taking spectatorship seriously, and doing so allows us to watch politics through sport.

Finally, this points toward a way of recognizing when sport is affecting politics. As I have shown, politics often infiltrate baseball, and baseball becomes a site for politics as well. I referenced a few examples of this happening in other sports, and it is plainly the case. There is a reason why NBA coaches spoke out against Donald Trump. They did so because of the community they take part in, and their speaking out in turn shapes how people who follow their sport understand politics. Political issues like labor laws can also be changed by sport. It is clear that not only can sport reflect politics but shape them as well.

One element perhaps unique to baseball is its rhetorical appeal as America's pastime. There is a link between American democracy and baseball not present in other sports. This particularly makes baseball more resonant when thinking about patriotism and nationalism, but it is not wholly unique. In fact, regarding the "paid patriotism" discussed in chapter 4, other leagues, primarily the National Football League, take far more money than MLB. Still, the symbolic power of this designation is unique to baseball.

The constant nature of baseball may also differentiate it from other sports. I have suggested that other sports, like football, have more of a Bacchic and festive feel than the routine experience of watching a baseball game. This is particularly true regarding spectatorship mediated through television or the radio. Watching football is a weekly experience, and often a celebration, whereas baseball is a daily affair. I am not alone in this claim. Barzun writes: "To watch a football game is to be in prolonged neurotic doubt as to what you are seeing. It's more like an emergency happening at a distance than a game. I don't wonder the spectators take to drink."[13] The constant nature of the game provides a more stable platform and a better opportunity for politics to emerge than other sports.

While there are reasons I chose to write about baseball, I hope that this project points toward the need to do a similar analysis for other sports. This work is meant to show the phenomenon and importance of the connection between sport and politics. This connection in turn merits further research into the relationship between politics and other sport. What can, say, soccer illuminate about American politics that we miss when looking at baseball? How does football shape one's understanding of politics in ways that baseball may not? What do small and local sports do to the politics of their communities? These are all important questions that lie beyond the scope of this project. However, it is my hope that this project raises these questions, among others.

SPORT AND DEMOCRATIC THEORY

As I mentioned in the Introduction, I have written this book at a time when American politics are marred by polarization, distrust, turmoil, and the rise of populist politics. A project like this may seem frivolous at a time when the political world is focused on core questions about liberal democracy. But by now it should be clear that examining sport provides insight into our democratic lives and, importantly, shows that sport and these seeming "diversions" are in fact a vital part of maintaining our liberal democratic order. This is the other possibility inherent in sport: that sport supplements democratic life and fosters concern, community, and educates citizens how to be citizens.

However, if we are on the verge of a populist era in which liberal democracy is in a constant state of threat, democracy at the ballpark only becomes more important when democracy at the ballot box and in our institutions is questioned, degraded, and assaulted. This highly visible realm of community spectatorship can become a site of resistance and empowerment as various protests, boycotts, and political discourse in sport shows. In 2019, America's populist leader, Donald Trump, attended a World Series game. The crowd booed the president roundly and threw his own anti-democratic language back at him, chanting "Lock him up! Lock him up!" Baseball is not by essence a platform that omits dissent and gives way to spectacle and populist forces. It is a site of pluralism, vibrant community, and resistance. It should not be surprising that a populist, anti-democratic leader would not fare well when exposed to democracy at the ballpark.

Indeed, looking at baseball reveals how everyday people confront politics. We know, for example, that many people are politically uninformed or do not follow politics. This type of person may follow sport. Sport provides a way to engage with political issues that citizens would otherwise ignore. For example, many people are uncomfortable thinking about racial inequality, but baseball has been and remains a place where this inequality is confronted. Arendt laments the blurring of the social and political sphere, but there is value in a social realm like baseball that provides a window into politics for people in their average, everyday lives.

Further, sport is part of what makes life in a liberal democratic society worth living. This is not true for everyone obviously, but free activity like sport and sport spectatorship is what distinguishes a liberal democracy from authoritarian regimes. Authoritarians often manipulate sport and attempt to use it to lend credibility to their regimes, and they do so because sport is indicative of a free society. Those manipulated spectacles of course do not offer the same genuine expression of freedom that authentic sporting events offer. To spend a Sunday afternoon surrounded by fellow citizens talking in the sun and watching grown men play a children's game—this type of leisure is not afforded everywhere, and it is an essential part of what it means to live freely in a liberal democratic world. This is partially why Roosevelt allowed baseball to continue during World War II. Giving up the sport would be giving up a large part of the reason they were fighting.

Regarding spectatorship, sport and baseball point toward a healthier understanding of spectatorship. The belief that when we watch something we are not doing something is misguided. Being a spectator helps cultivate judgment, and judgment is almost always political. When people watch a baseball game together, they absorb, think, judge, and change. Spectatorship informs how people understand the world around them, and helps create the narratives that people use to understand their lives and politics. Further, spectators of sport are often more active and engaged than we typically think. The crowd largely determines the character of the event, and the event is created by their participation.

Baseball offers a different type of democratic participation: anyone can watch the game and join the community of spectatorship, but it is not a community based on rationality or reason or even civic goals. It is a community that binds people together based on identification and interest and, once so bound, members then experience politics through the sport despite their lack of previous political connection. When people watch politics at the ballpark, or when the ballpark shapes politics, it does so before a political heterogeneous group of people. Politics, a force that seems often to drive people apart, unfolds within this sphere where something else brings people together. Democracy at the ballpark thus remains instructive as democracy outside of the ballpark becomes increasingly under threat.

As theories of routinized politics are eclipsed by political reality, this perspective of viewing politics as they emerge becomes increasingly important—both when studying political elites and when thinking about politics beyond those elite spaces. Democracy is about what people care about and what they do in public. Sport and baseball fill this need for meaning and show much about how people view themselves and their country. I take this everyday perspective seriously because democracy ultimately revolves around regular people and not the great men of history—democracy is about the spectators more than the spectacle. Baseball provides insight into this relationship. As Ernie Harwell, a veteran baseball announcer of fifty-five seasons said in his Hall of Fame speech, "In baseball democracy shines its clearest."[14]

NOTES

INTRODUCTION

1. For an analysis of the tyranny of the majority, see Alexis de Tocqueville, *Democracy in America*, ed. J.P. Mayer, trans. George Lawrence, First Harper Perennial Modern Classics ed., 2 vols. (New York: Harper Perennial Classics, 2006), 246–311. Accounts of democratic regimes undermining themselves through populist and authoritarian leaders are as old as democracy itself. See Plato, *The Republic*, trans. Richard W. Sterling and William C. Scott, 1st ed. (New York: Norton, 1985), books VIII and IX. For contemporary work on the relationship between populism and democracy, see William A. Galston, *Anti-Pluralism: The Populist Threat to Liberal Democracy* (New Haven, CT: Yale University Press, 2018); Ernesto Laclau, *On Populist Reason* (London; New York: Verso, 2005); Chantal Mouffe, *For a Left Populism* (London; New York: Verso, 2018); Yascha Mounk, *The People vs. Democracy: Why Our Freedom Is in Danger and How to Save It* (Cambridge, MA & London: Harvard University Press, 2018); Cas Mudde and Cristóbal Rovira Kaltwasser, *Populism: A Very Short Introduction*, Very Short Introductions (New York: Oxford University Press, 2017); Jan-Werner Müller, *What Is Populism?* (Philadelphia: University of Pennsylvania Press, 2016).

CHAPTER 1

1. www.baseball-almanac.com/hof/Ernie_Harwell_HOF_Induction.shtml
2. Michael L. Butterworth, *Baseball and Rhetorics of Purity: The National Pastime and American Identity During the War on Terror*, Rhetoric, Culture, and Social Critique (Tuscaloosa: University of Alabama Press, 2010), 4; Anthony Castrovince, "Baseball Symbolized Reiliency after 9/11" (2011). m.mlb.com/news/article/24200512

3. The famous quote by David Ortiz is, "This jersey that we wear today, it doesn't say Red Sox, it says Boston. We want to thank you, Mayor Menino, Governor Patrick, the whole police department for the great job they did this past week. This is our fucking city! And nobody [is] going to dictate our freedom. Stay strong." Indicative of how meaningful the moment was, the FCC chairman supported Ortiz's comments, despite his use of explicit language—transcending typical standards. Cork Gaines, "The Chairman of the Fcc Is Okay with David Ortiz Dropping an F-Bomb During Saturday's Red Sox Ceremony," (2013). www. businessinsider.com/fcc-david-ortiz-red-sox-ceremony-2013-4

4. Bill L. Weaver, "The Black Press and the Assault on Proffesional Baseball's 'Color Line,' October, 1945–April, 1947," *The Atlanta University Review of Race and Culture* 40, no. 4 (1979); Roger Kahn, "The Jackie Robinson I Remember," *The Journal of Blacks in Higher Education* 14 (1997); Tim Wendel, *Summer of '68: The Season That Changed Baseball—and America—Forever* (Cambridge, MA: Da Capo Press, 2012), 69; Patrick B. Miller and David Kenneth Wiggins, *Sport and the Color Line: Black Athletes and Race Relations in Twentieth-Century America* (New York: Routledge, 2004).

5. Cheryl Cooky, Ranissa Dycus, and Shari L. Dworkin, " 'What Makes a Woman a Woman?' Versus 'Our First Lady of Sport': A Comparative Analysis of the United States and the South African Media Coverage of Caster Semenya," *Journal of Sport & Social Issues* 37, no. 1 (2013); Jack Scott, *The Athletic Revolution* (New York: Free Press, 1971); Mark Edmundson, *Why Football Matters: My Education in the Game* (New York: Penguin, 2014).

6. For insights into why, see Thomas Gift and Andrew Miner, ""Dropping the Ball": The Understudied Nexus of Sports and Politics," *World Affairs* 180, no. 1 (2017).

7. time.com/3576090/midterm-elections-turnout-world-war-two/ and www. electproject.org/2014g

8. See for example, Nietzsche's "Homer's Contest," in which he attributes the fundamental drive for Greeks was distinction through competition, or Miller's argument about the connection between arête, athletics, and Greek society. Friedrich Wilhelm Nietzsche, *The Portable Nietzsche*, The Viking Portable Library 62 (New York: Viking Press, 1954), 38; Stephen G. Miller, *Arete: Greek Sports from Ancient Sources*, 3rd and expanded ed. (Berkeley: University of California Press, 2004).

9. See, for example, Pindar, *The Complete Odes*, trans. Anthony Verity, Oxford World's Classics (Oxford: Oxford University Press, 2007), 16, 122, 32.

10. Plato, *Symposium*, trans. Alexander Nehamas and Paul Woodruff (Indianapolis: Hackett, 1989), 72. Nichols too notes that Socrates is presented as superior to Alcibiades in war and philosophy while shirking the honor that he rightly earned for his prowess. Mary P. Nichols, "Philosophy and Empire: On Socrates and Alcibiades in Plato's 'Symposium,' " *Polity* 39, no. 4 (2007): 511.

11. Plato, *The Republic*, 403d–04.

12. *The Laws of Plato*, trans. Thomas L. Pangle, University of Chicago Press ed. (Chicago: University of Chicago Press, 1988), 829b–d.

13. Ibid., 831a.

14. Aristotle, *The Politics*, trans. Carnes Lord (Chicago: University of Chicago Press, 1984), 1337–39.

15. For example, Ajax attributes his to Athena, who Ajax blames for tripping him because she favors Odysseus. In athletic events, human and divinity mix. Homer, *The Iliad*, ed. Bernard Knox, trans. Robert Fagles (New York: Viking, 1990), Book 23, 860.

16. Miller gives a string of passages describing rituals involving oil, athletics, and religion in Miller, *Arete: Greek Sports from Ancient Sources*, 18–22.

17. David Sansone, *Greek Athletics and the Genesis of Sport* (Berkeley: University of California Press, 1988), 79.

18. Ulrich Sinn, *Olympia: Cult, Sport, and Ancient Festival*, 1st American ed. (Princeton, NJ: M. Wiener, 2000).

19. Thucydides, *The Peloponnesian War*, trans. Steven Lattimore (Indianapolis: Hackett, 1998), 6.16.

20. Xenophon, *Scripta Minora, with an English Translation*, trans. Edgar Cardew Marchant (London: W. Heinemann; G.P. Putnam's sons, 1925). *Agesilaus*, 9.6. *Hiero* 1.5 has a similar critique that chariot racing has nothing to do with, and should be regarded as inferior to, the wellness of the city. The objections of the philosophers were, of course, widely ignored.

21. Socrates famously references the "free meals for life" in Plato's *Apology* Plato and Aristophanes, *Four Texts on Socrates: Plato's Euthyphro, Apology, and Crito, and Aristophanes' Clouds*, trans. Thomas G. West and Grace Starry West, Rev. ed. (Ithaca, NY: Cornell University Press, 1998), 36d. Odysseus's athletic feats in Book VIII of *The Odyssey* are particularly fitting of a Homeric Hero. For an idea of the training required and the necessary status, see Tony Perrottet, *The Naked Olympics: The True Story of the Ancient Games* (New York: Random House, 2004), 47–59.

22. Donald G. Kyle, *Sport and Spectacle in the Ancient World*, Ancient Cultures (Malden, MA: Blackwell Pub., 2007), 249.

23. Harold Arthur Harris, *Sport in Greece and Rome*, Aspects of Greek and Roman Life (Ithaca, NY: Cornell University Press, 1972), 185.

24. Kyle, *Sport and Spectacle in the Ancient World*, 251–53.

25. Johan Huizinga, *Homo Ludens: A Study of the Play Element in Culture* (London: Maurice Temple Smith Ltd., 1970).

26. Josef Pieper, *Leisure: The Basis of Culture; the Philosophical Act* (San Francisco: Ignatius Press, 2009), 65.

27. Vukan Kuic, "Work, Leisure and Culture," *The Review of Politics* 43, no. 3 (1981): 438.

28. Jean-Jacques Rousseau and Jean Le Rond d Alembert, *Politics and the Arts, Letter to M. D'alembert on the Theatre*, Agora Editions (Glencoe, IL: Free Press, 1960), 125.

29. Along with a former student, I have explored Rousseau's work on the role of entertainment in republican life at length in an article. See Thomas Bunting and Erin Evans, "Together under the Open Sky: Rousseau on the Value of Entertainment," *The Political Science Reviewer* 43, no. 1 (2019).

30. See Book VII in Plato, *The Republic*.

31. Gustave Le Bon, *The Crowd: A Study of the Popular Mind*, 2d ed. (Dunwoody, GA: N.S. Berg, 1968), 22–23.

32. Ibid., 31.

33. Elias Canetti, *Crowds and Power* (New York: Farrar Straus Giroux, 1984), 17–19.

34. Ibid., 29.

35. Guy Debord, *The Society of the Spectacle* (New York: Zone Books, 1994), Ch. 1, 24.

36. Jürgen Habermas, "Three Normative Models of Democracy," *Constellations* 1, no. 1 (1994): 7.

37. Jürgen Habermas, *Legitimation Crisis* (Boston: Beacon Press, 1975), 108.

38. Jürgen Habermas, "Reconciliation through the Public Use of Reason: Remarks on John Rawls's Political Liberalism," *The Journal of Philosophy* 92, no. 3 (1995): 131.

39. This critique is levied by many thinkers, notably Lynn M. Sanders, "Against Deliberation," *Political Theory* 25, no. 3 (1997).

40. Habermas, "Three Normative Models of Democracy," 150.

41. John Rawls, "Justice as Fairness: Political Not Metaphysical," *Philosophy and Public Affairs* 14, no. 3 (1985): 231.

42. Ibid., 230.

43. James S. Fishkin, *The Voice of the People: Public Opinion and Democracy* (New Haven, CT: Yale University Press, 1995), 40.

44. Ibid., 162.

45. James S. Fishkin, *Democracy and Deliberation: New Directions for Democratic Reform* (New Haven, CT: Yale University Press, 1991), 25, 29.

46. Amy Gutmann and Dennis Thompson, *Why Deliberative Democracy?* (Princeton, NJ: Princeton University Press, 2004), 7.

47. Jeffrey E. Green, *The Eyes of the People: Democracy in an Age of Spectatorship* (Oxford: Oxford University Press, 2010), 128.

48. Ibid., 15.

49. Max Weber, *The Theory of Social and Economic Organization*, ed. Talcott Parsons, trans. A. M. Henderson, 1st American ed. (New York: Oxford University Press, 1947), 359.

50. For Schmitt, this friend and enemy distinction relies at the heart of any true conception of politics. Carl Schmitt, *The Concept of the Political*, Expanded ed. (Chicago: University of Chicago Press, 2007), 26–27.

51. Book VII of the *Prince* in Niccolò Machiavelli, *Machiavelli: The Chief Works and Others*, trans. Allan Gilbert (Durham, NC: Duke University Press, 1999).

52. The most famous advocate of this model is Samuel Kernell, *Going Public: New Strategies of Presidential Leadership*, 4th ed. (Washington, DC: CQ Press, 2007).

53. Kenneth R. Mayer, *With the Stroke of a Pen: Executive Orders and Presidential Power* (Princeton, NJ: Princeton University Press, 2001).

54. Nadia Urbinati, *Democracy Disfigured: Opinion, Truth, and the People* (Cambridge, MA: Harvard University Press, 2014), 172.

55. Ibid., 174.

56. Nadia Urbinati, "Unpolitical Democracy," *Political Theory* 38, no. 1 (2010).

57. See Sheldon S. Wolin, "Fugitive Democracy," *Constellations* 1, no. 1 (1994); "Norm and Form: The Constitutionalizing of Democracy," in *Athenian Political Thought and the Reconstruction of American Democracy*, ed. J. Peter Euben, John R. Wallach, and Josiah Ober (Ithaca, NY: Cornell University Press, 1994).

58. Mounk, for example, thinks populism is hostile to liberal democracy, whereas Müller argues populism is hostile to democracy writ large. See Mounk, *The People vs. Democracy: Why Our Freedom Is in Danger and How to Save It*; Müller, *What Is Populism?*

59. Galston, *Anti-Pluralism: The Populist Threat to Liberal Democracy*.

60. For information on populists owning sports teams, see Mudde and Rovira Kaltwasser, *Populism: A Very Short Introduction*, 71.

61. Jacques Rancière, *The Emancipated Spectator* (London: Verso, 2009), 2.

62. Ibid., 6.

63. Ibid., 12.

64. Ibid., 13.

65. Ibid., 17.

66. Richard Lipsky, *How We Play the Game: Why Sports Dominate American Life* (Boston: Beacon Press, 1981), 9.

67. Allen Guttmann, *Sports Spectators* (New York: Columbia University Press, 1986), 152.

68. Ibid., 154.

69. Ibid., 157.

70. Jeffrey E. Green, "Max Weber and the Reinvention of Popular Power," *Max Weber Studies* 8, no. 2 (2008).

71. For a background on the value of dissensus in democratic life, see Jacques Rancière, *Dissensus: On Politics and Aesthetics*, trans. Steve Corcoran (London: Continuum, 2010).

72. Lipsky, for example, shows how and why sports dominate American political life and why the academic prejudice that neglects sports as trivial endeavors is flawed. See especially Lipsky, *How We Play the Game: Why Sports Dominate American Life*, 2–12.

73. For an academic source see Christopher H. Evans, "Baseball as Civil Religion: The Genesis of an American Creation Story," in *The Faith of Fifty Million: Baseball, Religion, and American Culture*, ed. Christopher Hodge Evans and William R. Herzog (Louisville, KY: Westminster John Knox Press, 2002). This aspect of sport has also been artfully captured by Chaim Potok in his novel *The Chosen* (New York: Simon and Schuster, 1967).

74. Butterworth, *Baseball and Rhetorics of Purity: The National Pastime and American Identity During the War on Terror*.

75. Sherri Grasmuck and Janet Goldwater, *Protecting Home: Class, Race, and Masculinity in Boys' Baseball* (New Brunswick, NJ: Rutgers University Press, 2005), 43.

76. Horace Traubel, *With Walt Whitman in Camden* (New York: Rowman and Littlefield, 1961), Letter on Sunday April 7th, 1889.

77. Jacques Barzun, *God's Country and Mine: A Declaration of Love Spiced with a Few Harsh Words*, 1st ed. (Boston: Little, Brown, 1954), 159.

78. These conversations on the role and acceptance of gay players in baseball happen often. See, for example, Josh Slagter, "Detroit Tigers' Justin Verlander Tells CNN He's Open to Gay Teammate, Says Tigers Could Deal with It" (2013). www.mlive.com/tigers/index.ssf/2013/03/justin_verlander_tells_cnn_hes.html

79. Green, *The Eyes of the People: Democracy in an Age of Spectatorship*, 200.

80. See Aristotle, *The Politics*, 1337–39; Plato, *The Laws of Plato*, 831a.

81. For the formation of a "we" in war, see Michael Gelven, *War and Existence: A Philosophical Inquiry* (University Park: Pennsylvania State University Press, 1994); Schmitt, *The Concept of the Political*; Richard Avramenko, *Courage: The Politics of Life and Limb* (South Bend, IN: University of Notre Dame Press, 2011).

82. For academic work on the importance of communities created by sport, see Daniel A. Nathan, *Rooting for the Home Team: Sport, Community, and Identity* (Urbana: University of Illinois Press, 2013).

83. Al Filreis, "The Baseball Fan," in *The Cambridge Companion to Baseball*, ed. Leonard Cassuto and Stephen Partridge (Cambridge: Cambridge University Press, 2011).

84. Kyle, *Sport and Spectacle in the Ancient World*.

CHAPTER 2

1. Albert Borgmann, *Crossing the Postmodern Divide* (Chicago: University of Chicago Press, 1992), 135.

2. See, for example, Vered Amit and Nigel Rapport, *Community, Cosmopolitanism and the Problem of Human Commonality*, Anthropology, Culture and Society (London: Pluto Press, 2012). Edith L.B. Turner, *Communitas: The Anthropology of Collective Joy*. Contemporary Anthropology of Religion (New York: Palgrave Macmillan, 2012).

3. Sheila Croucher highlights many of these issues that arise in the increasingly globalized world and the human need for a sense of belonging and community. Sheila L. Croucher, *Globalization and Belonging: The Politics of Identity in a Changing World*, New Millennium Books in International Studies (Lanham, MD: Rowman & Littlefield, 2004).

4. See Schmitt, *The Concept of the Political*.

5. *The Crisis of Parliamentary Democracy*. Studies in Contemporary German Social Thought (Cambridge, MA: MIT Press, 1985), 12.

6. Michael Gelven also looks at war and its ability to form identities and its place in identity politics. Gelven, *War and Existence: A Philosophical Inquiry*.

7. See, for example, Michael Oriard, "Football Town under Friday Night Lights: High School Football and American Dreams," in *Rooting for the Home Team: Sport, Community, and Identity*, ed. Daniel A. Nathan (Urbana: University of Illinois Press, 2013).

8. Nathan, *Rooting for the Home Team*, 2.

9. See, for example, Michael J. Sandel, *Liberalism and the Limits of Justice* (Cambridge: Cambridge University Press, 1982); Michael Walzer, *Spheres of Justice: A Defense of Pluralism and Equality* (New York: Basic Books, 1983); Michael J. Sandel, *Democracy's Discontent: America in Search of a Public Philosophy* (Cambridge, MA: Belknap Press of Harvard University Press, 1996); Amitai Etzioni, *The Essential Communitarian Reader* (Lanham, MD: Rowman & Littlefield, 1998).

10. Alasdair C. MacIntyre, *After Virtue: A Study in Moral Theory* (South Bend, IN: University of Notre Dame Press, 1981).

11. Charles Taylor, *The Ethics of Authenticity* (Cambridge, MA: Harvard University Press, 1992).

12. Chantal Mouffe, *The Democratic Paradox* (London: Verso, 2000), 22.

13. Miranda Joseph, *Against the Romance of Community* (Minneapolis: University of Minnesota Press, 2002).

14. Rancière, *The Emancipated Spectator*, 16–17.

15. Nathan, *Rooting for the Home Team*, 2.

16. Josef Pieper, *Leisure: The Basis of Culture and the Philosophical Act*, trans. Alexander Dru (San Francisco: Ignatius, 2009), 66.

17. Ibid., 53.

18. Rousseau and Alembert, *Politics and the Arts, Letter to M. D'alembert on the Theatre*, 126.

19. Isaiah Berlin, *Four Essays on Liberty*. Oxford Paperbacks, 116 (London & New York: Oxford University Press, 1969).

20. Hubert L. Dreyfus and Sean Kelly, *All Things Shining: Reading the Western Classics to Find Meaning in a Secular Age*, 1st Free Press hardcover ed. (New York: Free Press, 2011), 192–93.

21. Lipsky, *How We Play the Game: Why Sports Dominate American Life*, 136.

22. Ibid., 141.

23. Bryan Curtis, "Barack/Nixon." grantland.com/features/the-eerie-similarities-barack-obama-richard-nixon-two-our-biggest-sports-fans-chief

24. Borgmann, *Crossing the Postmodern Divide*, 135.

25. See also Olivier Bauer's work that draws on the Canadiens in Montreal to develop a theory on how sport can become a religion. Olivier Bauer, *Hockey as a Religion: The Montreal Canadians*. Sport and Society Series (Champaign, IL: Common Ground Pub., 2011).

26. The old diamond was left intact for many years, but now the Detroit Police Athletic League is converting the space into a resource for Detroit children that connects them with the history of the baseball team in Detroit. Ian Thibodeau, "Tiger Stadium Project Brings Neighborhoods, Kids into Detroit's Resurgence, Pal Ceo Says" (2016). www.mlive.com/news/index.ssf/2016/06/tiger_stadium_project_brings_n.html

27. This union of the fourfold is important for understanding the character of baseball. The fourfold is a concept described by Martin Heidegger in "Building, Dwelling, Thinking." The fourfold consists of the earth, the sky, divinities, and mortals. For Heidegger, proper dwelling requires attuning these four together. Ballparks connect this fourfold with (1) their pastoral focus on the earth, (2) their reliance on the sky (rainouts cancel games), (3) the necessity of human participants and spectators, and (4) the lingering belief in an unfathomable force, be it the baseball gods, chance, or luck. The essential blend of these four forces constitutes a union of the fourfold. This provides an oasis of communal being-together outside of a technological mindset, which will be discussed in the final chapter. By uniting these four elements, baseball provides an opportunity to properly dwell as Heidegger understands the term, which implies an openness and acceptance of the fourfold as they present themselves. See "Building, Dwelling, Thinking," Martin Heidegger, *Poetry, Language, Thought*, His Works (New York: Harper & Row, 1971), 143–63.

28. Borgmann, *Crossing the Postmodern Divide*, 135.

29. Richard Skolnik, *Baseball and the Pursuit of Innocence: A Fresh Look at the Old Ball Game* (College Station: Texas A&M University, 1994), 173.

30. Le Bon, *The Crowd: A Study of the Popular Mind*.

31. Canetti, *Crowds and Power*, 18.

32. This tradition may be changing with the introduction of a pitch clock, much to this author's chagrin.

33. For an analysis of baseball demographics, see Mark Armour and Daniel R. Levitt, "Baseball Demographics. 1947–2012" (2013). sabr.org/bioproj/topic/baseball-demographics-1947-2012

34. It is not hard to come across this type of stunt food, but the ones cited here came from "23 Insane Things You Can Eat at the Ballpark" (2015). www.cbssports.com/mlb/photos/17-disgustingly-incredible-ballpark-foods/15

35. See notably Grasmuck and Goldwater, *Protecting Home: Class, Race, and Masculinity in Boys' Baseball.*

36. Benjamin G. Rader, *American Sports: From the Age of Folk Games to the Age of Spectators* (Englewood Cliffs, NJ: Prentice-Hall, 1983), 243.

37. For baseball fan demographics, see Danielle Eby, "2013 Sports Fan Demographics," (2014). opendorse.com/blog/2013-sports-fan-demographics

38. Donald Hall, *Fathers Playing Catch with Sons: Essays on Sport, Mostly Baseball* (San Francisco: North Point Press, 1985), 117.

39. www.forbes.com/mlb-valuations

40. Ken Burns and Lynn Novick, "5th Inning: Shadow Ball," in *Baseball* (PBS, 1994).

41. Roger Kahn, *The Boys of Summer* (New York: Harper & Row, 1972).

42. Fernando Valenzuela and Fernandomania in the 1980s first showed the power of tapping into local demographics in this way. The Dodgers also acquired Mexican slugger Adrian Gonzalez in 2012, and more recently, a young Mexican left-handed pitcher, Julio Urias. The potential of another young Mexican star that represents the Mexican and Mexican-American communities was certainly a factor in the Dodgers investing in Urias. See Dylan Hernandez, "Los Angeles Has a Lot Riding on 19-Year-Old Julio Urias' Dodgers Debut Tonight," *Los Angeles Times*, May 26, 2016.

43. Kathleen Gier, "Royals Salute the Negro Leagues with 'Dressed to the Nines at the K,'" *The Kansas City Star*, May 17, 2015.

44. Michael J. Sandel, *Public Philosophy: Essays on Morality in Politics* (Cambridge, MA: Harvard University Press, 2005), 81.

45. "The Vocabularist: Are Fans Fanatical or Fanciful?" *BBC News Magazine Monitor* (2015). www.bbc.com/news/blogs-magazine-monitor-34298659

46. All of these and more can be found on the MLB Community website at web.mlbcommunity.org/index.jsp.

47. Patricia Strach, *Hiding Politics in Plain Sight: Cause Marketing, Corporate Influence, and Breast Cancer Policymaking* (New York: Oxford University Press, 2016), 180.

48. This information all comes from Matt Hamilton and Tony Barboza, "Major League Baseball Investigation San Diego Gay Men's Chorus Controversy at Padres' Game," *Los Angeles Times*, 2016.

49. This description and these programs can be found at arizona.diamond-backs.mlb.com/ari/community/index.jsp.

50. For info on these Braves charities, see atlanta.braves.mlb.com/atl/community/index.jsp.

51. seattle.mariners.mlb.com/sea/community/programs.jsp

52. Adam Berry, "Mccutchen Carries on Clemente's Legacy" (2015). m.mlb. com/news/article/158069092/andrew-mccutchen-involved-in-charity-work

53. Bill Shea, "New Funds Help Athletes Score in Philanthropy" (2014). www. crainsdetroit.com/article/*20141026*/NEWS/310269927/new-funds-help-athletes-score-in-philanthropy

54. Dan Martin, "Yankees, A-Rod Play Ball: Home Run Millions Going to Charity," *New York Post*, July 3, 2015.

55. Nola Agha, "The Economic Impact of Stadia and Teams: The Case of Minor League Baseball," *Journal of Sports Economics* 14, no. 3 (2013).

56. Nola Agha and Dennis Coates, "A Compensating Differential Approach to Valuing the Social Benefit of Minor League Baseball," *Contemporary Economic Policy* 33, no. 2 (2015).

57. For a detailed analysis of why economists generally do not support public financing of stadiums, see Dennis Coates and Brad R. Humphreys, "Do Economists Reach a Conclusion on Subsidies for Sports Franchises, Stadiums, and Mega-Events?," *Econ Journal Watch* 5, no. 3 (2008).

58. Bob Herbert, "Wish Fulfillment for Woody," *The New York Times*, March 29, 2004.

59. Sean Dinces, "The Attrition of the Common Fan: Class, Spectatorship, and Major League Stadiums in Postwar Maerica," *Social Science History* 40, no. 2 (2016).

60. Ibid., 358–59.

61. Sandel, *Public Philosophy: Essays on Morality in Politics*, 82.

62. For an analysis of the stadium's architecture, see Michael Kimmelman, "A Ballpark That May Be Louder Than the Fans," *New York Times*, April 27, 2012.

63. Barry Jackson, "Despite New Park, Miami Marlins Enter Season among MLB's Lowest in Payroll," *Miami Herald*, March 31, 2016.

64. See Barry Petchesky, "The Real Cost to Miami for Marlins Park Is in the Billions." deadspin.com/5978964/the-real-cost-to-miami-for-marlins-park-is-in-the-billions; Mike Ozanian, "Miami Marlins Have Become Baseball's Most Expensive Stadium Disaster." www.forbes.com/sites/mikeozanian/2013/01/27/miami-mar-lins-have-become-baseballs-most-expensive-stadium-disaster/#2c3d48e342fe.

65. Ira Boudway and Kate Smith, "The Braves Play Taxpayers Better Than They Play Baseball," *Bloomberg Businessweek* (2016). www.bloomberg.com/features/2016-atlanta-braves-stadium

66. Dan Klepal, "Braves Bridge Budget Shows $2.2 Million in Additional Costs," *Atlanta Journal-Constitution* (2015). www.myajc.com/news/news/local-govt-politics/bridge-budget-shows-22-million-in-additional-costs/nnwBQ

67. Angie Schmitt, "Braves Stadium Relocation Shaping up to Be a Disaster," *Streets Blog USA* (2015). usa.streetsblog.org/2015/10/30/braves-stadium-relocation-shaping-up-to-be-a-disaster

68. Jeff Mosier, "Rangers New Stadium Plans Unveiled; Find out What It Will Cost and Timeline for Its Construction," *Dallas News* (2016). sportsday.dallas

news.com/texas-rangers/rangers/2016/05/20/live-video-rangers-unveil-early-plans-new-arlington-stadium

69. Sandel, *Public Philosophy: Essays on Morality in Politics*, 82.

70. Joanna Cagan and Neil DeMause, *Field of Schemes: How the Great Stadium Swindle Turns Public Money into Private Profit* (Monroe, ME: Common Courage Press, 1998), 33.

71. Adam Poulisse, "How the Los Angelos Dodgers Became Known as 'Los Doyers,'" *Pasadena Star-News* (2013). www.pasadenastarnews.com/sports/20131014/latinos-rocky-relationship-with-their-doyers-over-chavez-ravine-now-a-distant-memory

72. Borgmann, *Crossing the Postmodern Divide*, 135.

73. Sandel, *Public Philosophy: Essays on Morality in Politics*, 83.

74. Wolin, "Fugitive Democracy," 23.

75. "Norm and Form: The Constitutionalizing of Democracy," 37.

76. Dreyfus and Kelly, *All Things Shining: Reading the Western Classics to Find Meaning in a Secular Age*, 205.

77. Hall, *Fathers Playing Catch with Sons*.

78. Borgmann, *Crossing the Postmodern Divide*, 143.

79. Ken Rosenthal, "Study Shows Youth Baseball, Softball Participation on the Rise," *FoxSports.com* (2017). www.foxsports.com/mlb/story/study-shows-youth-baseball-softball-participation-on-the-rise-051817

80. Cited from FDR Library, "Presidents and America's Pastime: A Selection of Baseball Documents from the Nation's Presidential Libraries."

81. Nathan, *Rooting for the Home Team: Sport, Community, and Identity*, 3.

CHAPTER 3

1. Jackie Robinson and Alfred Duckett, *I Never Had It Made: An Autobiography* (Hopewell, NJ: Ecco Press, 1995), 75.

2. See Peter M. Nardi and Beth E. Schneider, *Social Perspectives in Lesbian and Gay Studies: A Reader* (London: Routledge, 1998); Iris Marion Young, *On Female Body Experience "Throwing Like a Girl" and Other Essays*, Studies in Feminist Philosophy (New York: Oxford University Press, 2005); Robert C. Lieberman, *Shaping Race Policy: The United States in Comparative Perspective*, Princeton Studies in American Politics (Princeton, NJ: Princeton University Press, 2005); Larry M. Bartels, *Unequal Democracy: The Political Economy of the New Gilded Age* (Princeton, NJ: Princeton University Press, 2008).

3. John Rawls, *A Theory of Justice* (Cambridge, MA: Belknap Press of Harvard University Press, 1971), "Justice as Fairness: Political Not Metaphysical," *Political Liberalism*, Expanded ed., Columbia Classics in Philosophy (New York: Columbia University Press, 2005).

4. Habermas, *Legitimation Crisis*; Fishkin, *Democracy and Deliberation: New Directions for Democratic Reform*; Habermas, "Reconciliation through the Public Use of Reason: Remarks on John Rawls's Political Liberalism"; Gutmann and Thompson, *Why Deliberative Democracy?*.

5. Diego Gambetta, "'Claro!': An Essay on Discursive Machismo," in *Deliberative Democracy*, ed. Jon Elster (Cambridge: Cambridge University Press, 1998); Seyla Benhabib, *The Claims of Culture: Equality and Diversity in the Global Era* (Princeton, NJ: Princeton University Press, 2002); Cheryl Hall, "Recognizing the Passion in Deliberation: Toward a More Democratic Theory of Democracy," *Hypatia* 22, no. 4 (2007); Joel Olson, "Friends and Enemies, Slaves and Masters: Fanaticism, Wendell Phillips, and the Limits of Democratic Theory," *The Journal of Politics* 71, no. 1 (2009).

6. While these thinkers also want pluralism within the realm of reason, there is a real tension to this aim. Benhabib's work shows this struggle between pluralism and the reasonable: she attempts to maintain fundamentalist claims of culture in a liberal democratic society and ultimately makes recourse to compromise and moral ambivalence. She refuses to acknowledge that competing visions of politics are sometimes not compatible. See Benhabib, *The Claims of Culture*.

7. Sheldon S. Wolin, "The Liberal/Democratic Divide. On Rawl's Political Liberalism," *Political Theory* 24, no. 1 (1996): 106.

8. "Democracy, Difference and Re-Cognition," *Political Theory* 21, no. 3 (1993): 479.

9. *Politics and Vision: Continuity and Innovation in Western Political Thought*, Expanded ed. (Princeton, NJ: Princeton University Press, 2004), 605.

10. Rancière, *Dissensus: On Politics and Aesthetics*, 42.

11. Ibid., 36.

12. Mouffe, *The Democratic Paradox*, 4. Connolly, also an agonistic democrat, focuses on a different paradox—that between identity and difference. People need a social form, common language, institutions, traditions, and political form, but each of these is a form of cruelty and subjugation. Connolly's liberalism is liberal because it desires neither overthrow nor idealization of tradition; it emphasizes rights and constitutional protections, but it is also skeptical about any "definitive resolution of the paradoxical relationship between identity and difference." William E. Connolly, *Identity/Difference: Democratic Negotiations of Political Paradox*, Expanded ed. (Minneapolis: University of Minnesota Press, 2002), 94.

13. Mouffe, *Democratic Paradox*, 8.

14. *On the Political*. Thinking in Action (London: Routledge, 2005), 3.

15. Mouffe argues that "an approach that reveals the impossibility of establishing a consensus without exclusion is of fundamental importance for democratic politics"—because such an approach can recognize instances of exclusion and come to grips with them, rather than "trying to disguise them under the veil of rationality or morality." "Deliberative Democracy or Agonistic Pluralism?," *Social Research* 66, no. 3 (1999): 757.

16. *Democratic Paradox*, 24–25.

17. Mouffe argues that a global reign of "Reason would only be a screen concealing the rule of a dominant power, which identifies its own interests with those of humanity and treats any disagreement as an illegitimate challenge to its *rational* leadership." "Which World Order: Cosmopolitan of Multipolar?," *Ethical Perspectives* 15, no. 4 (2008): 466.

18. *On the Political*, 20; *Democratic Paradox*, 13.

19. *Democratic Paradox*, 103.

20. Hanna Fenichel Pitkin, *The Concept of Representation* (Berkeley: University of California Press, 1967), 61.

21. Robert E. Goodin, "Representing Diversity," *British Journal of Political Science* 34, no. 3 (2004).

22. Leslie A. Schwindt-Bayer and William Mishler, "An Integrated Model of Women's Representation," *The Journal of Politics* 67, no. 2 (2005).

23. Jane Mansbridge, "Should Blacks Represent Blacks and Women Represent Women? A Contingent 'Yes,'" *The Journal of Politics* 61, no. 3 (1999).

24. Daniel Murphy, for example, was criticized for leaving the team to attend the birth of his child, prompting debate in sports media both ways about these types of work issues and gender roles. For coverage of this discussion, see Adam Rubin, "Daniel Murphy: Right to Take Leave," *ESPN* (2014). espn.go.com/new-york/mlb/story/_/id/10721495/daniel-murphy-new-york-mets-deflects-criticism-taking-paternity-leave

25. These conversations on the role and acceptance of gay players in baseball happen often. See, for example, Slagter, "Detroit Tigers' Justin Verlander Tells CNN He's Open to Gay Teammate, Says Tigers Could Deal with It."

26. This process is described at length by David Roediger in *Working toward Whiteness: How America's Immigrants Became White: The Strange Journey from Ellis Island to the Suburbs* (New York: Basic Books, 2005).

27. These nicknames and many, many others can be found at baseballreference.com.

28. Quoted from G. Edward White, *Creating the National Pastime: Baseball Transforms Itself, 1903-1953* (Princeton, NJ: Princeton University Press, 1996), 245.

29. Adrian Burgos, *Playing America's Game: Baseball, Latinos, and the Color Line*, American Crossroads (Berkeley: University of California Press, 2007), 96.

30. William M. Simons, "The Athlete as Jewish Standard Bearer: Media Images of Hank Greenberg," *Jewish Social Studies* 44, no. 2 (1982).

31. Vecsey claims the Negro league teams went 309–129 in documented barnstorming games and provides analysis of these barnstorming games. George Vecsey, *Baseball: A History of America's Favorite Game*, Modern Library Chronicles (New York: Modern Library, 2008), 92.

32. George Gmelch, for example, describes his experience playing in the Detroit Tigers' minor league system and becoming conscious for the first time about issues around race and class. He has since become well known as an

anthropologist. George Gmelch, *Playing with Tigers: A Minor League Chronicle of the Sixties* (Lincoln: University of Nebraska Press, 2016).

33. See, for example, Robert Curvin, "Remembering Jackie Robinson," *New York Times Magazine* (1982). www.nytimes.com/1982/04/04/magazine/remembering-jackie-robinson.html?pagewanted=all

34. Leslie Heaphy, "Baseball and the Color Line: From the Negro Leagues," in *The Cambridge Companion to Baseball*, ed. Leonard Cassuto and Stephen Partridge (Cambridge: Cambridge University Press, 2011), 73.

35. Jules Tygiel, *Baseball's Great Experiment: Jackie Robinson and His Legacy* (New York: Vintage Books, 1984), 182.

36. Much of the politics of the Pirates of that era and Ellis in particular are covered in Jeff Radice, "No No: A Dockumentary" (2014).

37. Mariano Rivera continued to wear number 42 after being grandfathered in until the end of 2013.

38. Hal Bodley, "Retiring No. 42 One of Baseball's Greatest Moments" (2013). m.mlb.com/news/article/44514982/retiring-no-42-one-of-baseballs-greatest-moments

39. Jordyn Phelps, "President Obama Explains Why He Attended MLB Exhibition Game in Cuba Despite Brussels Attacks" (2016). abcnews.go.com/Politics/president-obama-attend-mlb-exhibition-game-cuba/story?id=37842394

40. Robinson and Duckett, *I Never Had It Made*, 85.

41. Ibid., 76–77.

42. Ibid., 279.

43. Daniel McGraw, "Native Americans Protest Chief Wahoo at Cleveland Indians Home Opener," *The Guardian* (2015). www.theguardian.com/sport/2015/apr/11/native-americans-protest-chief-wahoo-logo-at-cleveland-indians-home-opener

44. Paul Lukas, "Hail to De-Chiefing" (2014). espn.go.com/mlb/story/_/id/10715887/uni-watch-some-fans-removing-chief-wahoo-logos-protest

45. See, for example, Ted Diadiun, "Let Chief Wahoo Opponents Be Offended on Their Own Time and Leave the Rest of Us Alone," *Cleveland.com* (2016). www.cleveland.com/opinion/index.ssf/2016/04/let_chief_wahoo_opponents_be_o.html

46. For analysis of the codes within baseball, see Ross Bernstein, *The Code: Baseball's Unwritten Rules and Its Ignore-at-Your-Own-Risk Code of Conduct* (Chicago: Triumph Books, 2008); Jason Turbow and Michael Duca, *The Baseball Codes: Beanballs, Sign Stealing, and Bench-Clearing Brawls: The Unwritten Rules of America's Pastime* (New York: Pantheon Books, 2010).

47. Steven Overman has undertaken just this analysis and has found that the virtues typically praised in sport taken from a Protestant ethic include things like "(I) worldly asceticism, (II) rationalization, (III) goal-directed behavior, (IV) achieved status, (V) individualism, (VI) work ethic, and (VII) time ethic." These virtues as interpreted often come with racial implications. Steven J. Overman, *The*

Protestant Ethic and the Spirit of Sport: How Calvinism and Capitalism Shaped America's Games (Macon, GA: Mercer University Press, 2011), 57.

48. David Tokiharu Mayeda, "From Model Minority to Economic Threat: Media Portrayals of Major League Baseball Pitchers Hideo Nomo and Hideki Irabu," *Journal of Sport & Social Issues* 23, no. 2 (1999).

49. For analysis on MLB announcers, see Adam Felder and Seth Amitin, "How MLB Announcers Favor American Players over Foreign Ones," *The Atlantic* (2012). www.theatlantic.com/entertainment/archive/2012/08/how-mlb-announcers-favor-american-players-over-foreign-ones/261265. Regarding magazine coverage, see Andrea M. Eagleman, "Stereotypes of Race and Nationality: A Qualitative Analysis of Sport Magazine Coverage of Mlb Players," *Journal of Sport Management* 25 (2011).

50. Ken Rosenthal, "Upton Not D-Backs Kind of Player" (2013). www.foxsports.com/mlb/story/quiet-justin-upton-not-the-kind-of-intense-player-arizona-diamondbacks-want-trade-to-atlanta-braves-hot-stove-012413

51. Sam Mellinger, "Times Are Changing, and So Should Major-League Baseball," *Kansas City Star* (2015). www.kansascity.com/sports/spt-columns-blogs/sam-mellinger/article18887139.html

52. McCarthy and Jones, for example, find that English Soccer announcers use coded racial language, while Mercurio and Filak find the same coded language is used in regards to quarterbacks in American football. David McCarthy and Robyn L. Jones, "Speed, Aggression, Strength and Tacitcal Naïveté: The Portrayal of the Black Soccer Player on Television," *Journal of Sport & Social Issues* 21, no. 4 (1997); Eugenio Mercurio and Vincent F. Filak, "Roughing the Passer: The Framing of Black and White Quarterbacks Prior to the NFL Draft," *Howard Journal of Communications* 21, no. 1 (2010).

53. Edwin Rios, "White People Could Learn a Thing or Two about Talking About Race from Orioles' Manager" (2015).

54. Eduardo A. Encina, "O's VP John Angelos: 'Ball Game Irrlelevant' When Compared to Poor's Plight," *The Baltimore Sun*, 2015.

55. James Wagner, "After a Long Lull, Protesting Is Taking Hold across Baseball," *New York Times* August 28, 2020.

56. David Ogden and Randall A. Rose, "Using Giddens's Structuration Theory to Examine the Waning Participation of African American's in Baseball," *Journal of Black Studies* 35, no. 4 (2005).

57. David C. Ogden, "Baseball and Blacks: A Loss of Affinity, a Loss of Community," in *Baseball and American Culture: Across the Diamond*, ed. Edward J. Rielly (New York: Haworth Press, 2003), 95.

58. M. Ann Hall, *Feminism and Sporting Bodies: Essays on Theory and Practice* (Champaign, IL: Human Kinetics, 1996); Lisa Disch and Mary Jo Kane, "When a Looker Is Really a Bitch: Lisa Olson, Sport, and the Heterosexual Matrix," *Signs*

21, no. 2 (1996); Amanda Roth and Susan A. Basow, "Femininity, Sports, and Feminism," *Journal of Sport and Social Issues* 28, no. 3 (2004).

59. Lee Sigelman and Paul J. Wahlbeck, "Gender Proportionality in Intercollegiate Athletics: The Mathematics of Title Ix Compliance," *Social Science Quarterly* 80, no. 3 (1999); Patrick James Rishe, "Gender Gaps and the Presence and Profitability of College Football," *Social Science Quarterly* 80, no. 4 (1999); Sarah L. Stafford, "Progress toward Title IX Compliance: The Effect of Formal and Informal Enforcement Mechanisms," *Social Science Quarterly* 85, no. 5 (2004); Bonnie J. Morris, "Teaching Athletics and Gender: A Pedagogical Narrative," *Women's Studies Quarterly* 33, no. 1–2 (2005); Elizabeth A. Sharrow, " 'Female Athlete' Politic: Title IX and the Naturalization of Sex Difference in Public Policy," *Politics, Groups, and Identities* 5, no. 1 (2017).

60. Jennifer Ring, *Stolen Bases: Why American Girls Don't Play Baseball* (Urbana: University of Illinois Press, 2009), 33–42.

61. She also points out that "Take Me Out to the Ball Game" was written about an Irish girl. Ring, *Stolen Bases*, 27.

62. Ring, *Stolen* Bases, 55.

63. Ibid., 26.

64. Grasmuck and Goldwater, *Protecting Home: Class, Race, and Masculinity in Boys' Baseball.*

65. Gai Berlage, *Women in Baseball: The Forgotten History* (Westport, CT: Praeger, 1994), 45.

66. In Clement's case, being treated differently than other umpires was probably welcome, as the period was notorious for the physical and verbal abuse routinely heaped upon umpires. Berlage, *Women in* Baseball, 45–68.

67. These rules had the effect of excluding black women as well. Pierman writes, "League rules governing conduct, beauty, and femininity colluded against African-American players who would not have been considered beautiful or feminine by any white, middle-class standard." Carol J. Pierman, "Baseball, Conduct and True Womanhood," *Women's Studies Quarterly* 33, no. 1–2 (2005): 71, 73.

68. Berlage, *Women in Baseball*, 138.

69. Ibid., 147.

70. Ibid., 153.

71. Jennifer Ring, "Invisible Women in America's National Pastime . . . Or, 'She's Good. It's History, Man,'" *Journal of Sport & Social Issues* 37, no. 1 (2012): 57.

72. Berlage, *Women in Baseball*, 96–97.

73. Ibid., 91.

74. Ring, "Invisible Women," 69.

75. Ann Travers, "Thinking the Unthinkable: Imagining an 'Un-American,' Girl-Friendly, Women- and Trans-Inclusive Alternative for Baseball."

76. Matt Wilhalme, "Mo'ne Davis Helps Set Little League World Series TV Record for ESPN," *Los Angeles Times*, August 21, 2014.

77. Michael Clair, "The Sonoma Stompers Are Set to Make More History by Signing Two Women to Their Roster" (2016). m.mlb.com/cutfour/2016/06/29/186 947558/sonoma-stompers-sign-two-women?partnerId=as_mlb_20160630_63346 566&adbid=748496511755923458&adbpl=tw&adbpr=241544156

78. Justin McCurry and Lawrence Donegan, "Eri Yoshida Wins Plaudits as First Japanese Woman in US Baseball League" (2010). www.theguardian.com/world/2010/aug/08/eri-yoshida-japan-woman-us-baseball

79. Chris Arnold, "2 Women Play for Sonoma Stompers Baseball Team" (2016). www.npr.org/sections/thetwo-way/2016/07/01/484316791/two-women-play-for-sonoma-stompers-baseball-team

80. Chris Landers, "Five Women Playing Baseball Right Now That You Should Pay Attention To" (2017). m.mlb.com/cutfour/2017/03/08/218326644/null

81. Lindsay Berra, "Female French Teen Makes MLB History" (2015). m.mlb.com/news/article/132044338/melissa-mayeux-france-eligible-sign-mlb

82. Marilyn Cohen, No Girls in the Clubhouse: The Exclusion of Women from Baseball (Jefferson, NC: McFarland, 2009), 178.

83. Ibid.

84. Ibid.

85. The U.S. women's hockey team went on strike for better wages and was successful, making a move toward equal footing with their male counterparts. Dave Zirin, "Victory! USA Women's Hockey Team Just Won Their Strike" (2017). www.thenation.com/article/victory-usa-womens-hockey-team-just-won-their-strike

86. Dorothy Seymour Mills, Chasing Baseball: Our Obsession with Its History, Numbers, People and Places (Jefferson, NC: McFarland & Co., 2010), 178.

87. Betsy Morais, "Breaking into Baseball's Ultimate Boys' Club," The Atlantic (2016). www.theatlantic.com/magazine/archive/2016/09/the-girl-of-summer/492737

88. Evan Cooper, "Decoding Will and Grace: Mass Audience Reception of a Popular Network Situation Comedy," Sociological Perspectives 46, no. 4 (2003).

89. Meg Rowley, "Pitchf/Oxq" (2017). www.baseballprospectus.com/article.php?articleid=31736

90. John Branch, "Posthumus Recognition: MLB to Recognize Glenn Burke as Baseball's Gay Pioneer," The New York Times, July 15, 2014.

91. Keith Stern, Queers in History: The Comprehensive Encyclopedia of Historical Gays, Lesbians, Bisexuals, and Transgenders (Dallas, TX: BenBella, 2009. Distributed by Perseus Distribution), 78.

92. Ibid.

93. Branch, "Posthumus Recognition."

94. Cyd Zeigler, "Billy Bean Hired by Major League Baseball as Ambassador for Inclusion, Will Lead Gay Inclusion Program" (2014). www.outsports.com/2014/7/15/5898727/billy-bean-gay-baseball-mlb

95. The text reads: "Attorney General Eric T. Schneiderman, Major League Baseball (MLB) Commissioner Allan H. (Bud) Selig and Major League Baseball

Players Association (MLBPA) Executive Director Michael Weiner today announced new efforts to protect current and future MLB players from discrimination and harassment based on sexual orientation. Following discussions with the Attorney General's office, MLB and the MLBPA agreed to undertake new actions to reinforce its workplace discrimination policies, including the creation and dissemination of a Workplace Code of Conduct to be distributed to every Major and Minor League player and posted in each locker room conveying MLB's non-discrimination policies. The League also agreed to implement new training opportunities for team officials and create a centralized complaint system for reporting incidents involving harassment and discrimination. In November 2011, MLB and the MLBPA added sexual discrimination language into their collective bargaining agreement." MLB, "A.G Schneiderman, MLB Commissioner Selig & MLBPA Executive Director Michael Weiner Announce New Code of Conduct Strengthening Protections against Discrimination Based on Sexual Orientation," news release, July 16, 2013. mlb.mlb.com/news/print.jsp?ymd=20130716&content_id=53917834&vkey=pr_mlb&c_id=mlb

96. Ibid.

97. He writes, "What offended me most about the whole to-do was not the charge of being homosexual. It was the general insinuation that, if I *were* gay, I wouldn't want everybody knowing about it. That I'd perpetuate a lie in the interest of some personal agenda. I found it hugely insulting that people believed I'd go so far out of my way—living with Playmates, vacationing with actresses, showing up at nightclubs—to act out a lifestyle that would amount to a charade. If I was gay, I'd be gay all the way. I had plenty of faults and character flaws, but being fake was never one of them. I was proud of that." Mike Piazza and Lonnie Wheeler, *Long Shot* (New York: Simon & Schuster, 2013), 261–62.

98. Kevin Baxter, "In Pro Sports, Gay Athletes Still Feel Unwelcome," *Los Angeles Times*, December 29, 2012.

99. Slagter, "Detroit Tigers' Justin Verlander Tells CNN He's Open to Gay Teammate."

100. Ken Rosenthal, "Seven Asked, Seven Answered: Baseball Execs Would Sign Gay Player" (2014). www.foxsports.com/mlb/story/major-league-baseball-execs-open-to-signing-gay-player-021014

101. Peter Jackel, "Redemption," *Referee* Magazine, 2014.

102. Jim Buzinski, "MLB Umpire Dale Scott Comes Out as Gay in the Quietest Way Possible." www.outsports.com/2014/12/2/7295993/major-league-baseball-umpire-dale-scott-gay-coming-out

103. Michael Baumann, "Change We Can Believe In: The Importance of Brewers Minor Leaguer David Denson's Decision to Come Out" (2015).

104. Bob Nightengale, "Orioles' Adam Jones Berated by Racist Taunts at Fenway Park," *USA Today* (2017). www.usatoday.com/story/sports/mlb/2017/05/01/orioles-adam-jones-berated-racist-taunts-fenway-park-peanuts/101187172

105. Chuck Schilken, "Yankees' CC Sabathia on Playing in Boston: 'I've Neer Been Called the N-Word' Anywhee but There," *Los Angeles Times* (2017). www.latimes.com/sports/sportsnow/la-sp-sabathia-jones-fenway-racism-20170503-story.html

106. Kyle Hightower, "Jones Says Racial Taunts Speak to Wider Racial Issues," *AP* (2017). apnews.com/b5c9f839f8344b07ac20b63a881c5e16/Jones-says-racial-taunts-speak-to-wider-racial-issues

107. Jorge Castillo, " 'It Don't Shock Me': Dusty Baker on Racial Abuse Directed at Adam Jones at Fenway," *The Washington Post* (2017). www.washington post.com/news/nationals-journal/wp/2017/05/02/it-dont-shock-me-dusty-baker-on-racial-abuse-directed-at-adam-jones-at-fenway/?utm_term=.ce6539e92b95

108. Hightower, "Jones Says Racial Taunts Speak to Wider Racial Issues."

109. Ibid.

110. For info in the report, see "MLB Receives Overall C+ in Racial, Gender Hiring Practices," *Associated Press* (2017). www.espn.com/mlb/story/_/id/19186207/mlb-receives-overall-c+-racial-gender-hiring-practices

CHAPTER 4

1. Barzun, *God's Country and Mine: A Declaration of Love Spiced with a Few Harsh Words*, 159.

2. For the importance of these qualities in childhood education, see Paul Tough, *How Children Succeed: Grit, Curiosity, and the Hidden Power of Character* (Boston: Houghton Mifflin Harcourt, 2012).

3. Galston notes that *arête* encompasses both excellence and individual or moral virtue. William A. Galston, *Liberal Purposes: Goods, Virtues, and Diversity in the Liberal State*, Cambridge Studies in Philosophy and Public Policy (Cambridge: Cambridge University Press, 1991), 218.

4. Debra Hawhee, for example, shows how the concepts of the *agon* and *arête* were at the center of Greek life. She also notes that the *agon* extends beyond simply competitions aimed at victory. There is a gathering capacity to the *agon* that exists outside of the victory/defeat dynamic. Debra Hawhee, "Agonism and Arete," *Philosophy & Rhetoric* 35, no. 3 (2002).

5. Kyle, *Sport and Spectacle in the Ancient World*, 54–55.

6. See, for example, Nancy B. Reed, *More Than Just a Game: The Military Nature of Greek Athletic Contests* (Chicago, IL: Ares Publishers, 1998).

7. Steven Johnstone, "Virtuous Toil, Vicious Work: Xenophon on Aristocratic Style," *Classical Philology* 89, no. 3 (1994).

8. Kyle, *Sport and Spectacle*, 84.

9. See book 23 of *The Iliad*.

10. Ajax slips and falls face-first in a pile of dung, and laments, saying, "'Foul, by heaven! The goddess fouled my finish! Always beside Odysseus—just like the man's mother, rushing to put his rivals in the dust.'" The spectators in turn laugh at Ajax's expense. Robert Fagles, *The Rage of Achilles from the Iliad*, Penguin 60s Classics (New York: Penguin Books, 1995), 583.

11. See, for example, Cedric Hubbell Whitman, *Homer and the Heroic Tradition* (Cambridge, MA: Harvard University Press, 1958).

12. Lynn E. Roller, "Funeral Games in Greek Art," *American Journal of Archaeology* 85, no. 2 (1981).

13. Hawhee, "Agonism and Arete," 191.

14. Ibid.

15. In addition, this taste for excellence transcends athletics. As they write, "far from narrowly focusing on elite athletic competitions, the rhetoric of each ode encourages all interpreters, by practicing excellence, to experience in their own lives 'a gleam of splendor given of heaven' (Pythian 8.98)" Nancy Felson and Richard J. Parmentier, "The 'Savy Interpreter': Performance and Interpretation in Pindar's Victory Odes," *Signs and Society* 3, no. 2 (2015): 265.

16. Nemean 8.40 Pindar, *The Complete Odes*, 110.

17. Plato, *The Republic*, 410c–d.

18. Ibid., 404.

19. Plato, *The Laws of Plato*, 796d.

20. Ibid., 797b.

21. Richard Avramenko and Thomas Bunting, "Sportsmanship and Politics: Xenophon on Ponos and Democratic Competition," *Perspectives on Political Science* (2017).

22. Xenophon, *Scripta Minora, with an English Translation*, On Hunting, XII.18.

23. See especially Aristotle, *Nicomachean Ethics*, trans. Terence Irwin, 2nd ed. (Indianapolis: Hackett, 1999).

24. *The Politics*, 1337b15.

25. She also notes that Aristotle's understanding of *arête* shifts within the context of rhetoric, but in *The Ethics arête* is a *hexis*, a state or condition that one attains Susan K. Allard-Nelson, "Virtue in Aristotle's Rhetoric: A Metaphysical and Ethical Capacity," *Philosophy & Rhetoric* 34, no. 3 (2001): 252.

26. For a discussion on a "complete life" in Aristotle's work, see Paul Farwell, "Aristotle and the Complete Life," *History of Philosophy Quarterly* 12, no. 3 (1995).

27. This passage is from Cato 5, written on November 22, 1787, quoted from David Wootton, *The Essential Federalist and Anti-Federalist Papers* (Indianapolis: Hackett, 2003), 62.

28. *Federalist 55*, 255.

29. Rawls, *Political Liberalism*, 139.

30. Judith N. Shklar, *Ordinary Vices* (Cambridge, MA: Belknap Press of Harvard University Press, 1984).

31. Judith Shklar, "The Liberalism of Fear," *Political Liberalism: Variations on a Theme* (1989).

32. Sharon R. Krause, *Liberalism with Honor* (Cambridge, MA: Harvard University Press, 2002), 8–21.

33. Peter Berkowitz, *Virtue and the Making of Modern Liberalism*, New Forum Books (Princeton, NJ: Princeton University Press, 1999), 173–84.

34. Galston, *Liberal Purposes*, 213.

35. Alasdair C. MacIntyre, *After Virtue: A Study in Moral Theory*, 3rd ed. (South Bend, IN: University of Notre Dame Press, 2007), 226.

36. Ibid., 259.

37. Robert P. George, *Making Men Moral: Civil Liberties and Public Morality* (Oxford: Oxford University Press, 1993).

38. See Norbert Campagna, "Virtue in Tocqueville's America," *Amerikastudien / American Studies* 52, no. 2 (2007).

39. Tocqueville, *Democracy in America*, 122.

40. Richard Avramenko and Richard Boyd, "Subprime Virtues: The Moral Dimensions of American Housing and Mortgage Policy," *Perspectives on Politics* 11, no. 1 (2013).

41. Richard Avramenko, *Courage: The Politics of Life and Limb*.

42. Richard Boyd, "The Value of Civility?," *Urban Studies* 43, no. 5–6 (2006).

43. John Lombardini, "Civic Laughter: Aristotle and the Political Virtue of Humor," *Political Theory* 41, no. 2 (2013).

44. Galston, *Liberal Purposes*, 220–37.

45. Stephen Macedo, *Liberal Virtues: Citizenship, Virtue, and Community in Liberal Constitutionalism* (Oxford: Oxford University Press, 1991), 266.

46. Philip Selznick, "Foundations of Communitarian Liberalism," in *The Essential Communitarian Reader*, ed. Amitai Etzioni (Lanham, MD: Rowman & Littlefield, 1998), 3.

47. Sheryle Bergmann Drewe, *Socrates, Sport, and Students: A Philosophical Inquiry into Physical Education and Sport* (New York: University Press of America, 2001), 85.

48. Studies have shown that this bodily education actually helps improve other areas of student education as well. See Robert R Rauner et al., "Evidence That Aerobic Fitness Is More Salient Than Weight Status in Predicting Standardized Math and Reading Outcomes in Fourth-through Eighth-Grade Students," *The Journal of Pediatrics* 163, no. 2 (2013).

49. It should be noted that while virtues in sport are often reflective of social values, there are also virtues that exist in sport independently. Robert Simon describes this concept, calling it "the inner morality of sport." The idea is

essentially this: while sport reflects societal values, there are inherent values within sport. Even if a society does not value hard work, for example (and aristocratic societies do not), sport would still inculcate one with the value or virtue of hard work because it is essential to excelling in sport. See Robert L. Simon, *Fair Play: The Ethics of Sport*, 3rd ed. (Boulder, CO: Westview Press, 2010), 195–97.

50. Overman, *The Protestant Ethic and the Spirit of Sport: How Calvinism and Capitalism Shaped America's Games*, 210.

51. Library, "Presidents and America's Pastime: A Selection of Baseball Documents from the Nation's Presidential Libraries."

52. Lipsky, *How We Play the Game: Why Sports Dominate American Life*, 22.

53. Barzun, *God's Country and Mine*, 161–62.

54. Cited from "Presidents and America's Pastime: A Selection of Baseball Documents from the Nation's Presidential Libraries."

55. Lipsky, *How We Play the Game*, 56–57.

56. Overman, *The Protestant Ethic*, 57.

57. See Ariel Kohen, *Untangling Heroism: Classical Philosophy and the Concept of the Hero*, Routledge Innovations in Political Theory (New York: Routledge, 2014).

58. Katz et al. describe a three-game series in New York in 1857 in which thousands of spectators paid fifty cents to watch the games. Harry L. Katz and Library of Congress., *Baseball Americana: Treasures from the Library of Congress* (New York: Smithsonian Books, 2009), 16–19.

59. Ibid., 18–19.

60. Bill James, *The New Bill James Historical Baseball Abstract* (New York: Free Press, 2001), 36.

61. Quoted in ibid., 70.

62. David Quentin Voigt, *America through Baseball* (Chicago: Nelson-Hall, 1976), 155–56.

63. This portrait of Cobb is presented by his biographer Al Stump, though recent work by Charles Leerhsen shows why this portrait may be incorrect. Unfortunately for Cobb, the vision of him as a villain and anti-hero has been the prevailing narrative until possibly today and explains why he could not be widely loved. To read a more fair portrait of Cobb, see Charles Leerhsen, *Ty Cobb: A Terrible Beauty* (New York: Simon & Schuster Paperbacks, 2016).

64. Quoted in Voigt, *America through Baseball*, 156.

65. For an account of the Black Sox scandal, see Eliot Asinof, *Eight Men Out: The Black Sox and the 1919 World Series* (New York: H. Holt, 1987).

66. Robert Fredrick Burk, *Much More Than a Game: Players, Owners, & American Baseball since 1921* (Chapel Hill: University of North Carolina Press, 2001), 13.

67. Ibid.

68. Leonard Cassuto and David Grant, "Babe Ruth, Sabermetrics, and Baseball's Politics of Greatness," in *The Cambridge Companion to Baseball*, ed. Leonard

Cassuto and Stephen Partridge (Cambridge: Cambridge University Press, 2011), 37.

69. Amber Roessner, *Inventing Baseball Heroes: Ty Cobb, Christy Mathewson, and the Sporting Press in America* (Baton Rouge: Louisiana State University Press, 2014), 148.

70. Leonard Cassuto, "Interchapter: Babe Ruth," in *The Cambridge Companion to Baseball*, ed. Leonard Cassuto and Stephen Partridge (Cambridge: Cambridge University Press, 2011), 47.

71. Ibid.

72. Library, "Presidents and America's Pastime: A Selection of Baseball Documents from the Nation's Presidential Libraries."

73. Mark Kurlansky, "Greenberg's Time," in *Hank Greenberg: The Hero Who Didn't Want to Be One*, ed. Mark Kurlansky (New Haven, CT: Yale University Press, 2011).

74. Simons, "The Athlete as Jewish Standard Bearer: Media Images of Hank Greenberg."

75. John Updike, "Hub Fans Bid Kid Adieu," in *The Only Game in Town: Sportswriting from the New Yorker*, ed. David Remnick (New York: Random House, 2010), 51.

76. Robinson and Duckett, *I Never Had It Made: An Autobiography*, 75.

77. Ibid., 269.

78. Ibid., 97.

79. It should also be noted that this account, focusing on MLB, overlooks the heroes of the Negro Leagues. Players like Satchel Paige, Josh Gibson, Cool Papa Bell, Rube Foster, and many, many more never had the chance to be national heroes in the same fashion. Paige did ultimately get to play in the majors, but it was well after his prime. Still, these players were heroes within their communities, and their style and deeds provided a meaningful vision of virtue for their community.

80. See Scott, *The Athletic Revolution*.

81. "Vin Scully's Greatest Calls: Hand Aaron's Historic 715th Home Run" (2016). www.usatoday.com/story/sports/mlb/2016/04/08/vin-scully-calls-hank-aaron-historic-715th-home-run-babe-ruth/82799928

82. Ibid.

83. This claim is likely false, but the arguments for and against can be seen here: David Leonhardt, "Myth of Men Who Saved Baseball," *New York Times* (2005). www.nytimes.com/2005/03/30/sports/myth-of-men-who-saved-baseball.html?mcubz=0&_r=0

84. Butterworth, *Baseball and Rhetorics of Purity: The National Pastime and American Identity During the War on Terror*, 81.

85. Indeed, Steven Smith suggests that patriotism should but thought of as an Aristotelian virtue in this manner. See Steven B. Smith, "In Defense of Patriotism,"

in *Political Philosophy*, ed. Steven B. Smith (New Haven, CT: Yale University Press, 2012).

86. Tocqueville, *Democracy in America*, 235.

87. Rupert H. Gordon, "Modernity, Freedom, and the State: Hegel's Concept of Patriotism," *The Review of Politics* 62, no. 2 (2000).

88. Jeffrey A. Smith, "Nationalism, Virtue, and the Spirit of Liberty in Rousseau's 'Government of Poland,'" *The Review of Politics* 65, no. 3 (2003).

89. Sean Richey, "Civic Engagement and Patriotism," *Social Science Quarterly* 92, no. 4 (2011).

90. Traubel, *With Walt Whitman in Camden*. Letter of April 7, 1889.

91. William B. Mead and Paul Dickson, *Baseball: The Presidents' Game* (Washington, DC: Farragut, 1993), 3.

92. Ibid.

93. Voigt, *America through Baseball*, 79.

94. Ibid., 90.

95. Michael L. Butterworth, "Ritual in the "Church of Baseball": Suppressing the Discourse of Democracy after 9/11," *Communication and Critical/Cultural Studies* 2, no. 2 (2005): 109.

96. John McCain and Jeff Flake, "Tackling Paid Patriotism: A Joint Oversight Report" (2015), 8.

97. Ibid.

98. Colin Kaepernick was a quarterback for the San Francisco 49ers who famously drew both criticism and support for his boycott of the national anthem. Kaepernick took a knee during the singing of the anthem to protest racial injustice.

99. Bob Nightengale, "Adam Jones on MLB's Lack of Kaepernick Protest: 'Baseball Is a White Man's Sport'" (2016). www.usatoday.com/story/sports/mlb/columnist/bob-nightengale/2016/09/12/adam-jones-orioles-colin-kaepernick-white-mans-sport/90260326

100. William C. Rhoden, "Sports of the Times; Delgado Makes a Stand by Taking a Seat," *New York Times* (2004). www.nytimes.com/2004/07/21/sports/sports-of-the-times-delgado-makes-a-stand-by-taking-a-seat.html?_r=0

101. Much of the information for the following description comes from excellent reporting, including Ben Reiter's podcast on the Astros' cheating scandal, "The Edge: Houston Astros," as well as an excellent report from *The Athletic* and *Wall Street Journal*. See Ken Rosenthal and Evan Drellich, "The Astros Stole Signs Electronically in 2017—Part of a Much Broader Issue for Major League Baseball," *The Athletic*; Jared Diamond, "Rule Breaking Permeated the Astros—Houston's Front Office Created 'Codebreaker' for the Purpose of Decoding Signs. The Players Took It from There," *The Wall Street Journal*, 2020.

102. For Bolsinger's perspective on this incident, see "The Astros' Cheating Derailed My Career. So I'm Suing," *The Washington Post*, 2020.

103. Des Bieler and Jacob Bogage, "Los Angeles City Council Calls on MLB to Give Dodgers 2017 and 2018 World Series Title," *The Washington Post*, 2020.

104. Quoted from R.J. Anderson, "MLB Commisioner Rob Manfred Apologies for Referring to World Series Trophy as 'a Piece of Metal'" (2020).

CHAPTER 5

1. Hannah Arendt, *The Human Condition*, 2nd ed. (Chicago: University of Chicago Press, 1998), 324.

2. For example, the thrust of Plato's critique of democracy is the mindless nature of the many. As he says in Crito, the many are those who would mindlessly kill someone only to wish that they could bring them back to life. See Plato and Aristophanes, *Four Texts on Socrates: Plato's Euthyphro, Apology, and Crito, and Aristophanes' Clouds*, 48d.

3. James Surowiecki, *The Wisdom of Crowds: Why the Many Are Smarter Than the Few and How Collective Wisdom Shapes Business, Economies, Societies, and Nations* (New York: Doubleday, 2004); David M. Estlund, *Democratic Authority: A Philosophical Framework* (Princeton, NJ: Princeton University Press, 2008); Hélène Landemore and Jon Elster, *Collective Wisdom: Principles and Mechanisms* (Cambridge: Cambridge University Press, 2012); Hélène Landemore, *Democratic Reason: Politics, Collective Intelligence, and the Rule of the Many* (Princeton, NJ: Princeton University Press, 2013).

4. Many writers have dealt with the problems presented by dominant epistemologies. For example, Michel Foucault developed the notion of *"epistemes"* to describe the groundwork of prevailing knowledge and uncovered shifting *epistemes* in *The Order of Things*. Michel Foucault, *The Order of Things: An Archaeology of the Human Sciences*, World of Man (London: Tavistock Publications, 1970). Similarly, Thomas Kuhn, looking at scientific revolutions, shows the rise and fall of "paradigms" in science and how the incommensurable paradigms change how we view the world. Thomas S. Kuhn, *The Structure of Scientific Revolutions* (Chicago: University of Chicago Press, 1962). While *epistemes*, paradigms, or epistemologies change over time, they can represent the predominant way of viewing the world during a period of time.

5. Martin Heidegger, *Being and Time*, trans. John Macquarrie and Edward Robinson (New York: Harper Perennial/Modern Thought, 2008); Eric Voegelin, *The New Science of Politics: An Introduction*, Pbk. ed., Charles R Walgreen Foundation Lectures (Chicago: University of Chicago Press, 1987); Arendt, *The Human Condition*; Jacques Ellul, *The Technological Society* (New York: Knopf, 1964).

6. Classical liberals like John Stuart Mill emphasize the importance of diversity of thinking to democratic life, suggesting that the mental well-being of mankind

relies on freedom of opinion and to stigmatize those with contrary opinions as immoral is polemical and dangerous for democracy. John Stuart Mill, *On Liberty and the Subjection of Women*, Alan Ryan ed. (London: Penguin Classics, 2006), 60, 62.

7. Joshua Cohen, "An Epistemic Conception of Democracy," *Ethics* 97, no. 1 (1986).

8. Jeremy Waldron, "The Wisdom of the Multitude: Some Reflections on Book 3, Chapter 11 of Aristotle's Politics," *Political Theory* 23, no. 4 (1995).

9. Josiah Ober, "Democracy's Wisdom: An Aristotelian Middle Way for Collective Judgment," *American Political Science Review* 107, no. 1 (2013).

10. James Bohman, "Deliberative Democracy and the Epistemic Benefits of Diversity," *Episteme* 3, no. 3 (2006).

11. Robert E. Goodin, "The Epistemic Benefits of Multiple Biased Observers," James Bohman, "Deliberative Democracy and the Epistemic Benefits of Diversity," *Episteme* 3, no. 3 (2006).

12. Richard Bradley, "Taking Advantage of Difference in Opinion," ibid.

13. Surowiecki, *The Wisdom of Crowds*, 47–58.

14. Ibid., xiii.

15. Christian List shows the difficulty of establishing such a standard. See Christian List, "Lessons from the Theory of Judgment Aggregation," in *Collective Wisdom: Principles and Mechanisms*, ed. Hélène Landemore and Jon Elster (Cambridge: Cambridge University Press, 2012).

16. Hélène Landemore, "Collective Wisdom: Old and New," ibid., 6–9.

17. See Daniel Andler, "What Has Collective Wisdom to Do with Wisdom?," ibid.

18. Elizabeth Anderson, "The Epistemology of Democracy," *Episteme* 3, no. 3 (2006): 12.

19. For issues with Condorcet's theorem, see Franz Dietrich, "The Premises of Condorcet's Jury Theorem Are Not Simultaneously Justified," *Episteme* 5, no. 1 (2008).

20. See William Nelson, "The Epistemic Value of the Democratic Process," ibid.

21. Urbinati, *Democracy Disfigured: Opinion, Truth, and the People*, 93–106.

22. Ibid., 82.

23. See primarily Rawls, *A Theory of Justice*; "Justice as Fairness: Political Not Metaphysical"; Habermas, "Reconciliation through the Public Use of Reason: Remarks on John Rawls's Political Liberalism"; Gutmann and Thompson, *Why Deliberative Democracy?*

24. Sandra Braman, for example, documents exactly how technology presents a myriad of epistemological problems. See Sandra Braman, "Technology and Epistemology: Information Policy and Desire," in *Cultural Technologies in Cultures of Technology: Culture as Means and Ends in Technologically Advanced Media World*, ed. G Golin (2012).

25. Ellul, *The Technological Society*, 432.

26. Arendt, *The Human Condition*, 257–68.

27. Taylor, *The Ethics of Authenticity*, 106.

28. Ellul, *The Technological Society*, 317.

29. Martin Heidegger, *The Question Concerning Technology, and Other Essays*, Harper Colophon Books (New York: Harper & Row, 1977), 14–15.

30. Ibid., 15.

31. Arendt, *The Human Condition*, 154.

32. Ibid., 155.

33. Voegelin, *The New Science of Politics: An Introduction*, 11.

34. Taken from baseballreference.com, 2,632 is Cal Ripken's consecutive games played streak, 56 is Joe DiMaggio's hit streak, 755 is Henry Aaron's career home run total, 714 is Babe Ruth's career home run total, 73 is the most home runs in a season set by Barry Bonds in 2001, 60 is Babe Ruth's long-standing single season home run record, later broken by Roger Maris, and .400 is an iconic batting average last achieved in a season by Ted Williams in 1941.

35. Early critics of traditional statistics include Henry Chadwick, who proposed an alternative method of evaluating fielding in 1872, F.C. Lane, who denounced batting average in 1916 for omitting the value of walks and weighing singles, doubles, triples, and home runs the same; and Allan Roth, who was the first statistician hired by a major league team whose work even affected the Dodgers lineups in the 1940s. Benjamin Baumer and Andrew S. Zimbalist, *The Sabermetric Revolution: Assessing the Growth of Analytics in Baseball* (Philadelphia: University of Pennsylvania Press, 2014), 12–14.

36. Surowiecki, for example, praises moneyball for disrupting the clubby culture of baseball and highlighting the merit of previously underappreciated players. Surowiecki, *The Wisdom of Crowds*, 48. Sabermetrics indeed have destroyed previous bias about players that revolve around height, the "good face," and other discriminatory policies that exclude players on grounds unrelated to merit.

37. This claim is in keeping with political theory that is less interested in the use of analytics among economists and more concerned with the language of economy dominating everyday political life. There is a distinction to be made between experts and the masses.

38. This number is gathered from IMDB.

39. Roger Angell, *Five Seasons: A Baseball Companion* (New York: Simon and Schuster, 1977); A. Bartlett Giamatti and Kenneth S. Robson, *A Great and Glorious Game: Baseball Writings of A. Bartlett Giamatti* (Chapel Hill, NC: Algonquin Books, 1998).

40. Michael Lewis, *Moneyball: The Art of Winning an Unfair Game* (New York: W.W. Norton, 2003), xiv.

41. Ibid., 88.

42. Ibid., 213.

43. A notable scene in the film *Moneyball* comes when Paul DePodesta, after advocating releasing a player, is forced to release the player himself. Lewis

writes, "Now, suddenly, there is a difference between trading stocks and bonds and trading human beings. There's a discomfort." Ibid.

44. Paul Casella, "Statcast Primer: Baseball Will Never Be the Same" (2015).

45. Neil Paine, "On Deck: A Sabermetric Broadcast" (2014). fivethirtyeight. com/features/on-deck-a-sabermetric-broadcast

46. Lewis, *Moneyball*, 41.

47. Ibid., 133.

48. In the book, the chief trait that is undervalued is on-base percentage (the rest of the league values batting average) and the chief trait that is overvalued is a reliever who has saves—because saves are a situational statistic they have little bearing on the actual skill or ability of a given player.

49. Jonah Keri, *Baseball between the Numbers: Why Everything You Know About the Game Is Wrong* (New York: Basic Books, 2006), xxxiv.

50. Steve Kettman, "Don't Let Statistics Ruin Baseball," *New York Times*, 4/8/2015.

51. Keri, *Baseball between the Numbers: Why Everything You Know About the Game Is Wrong*.

52. For clutch hitting, see Nate Silver, "Is David Ortiz a Clutch Hitter," in *Baseball between the Numbers: Why Everything You Know about the Game Is Wrong*, ed. Jonah Keri (New York: Basic Books, 2006); regarding defense, see James Click, "Did Derek Jeter Deserve the Gold Glove?," ibid.; and for contracts and productivity, see Dayn Perry, "Do Players Perform Better in Contract Years?," ibid.

53. Manuel P. Teodoro and Jon R. Bond, "Presidents, Baseball, and Wins above Expectations: What Can Sabermetrics Tell Us About Presidential Success? Why Ronald Reagan Is Like Bobby Cox and Lyndon Johnson Is Like Joe Torre," *PS: Political Science & Politics* 50, no. 2 (2017).

54. Kettman, "Don't Let Statistics Ruin Baseball."

55. Ibid.

56. Ibid.

57. John Sexton, Thomas Oliphant, and Peter J. Schwartz, *Baseball as a Road to God: Seeing Beyond the Game* (New York: Gotham Books, 2013), 3.

58. Sexton likely gets this language of Scientism from Voegelin's essay "The Origins of Scientism," which describes the phenomenon that I call technological thinking. Voegelin's scientism is defined by "(1) The assumption that mathematized science of natural phenomena is a model science to which all other sciences ought to conform; (2) that all realms of being are accessible to the methods of the sciences of phenomena; and (3) that all reality which is not accessible to sciences of phenomena is either irrelevant or, in the more radical form of the dogma, illusionary." Eric Voegelin, "The Origins of Scientism," *Social Research* 15, no. 4 (1948): 462.

59. Sexton, Oliphant, and Schwartz, *Baseball as a Road to God*, 64.

60. Ibid., 65.

61. Ibid., 5.

62. Ibid., 185. Hubert Dreyfus and Sean Dorrance Kelly provide another example of this type of communal experience. They open their chapter titled "Lives Worth Living in a Secular Age" on Lou Gehrig's farewell speech and claim that "For the moments that led up to and were held together by Gehrig's speech, 62,000 people knew exactly what they were about. . . . Sports may be the place in contemporary life where Americans find sacred community most easily." Dreyfus and Kelly, *All Things Shining: Reading the Western Classics to Find Meaning in a Secular Age*, 192.

63. Sexton, Oliphant, and Schwartz, *Baseball as a Road to God*, 217.

64. This call for reveling in the simple things and the small moments in life echoes Heidegger's claim in *The Question Concerning Technology* that the saving power that turns away from technology exists "Here and now and in the little things." Heidegger, *The Question Concerning Technology, and Other Essays*, 33.

65. Ben Lindbergh, "The Art of Pitch Framing" (2013). grantland.com/features/studying-art-pitch-framing-catchers-such-francisco-cervelli-chris-stewart-jose-molina-others

66. Nick Cafardo, "John Henry Says Red Sox Will Rely Less on Analytics," *Boston Globe* (2016).

67. Bill James, "Underestimating the Fog," *Baseball Research Journal*, 33 (2004).

68. Ibid.

69. One could site an endless number of articles, debates, and discussions, but the interaction between Hawk Harrelson and Brian Kenny is emblematic of the divide. Bryan Curtis, "Brian Kenny Is Making Sense" (2013).

70. Michael Dunlop Young, *The Rise of the Meritocracy, 1870–2033: An Essay on Education and Equality* (London: Thames and Hudson, 1958).

71. Richard J. Shavelson et al., "Problems with the Use of Student Test Scores to Evaluate Teachers," Washington, DC: Economic Policy Institute (2010).

72. James E. Côté and Anton Allahar, *Lowering Higher Education: The Rise of Corporate Universities and the Fall of Liberal Education* (Toronto: University of Toronto Press, 2011). For a cursory look at the arguments for and against STEM, see, for example, Justin Brady, "Stem Is Incredibly Valuable, but If We Want the Best Innovators We Must Teach the Arts," *The Washington Post* (2014). www.washingtonpost.com/news/innovations/wp/2014/09/05/stem-is-incredibly-valuable-but-if-we-want-the-best-innovators-we-must-teach-the-arts

73. Davide Bonazzi, "The Life and Death of an Amazon Warehouse Temp" (2015). highline.huffingtonpost.com/articles/en/life-and-death-amazon-temp

74. See Christopher Hodge Evans and William R. Herzog, *The Faith of Fifty Million: Baseball, Religion, and American Culture* (Louisville, KY: Westminster John Knox Press, 2002); Michael Mandelbaum, *The Meaning of Sports: Why Americans Watch Baseball, Football, and Basketball, and What They See When They Do* (New York: Public Affairs, 2004).

75. Borgmann, *Crossing the Postmodern Divide*, 143.

76. For an analysis of the relational character of "things" and its importance, see Herbert Marcuse, *One-Dimensional Man: Studies in the Ideology of Advanced Industrial Society* (Boston: Beacon Press, 1991), 211.

CONCLUSION

1. A. Bartlett Giamatti and Kenneth S. Robson, *A Great and Glorious Game: Baseball Writings of A. Bartlett Giamatti* (Chapel Hill, NC: Algonquin Books, 1998), 98.

2. This is true notably of Jennifer Ring's excellent work on gender and baseball. Much of the importance of her analysis is brought home between chapters with narratives about her daughter's experience playing baseball in a world dominated by males and men. See Ring, *Stolen Bases: Why American Girls Don't Play Baseball*.

3. Arendt, *The Human Condition*, 97.

4. Lisa J. Disch, "More Truth Than Fact: Storytelling as Critical Understanding in the Writings of Hannah Arendt," *Political Theory* 21, no. 4 (1993): 665.

5. Arendt, *The Human Condition*, 184.

6. Ibid., 198.

7. Ibid., 181.

8. Michael Jackson, *Politics of Storytelling Variations on a Theme by Hannah Arendt* (Chicago: University of Chicago Press, 2013).

9. Arendt, *The Human Condition*, 192.

10. *Between Past and Future: Eight Exercises in Political Thought* (New York: Penguin, 2006), 258.

11. For an analysis of how baseball fiction contributes to American culture, see Timothy Morris, *Making the Team: The Cultural Work of Baseball Fiction* (Urbana: University of Illinois Press, 1997).

12. See, for example, Robert Staughton Lynd and Helen Merrell Lynd, *Middletown: A Study in American Culture*. Harvest Books (New York: Harcourt, 1959).

13. Barzun, *God's Country and Mine: A Declaration of Love Spiced with a Few Harsh Words*, 162.

14. www.baseball-almanac.com/hof/Ernie_Harwell_HOF_Induction.shtml

WORKS CITED

"23 Insane Things You Can Eat at the Ballpark." (2015). www.cbssports.com/mlb/photos/17-disgustingly-incredible-ballpark-foods/15

Agha, Nola. "The Economic Impact of Stadia and Teams: The Case of Minor League Baseball." *Journal of Sports Economics* 14, no. 3 (2013): 227–52.

Agha, Nola, and Dennis Coates. "A Compensating Differential Approach to Valuing the Social Benefit of Minor League Baseball." *Contemporary Economic Policy* 33, no. 2 (2015): 285–99.

Allard-Nelson, Susan K. "Virtue in Aristotle's Rhetoric: A Metaphysical and Ethical Capacity." *Philosophy & Rhetoric* 34, no. 3 (2001): 245–59.

Amit, Vered, and Nigel Rapport. *Community, Cosmopolitanism and the Problem of Human Commonality.* Anthropology, Culture and Society. London: Pluto Press, 2012.

Anderson, Elizabeth. "The Epistemology of Democracy." *Episteme* 3, no. 3 (2006): 8–22.

Anderson, R.J. "MLB Commisioner Rob Manfred Apologies for Referring to World Series Trophy as 'a Piece of Metal' " (2020).

Andler, Daniel. "What Has Collective Wisdom to Do with Wisdom?" In *Collective Wisdom: Principles and Mechanisms*, edited by Hélène Landemore and Jon Elster. Cambridge: Cambridge University Press, 2012.

Angell, Roger. *Five Seasons: A Baseball Companion.* New York: Simon and Schuster, 1977.

Arendt, Hannah. *Between Past and Future: Eight Exercises in Political Thought.* Penguin Classics. New York: Penguin, 2006.

———. *The Human Condition.* 2nd ed. Chicago: University of Chicago Press, 1998.

Aristotle. *Nicomachean Ethics.* Translated by Terence Irwin. 2nd ed. Indianapolis: Hackett Pub. Co., 1999.

———. *The Politics.* Translated by Carnes Lord. Chicago: University of Chicago Press, 1984.

Armour, Mark, and Daniel R. Levitt. "Baseball Demographics. 1947–2012" (2013). sabr.org/bioproj/topic/baseball-demographics-1947-2012

Arnold, Chris. "2 Women Play for Sonoma Stompers Baseball Team." July 1, 2016. www.npr.org/sections/thetwo-way/2016/07/01/484316791/two-women-play-for-sonoma-stompers-baseball-team

Asinof, Eliot. *Eight Men Out: The Black Sox and the 1919 World Series.* New York: H. Holt, 1987.

Avramenko, Richard. *Courage: The Politics of Life and Limb.* South Bend, IN: University of Notre Dame Press, 2011.

Avramenko, Richard, and Richard Boyd. "Subprime Virtues: The Moral Dimensions of American Housing and Mortgage Policy." *Perspectives on Politics* 11, no. 1 (2013): 111–31.

Avramenko, Richard, and Thomas Bunting. "Sportsmanship and Politics: Xenophon on Ponos and Democratic Competition." *Perspectives on Political Science* (2017): 1–12.

Bartels, Larry M. *Unequal Democracy: The Political Economy of the New Gilded Age.* Princeton, NJ: Princeton University Press, 2008.

Barzun, Jacques. *God's Country and Mine: A Declaration of Love Spiced with a Few Harsh Words.* Boston: Little, Brown, 1954.

Bauer, Olivier. *Hockey as a Religion: The Montreal Canadians.* Sport and Society Series. Champaign, IL: Common Ground, 2011.

Baumann, Michael. "Change We Can Believe In: The Importance of Brewers Minor Leaguer David Denson's Decision to Come Out." August 7, 2015. grantland.com/the-triangle/2015-mlb-milwaukee-brewers-prospect-david-denson-comes-out-as-gay

Baumer, Benjamin, and Andrew S. Zimbalist. *The Sabermetric Revolution: Assessing the Growth of Analytics in Baseball.* Philadelphia: University of Pennsylvania Press, 2014.

Baxter, Kevin. "In Pro Sports, Gay Athletes Still Feel Unwelcome." *Los Angeles Times.* December 29, 2012.

Benhabib, Seyla. *The Claims of Culture: Equality and Diversity in the Global Era.* Princeton, NJ: Princeton University Press, 2002.

Berkowitz, Peter. *Virtue and the Making of Modern Liberalism.* New Forum Books. Princeton, NJ: Princeton University Press, 1999.

Berlage, Gai. *Women in Baseball: The Forgotten History.* Westport, CT: Praeger, 1994.

Berlin, Isaiah. *Four Essays on Liberty.* Oxford Paperbacks, 116. London & New York: Oxford University Press, 1969.

Bernstein, Ross. *The Code: Baseball's Unwritten Rules and Its Ignore-at-Your-Own-Risk Code of Conduct.* Chicago: Triumph Books, 2008.

Berra, Lindsay. "Female French Teen Makes MLB History." July 22, 2015. m.mlb.com/news/article/132044338/melissa-mayeux-france-eligible-sign-mlb

Berry, Adam. "Mccutchen Carries on Clemente's Legacy" (2015). m.mlb.com/news/article/158069092/andrew-mccutchen-involved-in-charity-work

Bieler, Des, and Jacob Bogage. "Los Angeles City Council Calls on MLB to Give Dodgers 2017 and 2018 World Series Title." *The Washington Post* (2020).

Bodley, Hal. "Retiring No. 42 One of Baseball's Greatest Moments." April 11, 2013. m.mlb.com/news/article/44514982/retiring-no-42-one-of-baseballs-greatest-moments

Bohman, James. "Deliberative Democracy and the Epistemic Benefits of Diversity." *Episteme* 3, no. 3 (2006): 175–91.

Bolsinger, Mike. "The Astros' Cheating Derailed My Career. So I'm Suing." *The Washington Post*. February 15, 2020. sportsbetforum.net/2020/02/15/the-astros-cheating-derailed-my-career-so-im-suing

Bonazzi, Davide. "The Life and Death of an Amazon Warehouse Temp" (2015). highline.huffingtonpost.com/articles/en/life-and-death-amazon-temp

Borgmann, Albert. *Crossing the Postmodern Divide*. Chicago: University of Chicago Press, 1992.

Boudway, Ira, and Kate Smith. "The Braves Play Taxpayers Better Than They Play Baseball." *Bloomberg Businessweek*. April 27, 2016. www.bloomberg.com/features/2016-atlanta-braves-stadium

Boyd, Richard. " 'The Value of Civility?' " *Urban Studies* 43, no. 5–6 (2006): 863–78.

Bradley, Richard. "Taking Advantage of Difference in Opinion." *Episteme* 3, no. 3 (2006): 141–55.

Brady, Justin. "Stem Is Incredibly Valuable, but If We Want the Best Innovators We Must Teach the Arts." *The Washington Post*. September 5, 2014. www.washingtonpost.com/news/innovations/wp/2014/09/05/stem-is-incredibly-valuable-but-if-we-want-the-best-innovators-we-must-teach-the-arts

Braman, Sandra. "Technology and Epistemology: Information Policy and Desire." In *Cultural Technologies in Cultures of Technology: Culture as Means and Ends in Technologically Advanced Media World*, edited by G. Golin, 2012.

Branch, John. "Posthumus Recognition: MLB to Recognize Glenn Burke as Baseball's Gay Pioneer." *New York Times*. July 15, 2014.

Bunting, Thomas, and Erin Evans. "Together under the Open Sky: Rousseau on the Value of Entertainment." *The Political Science Reviewer* 43, no. 1 (2019): 107–36.

Burgos, Adrian. *Playing America's Game: Baseball, Latinos, and the Color Line*. American Crossroads. Berkeley: University of California Press, 2007.

Burk, Robert Fredrick. *Much More Than a Game: Players, Owners, & American Baseball since 1921*. Chapel Hill: University of North Carolina Press, 2001.

Burns, Ken, and Lynn Novick. "5th Inning: Shadow Ball." In *Baseball*: PBS, 1994.

Butterworth, Michael L. *Baseball and Rhetorics of Purity: The National Pastime and American Identity During the War on Terror*. Rhetoric, Culture, and Social Critique. Tuscaloosa: University of Alabama Press, 2010.

————. "Ritual in the "Church of Baseball": Suppressing the Discourse of Democracy after 9/11." *Communication and Critical/Cultural Studies* 2, no. 2 (2005): 107–29.

Buzinski, Jim. "MLB Umpire Dale Scott Comes out as Gay in the Quietest Way Possible." December 2, 2014. www.outsports.com/2014/12/2/7295993/major-league-baseball-umpire-dale-scott-gay-coming-out

Cafardo, Nick. "John Henry Says Red Sox Will Rely Less on Analytics." *Boston Globe.* February 24, 2016.

Cagan, Joanna, and Neil DeMause. *Field of Schemes: How the Great Stadium Swindle Turns Public Money into Private Profit.* Monroe, ME: Common Courage Press, 1998.

Campagna, Norbert. "Virtue in Tocqueville's America." *Amerikastudien / American Studies* 52, no. 2 (2007): 169–86.

Canetti, Elias. *Crowds and Power.* New York: Farrar Straus Giroux, 1984.

Casella, Paul. "Statcast Primer: Baseball Will Never Be the Same." (2015).

Cassuto, Leonard. "Interchapter: Babe Ruth." In *The Cambridge Companion to Baseball*, edited by Leonard Cassuto and Stephen Partridge. Cambridge: Cambridge University Press, 2011.

Cassuto, Leonard, and David Grant. "Babe Ruth, Sabermetrics, and Baseball's Politics of Greatness." In *The Cambridge Companion to Baseball*, edited by Leonard Cassuto and Stephen Partridge. Cambridge: Cambridge University Press, 2011.

Castillo, Jorge. " 'It Don't Shock Me': Dusty Baker on Racial Abuse Directed at Adam Jones at Fenway." *The Washington Post.* May 2, 2017. www.washingtonpost.com/news/nationals-journal/wp/2017/05/02/it-dont-shock-me-dusty-baker-on-racial-abuse-directed-at-adam-jones-at-fenway/?utm_term=.ce6539e92b95

Castrovince, Anthony. "Baseball Symbolized Reiliency after 9/11." September 7, 2011. m.mlb.com/news/article/24200512

Clair, Michael. "The Sonoma Stompers Are Set to Make More History by Signing Two Women to Their Roster." June 29, 2016. m.mlb.com/cutfour/2016/06/29/186947558/sonoma-stompers-sign-two-women?partnerId=as_mlb_20160630_63346566&adbid=748496511755923458&adbpl=tw&adbpr=241544156

Click, James. "Did Derek Jeter Deserve the Gold Glove?" In *Baseball between the Numbers: Why Everything You Know About the Game Is Wrong*, edited by Jonah Keri. New York: Basic Books, 2006.

Coates, Dennis, and Brad R. Humphreys. "Do Economists Reach a Conclusion on Subsidies for Sports Franchises, Stadiums, and Mega-Events?" *Econ Journal Watch* 5, no. 3 (2008): 294–315.

Cohen, Joshua. "An Epistemic Conception of Democracy." *Ethics* 97, no. 1 (1986): 26–38.

Cohen, Marilyn. *No Girls in the Clubhouse: The Exclusion of Women from Baseball.* Jefferson, NC: McFarland, 2009.

Connolly, William E. *Identity/Difference: Democratic Negotiations of Political Paradox.* Expanded ed. Minneapolis: University of Minnesota Press, 2002.

Cooky, Cheryl; Dycus, Ranissa; Dworkin, Shari L. " 'What Makes a Woman a Woman?' Versus 'Our First Lady of Sport': A Comparative Analysis of the United States and the South African Media Coverage of Caster Semenya." *Journal of Sport & Social Issues* 37, no. 1 (2013): 31–56.

Cooper, Evan. "Decoding *Will and Grace*: Mass Audience Reception of a Popular Network Situation Comedy." *Sociological Perspectives* 46, no. 4 (2003): 513–33.

Côté, James E., and Anton Allahar. *Lowering Higher Education: The Rise of Corporate Universities and the Fall of Liberal Education.* Toronto: University of Toronto Press, 2011.

Croucher, Sheila L. *Globalization and Belonging: The Politics of Identity in a Changing World.* New Millennium Books in International Studies. Lanham, MD: Rowman & Littlefield, 2004.

Curtis, Bryan. "Barack/Nixon." May 18, 2012. grantland.com/features/the-eerie-similarities-barack-obama-richard-nixon-two-our-biggest-sports-fans-chief
———. "Brian Kenny Is Making Sense" (2013).

Curvin, Robert. "Remembering Jackie Robinson." *New York Times Magazine* (1982). www.nytimes.com/1982/04/04/magazine/remembering-jackie-robinson.html?pagewanted=all

Debord, Guy. *The Society of the Spectacle.* New York: Zone Books, 1994.

Diadiun, Ted. "Let Chief Wahoo Opponents Be Offended on Their Own Time and Leave the Rest of Us Alone." *Cleveland.com.* April 12, 2016. www.cleveland.com/opinion/index.ssf/2016/04/let_chief_wahoo_opponents_be_o.html.

Diamond, Jared. "Rule Breaking Permeated the Astros—Houston's Front Office Created 'Codebreaker' for the Purpose of Decoding Signs. The Players Took It from There." *The Wall Street Journal* 2020.

Dietrich, Franz. "The Premises of Condorcet's Jury Theorem Are Not Simultaneously Justified." *Episteme* 5, no. 1 (2008): 56–73.

Dinces, Sean. "The Attrition of the Common Fan: Class, Spectatorship, and Major League Stadiums in Postwar Maerica." *Social Science History* 40, no. 2 (2016): 339–65.

Disch, Lisa J. "More Truth Than Fact: Storytelling as Critical Understanding in the Writings of Hannah Arendt." *Political Theory* 21, no. 4 (1993): 665–94.

Disch, Lisa, and Mary Jo Kane. "When a Looker Is Really a Bitch: Lisa Olson, Sport, and the Heterosexual Matrix." *Signs* 21, no. 2 (1996): 278–308.

Drewe, Sheryle Bergmann. *Socrates, Sport, and Students: A Philosophical Inquiry into Physical Education and Sport.* New York: University Press of America, 2001.

Dreyfus, Hubert L., and Sean Kelly. *All Things Shining: Reading the Western Classics to Find Meaning in a Secular Age.* New York: Free Press, 2011.

Eagleman, Andrea M. "Stereotypes of Race and Nationality: A Qualitative Analysis of Sport Magazine Coverage of MLB Players." *Journal of Sport Management* 25 (2011): 156–68.

Eby, Danielle. "2013 Sports Fan Demographics" (2014). opendorse.com/blog/2013-sports-fan-demographics

Edmundson, Mark. *Why Football Matters: My Education in the Game.* New York: Penguin, 2014.

Ellul, Jacques. *The Technological Society.* New York: Knopf, 1964.

Encina, Eduardo A. "O's VP John Angelos: 'Ball Game Irrlelevant' When Compared to Poor's Plight." *The Baltimore Sun*, 2015.

Estlund, David M. *Democratic Authority: A Philosophical Framework.* Princeton, NJ: Princeton University Press, 2008.

Etzioni, Amitai. *The Essential Communitarian Reader.* Lanham, MD: Rowman & Littlefield, 1998.

Evans, Christopher H. "Baseball as Civil Religion: The Genesis of an American Creation Story." In *The Faith of Fifty Million: Baseball, Religion, and American Culture*, edited by Christopher Hodge Evans and William R. Herzog. Louisville, KY: Westminster John Knox Press, 2002.

Evans, Christopher Hodge, and William R. Herzog. *The Faith of Fifty Million: Baseball, Religion, and American Culture.* Louisville, KY: Westminster John Knox Press, 2002.

Farwell, Paul. "Aristotle and the Complete Life." *History of Philosophy Quarterly* 12, no. 3 (1995): 247–63.

Felder, Adam, and Seth Amitin. "How MLB Announcers Favor American Players over Foreign Ones." *The Atlantic.* August 27, 2012. www.theatlantic.com/entertainment/archive/2012/08/how-mlb-announcers-favor-american-players-over-foreign-ones/261265

Felson, Nancy, and Richard J. Parmentier. "The "Savy Interpreter": Performance and Interpretation in Pindar's Victory Odes." *Signs and Society* 3, no. 2 (2015): 261–305.

Filreis, Al. "The Baseball Fan." In *The Cambridge Companion to Baseball*, edited by Leonard Cassuto and Stephen Partridge. Cambridge: Cambridge University Press, 2011.

Fishkin, James S. *Democracy and Deliberation: New Directions for Democratic Reform.* New Haven, CT: Yale University Press, 1991.

———. *The Voice of the People: Public Opinion and Democracy.* New Haven, CT: Yale University Press, 1995.

Foucault, Michel. *The Order of Things: An Archaeology of the Human Sciences.* World of Man. London: Tavistock Publications, 1970.

Gaines, Cork. "The Chairman of the FCC Is Okay with David Ortiz Dropping an F-Bomb During Saturday's Red Sox Ceremony." April 22, 2013. www.businessinsider.com/fcc-david-ortiz-red-sox-ceremony-2013-4

Galston, William A. *Anti-Pluralism: The Populist Threat to Liberal Democracy.* New Haven: Yale University Press, 2018.

———. *Liberal Purposes: Goods, Virtues, and Diversity in the Liberal State.* Cambridge Studies in Philosophy and Public Policy. Cambridge: Cambridge University Press, 1991.

Gambetta, Diego. "'Claro!': An Essay on Discursive Machismo." In *Deliberative Democracy*, edited by Jon Elster. Cambridge: Cambridge University Press, 1998.

Gelven, Michael. *War and Existence: A Philosophical Inquiry.* University Park, PA: Pennsylvania State University Press, 1994.

George, Robert P. *Making Men Moral: Civil Liberties and Public Morality.* Oxford: Oxford University Press, 1993.

Giamatti, A. Bartlett, and Kenneth S. Robson. *A Great and Glorious Game: Baseball Writings of A. Bartlett Giamatti.* Chapel Hill, N.C.: Algonquin Books, 1998.

———. *A Great and Glorious Game: Baseball Writings of A. Bartlett Giamatti.* Chapel Hill, NC: Algonquin Books, 1998.

Gier, Kathleen. "Royals Salute the Negro Leagues with 'Dressed to the Nines at the K.'" *The Kansas City Star.* May 17, 2015.

Gift, Thomas, and Andrew Miner. "'Dropping the Ball': The Understudied Nexus of Sports and Politics." *World Affairs* 180, no. 1 (2017): 127–61.

Gmelch, George. *Playing with Tigers: A Minor League Chronicle of the Sixties.* Lincoln, NE: University of Nebraska Press, 2016.

Goodin, Robert E. "The Epistemic Benefits of Multiple Biased Observers." *Episteme* 3, no. 3 (2006): 166–74.

———. "Representing Diversity." *British Journal of Political Science* 34, no. 3 (2004): 453–68.

Gordon, Rupert H. "Modernity, Freedom, and the State: Hegel's Concept of Patriotism." *The Review of Politics* 62, no. 2 (2000): 295–325.

Grasmuck, Sherri, and Janet Goldwater. *Protecting Home: Class, Race, and Masculinity in Boys' Baseball.* New Brunswick, NJ: Rutgers University Press, 2005.

Green, Jeffrey E. *The Eyes of the People: Democracy in an Age of Spectatorship.* Oxford: Oxford University Press, 2010.

———. "Max Weber and the Reinvention of Popular Power." *Max Weber Studies* 8, no. 2 (2008): 187–224.

Gutmann, Amy, and Dennis Thompson. *Why Deliberative Democracy?* Princeton, NJ: Princeton University Press, 2004.

Guttmann, Allen. *Sports Spectators.* New York: Columbia University Press, 1986.

Habermas, Jürgen. "Reconciliation through the Public Use of Reason: Remarks on John Rawls's Political Liberalism." *The Journal of Philosophy* 92, no. 3 (1995): 109–31.

———. "Three Normative Models of Democracy." *Constellations* 1, no. No 1 (1994): 1–10.

Habermas, Jürgen. *Legitimation Crisis.* Boston: Beacon Press, 1975.

Hall, Cheryl. "Recognizing the Passion in Deliberation: Toward a More Democratic Theory of Democracy." *Hypatia* 22, no. 4 (2007): 81–95.

Hall, Donald. *Fathers Playing Catch with Sons: Essays on Sport, Mostly Baseball.* San Francisco: North Point Press, 1985.

Hall, M. Ann. *Feminism and Sporting Bodies: Essays on Theory and Practice.* Champaign, IL: Human Kinetics, 1996.

Hamilton, Matt;, and Tony Barboza. "Major League Baseball Investigation San Diego Gay Men's Chorus Controversy at Padres' Game." *Los Angeles Times,* 2016.

Harris, Harold Arthur. *Sport in Greece and Rome.* Aspects of Greek and Roman Life. Ithaca, NY: Cornell University Press, 1972.

Hawhee, Debra. "Agonism and Arete." *Philosophy & Rhetoric* 35, no. 3 (2002): 185–207.

Heaphy, Leslie. "Baseball and the Color Line: From the Negro Leagues." In *The Cambridge Companion to Baseball,* edited by Leonard Cassuto and Stephen Partridge. Cambridge: Cambridge University Press, 2011.

Heidegger, Martin. *Being and Time.* Translated by John Macquarrie and Edward Robinson. New York: Harper Perennial/Modern Thought, 2008.

———. *Poetry, Language, Thought.* His Works. New York: Harper & Row, 1971.

———. *The Question Concerning Technology, and Other Essays.* New York: Harper & Row, 1977.

Herbert, Bob. "Wish Fulfillment for Woody." *New York Times.* March 29, 2004.

Hernandez, Dylan. "Los Angeles Has a Lot Riding on 19-Year-Old Julio Urias' Dodgers Debut Tonight." *Los Angeles Times.* May 26, 2016.

Hightower, Kyle. "Jones Says Racial Taunts Speak to Wider Racial Issues." *AP* (2017). 5/3/2017. apnews.com/b5c9f839f8344b07ac20b63a881c5e16/Jones-says-racial-taunts-speak-to-wider-racial-issues

Homer. *The Iliad.* Translated by Robert Fagles. Edited by Bernard Knox. New York: Viking, 1990.

Homer, and Robert Fagles. *The Rage of Achilles from the Iliad.* Penguin 60s Classics. New York: Penguin Books, 1995.

Homer. *The Iliad, Classics on cassette.* Sound recording on six cassettes. St. Paul: Penguin-HighBridge Audio, 1992.

Huizinga, Johan. *Homo Ludens: A Study of the Play Element in Culture.* London: Maurice Temple Smith Ltd., 1970.

Jackel, Peter. "Redemption." *Referee Magazine,* 2014, 21–24.

Jackson, Barry. "Despite New Park, Miami Marlins Enter Season among MLB's Lowest in Payroll." *Miami Herald*. March 31, 2016.

Jackson, Michael. *Politics of Storytelling Variations on a Theme by Hannah Arendt*. Chicago: University of Chicago Press, 2013.

James, Bill. *The New Bill James Historical Baseball Abstract*. New York: Free Press, 2001.

———. "Underestimating the Fog." *Baseball Research Journal* 33 (2004).

Johnstone, Steven. "Virtuous Toil, Vicious Work: Xenophon on Aristocratic Style." *Classical Philology* 89, no. 3 (1994): 219–40.

Joseph, Miranda. *Against the Romance of Community*. Minneapolis: University of Minnesota Press, 2002.

Kahn, Roger. *The Boys of Summer*. New York: Harper & Row, 1972.

———. "The Jackie Robinson I Remember." *The Journal of Blacks in Higher Education* 14 (1997): 88–93.

Katz, Harry L., and Library of Congress. *Baseball Americana: Treasures from the Library of Congress*. New York: Smithsonian Books, 2009.

Keri, Jonah. *Baseball between the Numbers: Why Everything You Know About the Game Is Wrong*. New York: Basic Books, 2006.

Kernell, Samuel. *Going Public: New Strategies of Presidential Leadership*. 4th ed. Washington, DC: CQ Press, 2007.

Kettman, Steve. "Don't Let Statistics Ruin Baseball." *New York Times*. April 8, 2015.

Kimmelman, Michael. "A Ballpark That May Be Louder Than the Fans." *New York Times*, April 27, 2012.

Klepal, Dan. "Braves Bridge Budget Shows $2.2 Million in Additional Costs." *Atlantal Journal-Constitution*. October 5, 2015. www.myajc.com/news/news/local-govt-politics/bridge-budget-shows-22-million-in-additional-costs/nnwBQ

Kohen, Ariel. *Untangling Heroism: Classical Philosophy and the Concept of the Hero*. Routledge Innovations in Political Theory. New York: Routledge, 2014.

Krause, Sharon R. *Liberalism with Honor*. Cambridge, MA: Harvard University Press, 2002.

Kuhn, Thomas S. *The Structure of Scientific Revolutions*. Chicago: University of Chicago Press, 1962.

Kuic, Vukan. "Work, Leisure and Culture." *The Review of Politics* 43, no. 3 (1981): 436–65.

Kurlansky, Mark. "Greenberg's Time." In *Hank Greenberg: The Hero Who Didn't Want to Be One*, edited by Mark Kurlansky. New Haven, CT: Yale University Press, 2011.

Kyle, Donald G. *Sport and Spectacle in the Ancient World*. Ancient Cultures. Malden, MA: Blackwell Pub., 2007.

Laclau, Ernesto. *On Populist Reason*. London; New York: Verso, 2005.

Landemore, Hélène. "Collective Wisdom: Old and New." In *Collective Wisdom: Principles and Mechanisms*, edited by Hélène Landemore and Jon Elster. Cambridge: Cambridge University Press, 2012.

———. *Democratic Reason: Politics, Collective Intelligence, and the Rule of the Many*. Princeton, NJ: Princeton University Press, 2013.

Landemore, Hélène, and Jon Elster. *Collective Wisdom: Principles and Mechanisms*. Cambridge: Cambridge University Press, 2012.

Landers, Chris. "Five Women Playing Baseball Right Now That You Should Pay Attention To." March 8, 2017. m.mlb.com/cutfour/2017/03/08/218326644/null

Le Bon, Gustave. *The Crowd: A Study of the Popular Mind*. 2nd ed. Dunwoody, GA: N.S. Berg, 1968.

Leerhsen, Charles. *Ty Cobb: A Terrible Beauty*. New York: Simon & Schuster Paperbacks, 2016.

Leonhardt, David. "Myth of Men Who Saved Baseball." *New York Times*. March 30, 2005. www.nytimes.com/2005/03/30/sports/myth-of-men-who-saved-baseball.html?mcubz=0&_r=0

Lewis, Michael. *Moneyball: The Art of Winning an Unfair Game*. New York: W.W. Norton, 2003.

Library, FDR. "Presidents and America's Pastime: A Selection of Baseball Documents from the Nation's Presidential Libraries."

Lieberman, Robert C. *Shaping Race Policy: The United States in Comparative Perspective*. Princeton Studies in American Politics. Princeton, NJ: Princeton University Press, 2005.

Lindbergh, Ben. "The Art of Pitch Framing" (2013). grantland.com/features/studying-art-pitch-framing-catchers-such-francisco-cervelli-chris-stewart-jose-molina-others

Lipsky, Richard. *How We Play the Game: Why Sports Dominate American Life*. Boston: Beacon Press, 1981.

List, Christian. "Lessons from the Theory of Judgment Aggregation." In *Collective Wisdom: Principles and Mechanisms*, edited by Hélène Landemore and Jon Elster. Cambridge: Cambridge University Press, 2012.

Lombardini, John. "Civic Laughter: Aristotle and the Political Virtue of Humor." *Political Theory* 41, no. 2 (2013): 203–30.

Lukas, Paul. "Hail to De-Chiefing." April 2, 2014. espn.go.com/mlb/story/_/id/10715887/uni-watch-some-fans-removing-chief-wahoo-logos-protest

Lynd, Robert Staughton, and Helen Merrell Lynd. *Middletown: A Study in American Culture*. Harvest Books. New York: Harcourt, 1959.

Macedo, Stephen. *Liberal Virtues: Citizenship, Virtue, and Community in Liberal Constitutionalism*. Oxford: Oxford University Press, 1991.

Machiavelli, Niccolò. *Machiavelli: The Chief Works and Others*. Translated by Allan Gilbert. Durham, NC: Duke University Press, 1999.

MacIntyre, Alasdair C. *After Virtue: A Study in Moral Theory*. South Bend, IN: University of Notre Dame Press, 1981.

————. *After Virtue: A Study in Moral Theory.* 3rd ed. South Bend, IN: University of Notre Dame Press, 2007.

Mandelbaum, Michael. *The Meaning of Sports: Why Americans Watch Baseball, Football, and Basketball, and What They See When They Do.* New York: Public Affairs, 2004.

Mansbridge, Jane. "Should Blacks Represent Blacks and Women Represent Women? A Contingent 'Yes.'" *The Journal of Politics* 61, no. 3 (1999): 628–57.

Marcuse, Herbert. *One-Dimensional Man: Studies in the Ideology of Advanced Industrial Society.* Boston: Beacon Press, 1991.

Martin, Dan. "Yankees, a-Rod Play Ball: Home Run Millions Going to Charity." *New York Post.* July 3, 2015.

Mayeda, David Tokiharu. "From Model Minority to Economic Threat: Media Portrayals of Major League Baseball Pitchers Hideo Nomo and Hideki Irabu." *Journal of Sport & Social Issues* 23, no. 2 (1999): 203–17.

Mayer, Kenneth R. *With the Stroke of a Pen: Executive Orders and Presidential Power.* Princeton, NJ: Princeton University Press, 2001.

McCain, John, and Jeff Flake. "Tackling Paid Patriotism: A Joint Oversight Report." 2015.

McCarthy, David, and Robyn L. Jones. "Speed, Aggression, Strength and Tacitcal Naïveté: The Portrayal of the Black Soccer Player on Television." *Journal of Sport & Social Issues* 21, no. 4 (1997): 348–62.

McCurry, Justin;, and Lawrence Donegan. "Eri Yoshida Wins Plaudits as First Japanese Woman in Us Baseball League." August 8, 2010. www.theguardian.com/world/2010/aug/08/eri-yoshida-japan-woman-us-baseball

McGraw, Daniel. "Native Americans Protest Chief Wahoo at Cleveland Indians Home Opener." *The Guardian.* April 11, 2015. www.theguardian.com/sport/2015/apr/11/native-americans-protest-chief-wahoo-logo-at-cleveland-indians-home-opener

Mead, William B., and Paul Dickson. *Baseball: The Presidents' Game.* Washington, DC: Farragut Pub. Co., 1993.

Mellinger, Sam. "Times Are Changing, and So Should Major-League Baseball." *Kansas City Star.* April 18, 2015. www.kansascity.com/sports/spt-columns-blogs/sam-mellinger/article18887139.html

Mercurio, Eugenio, and Vincent F. Filak. "Roughing the Passer: The Framing of Black and White Quarterbacks Prior to the NFL Draft." *Howard Journal of Communications* 21, no. 1 (2010): 56–71.

Miller, Patrick B., and David Kenneth Wiggins. *Sport and the Color Line: Black Athletes and Race Relations in Twentieth-Century America.* New York: Routledge, 2004.

Miller, Stephen G. *Arete: Greek Sports from Ancient Sources.* Third and expanded ed. Berkeley: University of California Press, 2004.

Mills, Dorothy Seymour. *Chasing Baseball: Our Obsession with Its History, Numbers, People and Places.* Jefferson, NC: McFarland & Co., 2010.

MLB. "A.G Schneiderman, MLB Commissioner Selig & MLBPA Executive Director Michael Weiner Announce New Code of Conduct Strengthening Protections against Discrimination Based on Sexual Orientation." News release. July 16, 2013. mlb.mlb.com/news/print.jsp?ymd=20130716& content_id=53917834&vkey=pr_mlb&c_id=mlb

"MLB Receives Overall C+ in Racial, Gender Hiring Practices." *Associated Press*. April 18, 2017. www.espn.com/mlb/story/_/id/19186207/mlb-receives-overall-c+-racial-gender-hiring-practices

Morais, Betsy. "Breaking into Baseball's Ultimate Boys' Club." *The Atlantic* (2016). www.theatlantic.com/magazine/archive/2016/09/the-girl-of-summer/492737

Morris, Bonnie J. "Teaching Athletics and Gender: A Pedagogical Narrative." *Women's Studies Quarterly* 33, no. 12 (2005): 233–45.

Morris, Timothy. *Making the Team: The Cultural Work of Baseball Fiction*. Sport and Society. Urbana: University of Illinois Press, 1997.

Mosier, Jeff. "Rangers New Stadium Plans Unveiled; Find out What It Will Cost and Timeline for Its Construction." *Dallas News* (2016). sportsday. dallasnews.com/texas-rangers/rangers/2016/05/20/live-video-rangers-unveil-early-plans-new-arlington-stadium

Mouffe, Chantal. "Deliberative Democracy or Agonistic Pluralism?" *Social Research* 66, no. 3 (1999): 745–58.

———. *The Democratic Paradox*. London: Verso, 2000.

———. *For a Left Populism*. London & New York: Verso, 2018.

———. *On the Political*. Thinking in Action. London: Routledge, 2005.

———. "Which World Order: Cosmopolitan of Multipolar?" *Ethical Perspectives* 15, no. 4 (2008): 453–67.

Mounk, Yascha. *The People Vs. Democracy: Why Our Freedom Is in Danger and How to Save It*. Cambridge, MA & London: Harvard University Press, 2018.

Mudde, Cas, and Cristóbal Rovira Kaltwasser. *Populism: A Very Short Introduction*. Very Short Introductions. New York: Oxford University Press, 2017.

Müller, Jan-Werner. *What Is Populism?* Philadelphia: University of Pennsylvania Press, 2016.

Nardi, Peter M., and Beth E. Schneider. *Social Perspectives in Lesbian and Gay Studies: A Reader*. London: Routledge, 1998.

Nathan, Daniel A. *Rooting for the Home Team: Sport, Community, and Identity*. Urbana: University of Illinois Press, 2013.

Nelson, William. "The Epistemic Value of the Democratic Process." *Episteme* 5, no. 1 (2008): 19–32.

Nichols, Mary P. "Philosophy and Empire: On Socrates and Alcibiades in Plato's 'Symposium.'" *Polity* 39, no. 4 (2007): 502–21.

Nietzsche, Friedrich Wilhelm. *The Portable Nietzsche*. New York: Viking Press, 1954.

Nightengale, Bob. "Adam Jones on MLB's Lack of Kaepernick Protest: 'Baseball Is a White Man's Sport.'" September 12, 2016. www.usatoday.com/story/

sports/mlb/columnist/bob-nightengale/2016/09/12/adam-jones-orioles-colin-kaepernick-white-mans-sport/90260326

———. "Orioles' Adam Jones Berated by Racist Taunts at Fenway Park." *USA Today.* May 1, 2017. www.usatoday.com/story/sports/mlb/2017/05/01/orioles-adam-jones-berated-racist-taunts-fenway-park-peanuts/101187172

Ober, Josiah. "Democracy's Wisdom: An Aristotelian Middle Way for Collective Judgment." *American Political Science Review* 107, no. 1 (2013): 104–22.

Ogden, David C. "Baseball and Blacks: A Loss of Affinity, a Loss of Community." In *Baseball and American Culture: Across the Diamond*, edited by Edward J. Rielly. New York: Haworth Press, 2003.

Ogden, David, and Randall A. Rose. "Using Giddens's Structuration Theory to Examine the Waning Participation of African American's in Baseball." *Journal of Black Studies* 35, no. 4 (2005): 225–45.

Olson, Joel. "Friends and Enemies, Slaves and Masters: Fanaticism, Wendell Phillips, and the Limits of Democratic Theory." *The Journal of Politics* 71, no. 1 (2009): 82–95.

Oriard, Michael. "Football Town under Friday Night Lights: High School Football and American Dreams." In *Rooting for the Home Team: Sport, Community, and Identity*, edited by Daniel A. Nathan. Urbana: University of Illinois Press, 2013.

Overman, Steven J. *The Protestant Ethic and the Spirit of Sport: How Calvinism and Capitalism Shaped America's Games.* Macon, GA: Mercer University Press, 2011.

Ozanian, Mike. "Miami Marlins Have Become Baseball's Most Expensive Stadium Disaster." January 27, 2013. www.forbes.com/sites/mikeozanian/2013/01/27/miami-marlins-have-become-baseballs-most-expensive-stadium-disaster/#2c3d48e342fe

Paine, Neil. "On Deck: A Sabermetric Broadcast" (2014). fivethirtyeight.com/features/on-deck-a-sabermetric-broadcast

Perrottet, Tony. *The Naked Olympics: The True Story of the Ancient Games.* New York: Random House, 2004.

Perry, Dayn. "Do Players Perform Better in Contract Years?" In *Baseball between the Numbers: Why Everything You Know About the Game Is Wrong*, edited by Jonah Keri. New York: Basic Books, 2006.

Petchesky, Barry. "The Real Cost to Miami for Marlines Park Is in the Billions." January 25, 13. deadspin.com/5978964/the-real-cost-to-miami-for-marlins-park-is-in-the-billions

Phelps, Jordyn. "President Obama Explains Why He Attended MLB Exhibition Game in Cuba Despite Brussels Attacks." (2016). abcnews.go.com/Politics/president-obama-attend-mlb-exhibition-game-cuba/story?id=37842394

Piazza, Mike, and Lonnie Wheeler. *Long Shot.* New York: Simon & Schuster, 2013.

Pieper, Josef. *Leisure: The Basis of Culture and the Philosophical Act.* Translated by Alexander Dru. San Francisco: Ignatius, 2009.

Pierman, Carol J. "Baseball, Conduct and True Womanhood." *Women's Studies Quarterly* 33, no. 1–2 (2005): 68–85.

Pindar. *The Complete Odes.* Translated by Anthony Verity. Oxford: Oxford University Press, 2007.

Pitkin, Hanna Fenichel. *The Concept of Representation.* Berkeley: University of California Press, 1967.

Plato. *The Laws of Plato.* Translated by Thomas L. Pangle. Chicago: University of Chicago Press, 1988.

———. *The Republic.* Translated by Richard W. Sterling and William C. Scott. New York: Norton, 1985.

———. *Symposium.* Translated by Alexander Nehamas and Paul Woodruff. Indianapolis: Hackett, 1989.

Plato and Aristophanes. *Four Texts on Socrates: Plato's Euthyphro, Apology, and Crito, and Aristophanes' Clouds.* Translated by Thomas G. West and Grace Starry West. Rev. ed. Ithaca, NY: Cornell University Press, 1998.

Potok, Chaim. *The Chosen: A Novel.* New York: Simon and Schuster, 1967.

Poulisse, Adam. "How the Los Angelos Dodgers Became Known as 'Los Doyers.'" *Pasadena Star-News.* October 14, 2013. www.pasadenastarnews.com/sports/20131014/latinos-rocky-relationship-with-their-doyers-over-chavez-ravine-now-a-distant-memory

Rader, Benjamin G. *American Sports: From the Age of Folk Games to the Age of Spectators.* Englewood Cliffs, NJ: Prentice-Hall, 1983.

Rancière, Jacques. *Dissensus: On Politics and Aesthetics.* Translated by Steve Corcoran. London: Continuum, 2010.

———. *The Emancipated Spectator.* London: Verso, 2009.

Rauner, Robert R., Ryan W. Walters, Marybell Avery, and Teresa J Wanser. "Evidence That Aerobic Fitness Is More Salient Than Weight Status in Predicting Standardized Math and Reading Outcomes in Fourth-through Eighth-Grade Students." *The Journal of Pediatrics* 163, no. 2 (2013): 344–48.

Rawls, John. "Justice as Fairness: Political Not Metaphysical." *Philosophy and Public Affairs* 14, no. 3 (1985): 223–51.

———. *Political Liberalism.* Columbia Classics in Philosophy. Expanded ed. New York: Columbia University Press, 2005.

———. *A Theory of Justice.* Cambridge, MA: Harvard University Press (Belknap), 1971.

Reed, Nancy B. *More Than Just a Game: The Military Nature of Greek Athletic Contests.* Chicago: Ares Publishers, 1998.

Rhoden, William C. "Sports of the Times: Delgado Makes a Stand by Taking a Seat." *New York Times.* July 21, 2004. www.nytimes.com/2004/07/21/sports/sports-of-the-times-delgado-makes-a-stand-by-taking-a-seat.html?_r=0

Richey, Sean. "Civic Engagement and Patriotism." *Social Science Quarterly* 92, no. 4 (2011): 1044–56.

Ring, Jennifer. "Invisible Women in America's National Pastime . . . Or, 'She's Good. It's History, Man.'" *Journal of Sport & Social Issues* 37, no. 1 (2012): 57–77.

———. *Stolen Bases: Why American Girls Don't Play Baseball.* Urbana: University of Illinois Press, 2009.

Rios, Edwin. "White People Could Learn a Thing or Two About Talking About Race from Orioles' Manager." April 30, 2015. www.motherjones.com/politics/2015/04/orioles-manager-buck-showalter-baltimore-protests

Rishe, Patrick James. "Gender Gaps and the Presence and Profitability of College Football." *Social Science Quarterly* 80, no. 4 (1999): 702–17.

Robinson, Jackie, and Alfred Duckett. *I Never Had It Made: An Autobiography.* Hopewell, NJ: Ecco Press, 1995.

Roediger, David R. *Working toward Whiteness: How America's Immigrants Became White: The Strange Journey from Ellis Island to the Suburbs.* New York: Basic Books, 2005.

Roessner, Amber. *Inventing Baseball Heroes: Ty Cobb, Christy Mathewson, and the Sporting Press in America.* Baton Rouge: Louisiana State University Press, 2014.

Roller, Lynn E. "Funeral Games in Greek Art." *American Journal of Archaeology* 85, no. 2 (1981): 107–19.

Rosenthal, Ken. "Seven Asked, Seven Answered: Baseball Execs Would Sign Gay Player." February 10, 2014. www.foxsports.com/mlb/story/major-league-baseball-execs-open-to-signing-gay-player-021014

———. "Study Shows Youth Baseball, Softball Participation on the Rise." *FoxSports. com* May 18, 2017. www.foxsports.com/mlb/story/study-shows-youth-baseball-softball-participation-on-the-rise-051817

———. "Upton Not D-Backs Kind of Player." January 24, 2013. www.foxsports.com/mlb/story/quiet-justin-upton-not-the-kind-of-intense-player-arizona-diamondbacks-want-trade-to-atlanta-braves-hot-stove-012413

Rosenthal, Ken, and Evan Drellich. "The Astros Stole Signs Electronically in 2017—Part of a Much Broader Issue for Major League Baseball." *The Athletic.*

Roth, Amanda, and Susan A. Basow. "Femininity, Sports, and Feminism." *Journal of Sport and Social Issues* 28, no. 3 (2004): 245–65.

Rousseau, Jean-Jacques, and Jean Le Rond d Alembert. *Politics and the Arts, Letter to M. D'alembert on the Theatre.* Agora Editions. Glencoe, IL: Free Press, 1960.

Rowley, Meg. "Pitchf/Oxq." May 2, 2017. www.baseballprospectus.com/article.php?articleid=31736

Rubin, Adam. "Daniel Murphy: Right to Take Leave." *ESPN* (2014). April 4, 2014. espn.go.com/new-york/mlb/story/_/id/10721495/daniel-murphy-new-york-mets-deflects-criticism-taking-paternity-leave

Sandel, Michael J. *Democracy's Discontent: America in Search of a Public Philosophy.* Cambridge, MA: Harvard University Press (Belknap), 1996.

———. *Liberalism and the Limits of Justice.* Cambridge: Cambridge University Press, 1982.

———. *Public Philosophy: Essays on Morality in Politics.* Cambridge, MA: Harvard University Press, 2005.

Sanders, Lynn M. "Against Deliberation." *Political Theory* 25, no. 3 (1997): 347–76.

Sansone, David. *Greek Athletics and the Genesis of Sport.* Berkeley: University of California Press, 1988.

Schilken, Chuck. "Yankees' CC Sabathia on Playing in Boston: 'I've Neer Been Called the N-Word' Anywhere but There." *Los Angeles Times* (2017). May 3, 2017. www.latimes.com/sports/sportsnow/la-sp-sabathia-jones-fenway-racism-20170503-story.html

Schmitt, Angie. "Braves Stadium Relocation Shaping up to Be a Disaster." *Streets Blog USA.* October 30, 2015. usa.streetsblog.org/2015/10/30/braves-stadium-relocation-shaping-up-to-be-a-disaster

Schmitt, Carl. *The Concept of the Political.* Expanded ed. Chicago: University of Chicago Press, 2007.

———. *The Crisis of Parliamentary Democracy.* Studies in Contemporary German Social Thought. Cambridge, MA: MIT Press, 1985.

Schwindt-Bayer, Leslie A., and William Mishler. "An Integrated Model of Women's Representation." *The Journal of Politics* 67, no. 2 (2005): 407–28.

Scott, Jack. *The Athletic Revolution.* New York: Free Press, 1971.

Selznick, Philip. "Foundations of Communitarian Liberalism." In *The Essential Communitarian Reader,* edited by Amitai Etzioni. Lanham, MD: Rowman & Littlefield, 1998.

Sexton, John, Thomas Oliphant, and Peter J. Schwartz. *Baseball as a Road to God: Seeing Beyond the Game.* New York: Gotham Books, 2013.

Sharrow, Elizabeth A. " 'Female Athlete' Politic: Title Ix and the Naturalization of Sex Difference in Public Policy." *Politics, Groups, and Identities* 5, no. 1 (2017): 46–66.

Shavelson, Richard J., Robert L. Linn, Eva L. Baker, Helen F. Ladd, L. Darling-Hammond, L.A. Shepard, and Richard Rothstein. "Problems with the Use of Student Test Scores to Evaluate Teachers." *Washington, DC: Economic Policy Institute* (2010).

Shea, Bill. "New Funds Help Athletes Score in Philanthropy" (2014). www.crains detroit.com/article/20141026/NEWS/310269927/new-funds-help-athletes-score-in-philanthropy

Shklar, Judith. "The Liberalism of Fear." *Political Liberalism: Variations on a Theme* (1989): 149–66.

Shklar, Judith N. *Ordinary Vices.* Cambridge, MA: Harvard University Press (Belknap), 1984.

Sigelman, Lee, and Paul J. Wahlbeck. "Gender Proportionality in Intercollegiate Athletics: The Mathematics of Title Ix Compliance." *Social Science Quarterly* 80, no. 3 (1999): 518–38.

Silver, Nate. "Is David Ortiz a Clutch Hitter?" In *Baseball between the Numbers: Why Everything You Know About the Game Is Wrong*, edited by Jonah Keri. New York: Basic Books, 2006.

Simon, Robert L. *Fair Play: The Ethics of Sport*. 3rd ed. Boulder, CO: Westview Press, 2010.

Simons, William M. "The Athlete as Jewish Standard Bearer: Media Images of Hank Greenberg." *Jewish Social Studies* 44, no. 2 (1982): 95–112.

Sinn, Ulrich. *Olympia: Cult, Sport, and Ancient Festival*. Princeton, NJ: M. Wiener, 2000.

Skolnik, Richard. *Baseball and the Pursuit of Innocence: A Fresh Look at the Old Ball Game*. College Station: Texas A&M University, 1994.

Slagter, Josh. "Detroit Tigers' Justin Verlander Tells Cnn He's Open to Gay Teammate, Says Tigers Could Deal with It" (2013). www.mlive.com/tigers/index.ssf/2013/03/justin_verlander_tells_cnn_hes.html.

Smith, Jeffrey A. "Nationalism, Virtue, and the Spirit of Liberty in Rousseau's 'Government of Poland.'" *The Review of Politics* 65, no. 3 (2003): 409–37.

Smith, Steven B. "In Defense of Patriotism." In *Political Philosophy*, edited by Steven B. Smith. New Haven, CT: Yale University Press, 2012.

Stafford, Sarah L. "Progress toward Title Ix Compliance: The Effect of Formal and Informal Enforcement Mechanisms." *Social Science Quarterly* 85, no. 5 (2004): 1469–86.

Stern, Keith. *Queers in History: The Comprehensive Encyclopedia of Historical Gays, Lesbians, Bisexuals, and Transgenders*. Dallas, TX: BenBella, 2009. Distributed by Perseus Distribution.

Strach, Patricia. *Hiding Politics in Plain Sight: Cause Marketing, Corporate Influence, and Breast Cancer Policymaking*. New York: Oxford University Press, 2016.

Stuart Mill, John *On Liberty and the Subjection of Women*. London: Penguin Classics, 2006.

Surowiecki, James. *The Wisdom of Crowds: Why the Many Are Smarter Than the Few and How Collective Wisdom Shapes Business, Economies, Societies, and Nations*. New York: Doubleday, 2004.

Taylor, Charles. *The Ethics of Authenticity*. Cambridge, MA: Harvard University Press, 1992.

Teodoro, Manuel P., and Jon R. Bond. "Presidents, Baseball, and Wins above Expectations: What Can Sabermetrics Tell Us About Presidential Success?: Why Ronald Reagan Is Like Bobby Cox and Lyndon Johnson Is Like Joe Torre." *PS: Political Science & Politics* 50, no. 2 (2017): 339–46.

Thibodeau, Ian. "Tiger Stadium Project Brings Neighborhoods, Kids into Detroit's Resurgence, Pal Ceo Says." June 2, 2016. www.mlive.com/news/index.ssf/2016/06/tiger_stadium_project_brings_n.html

Thucydides. *The Peloponnesian War*. Translated by Steven Lattimore. Indianapolis: Hackett, 1998.

Tocqueville, Alexis de. *Democracy in America*. Translated by George Lawrence. Edited by J.P. Mayer. 2 vols. New York: Harper Perennial Classics, 2006.

Tough, Paul. *How Children Succeed: Grit, Curiosity, and the Hidden Power of Character*. Boston: Houghton Mifflin Harcourt, 2012.

Traubel, Horace. *With Walt Whitman in Camden*. New York: Rowman and Littlefield, 1961.

Travers, Ann. "Thinking the Unthinkable: Imagining an "Un-American," Girl-Friendly, Women- and Trans-Inclusive Alternative for Baseball." *Journal of Sport & Social Issues* 37, no. 1 (2012): 78–96.

Turbow, Jason, and Michael Duca. *The Baseball Codes: Beanballs, Sign Stealing, and Bench-Clearing Brawls: The Unwritten Rules of America's Pastime*. New York: Pantheon Books, 2010.

Turner, Edith L. B. *Communitas: The Anthropology of Collective Joy*. Contemporary Anthropology of Religion. New York: Palgrave Macmillan, 2012.

Tygiel, Jules. *Baseball's Great Experiment Jackie Robinson and His Legacy*. New York: Vintage Books, 1984.

Updike, John. "Hub Fans Bid Kid Adieu." In *The Only Game in Town: Sportswriting from the New Yorker*, edited by David Remnick. New York: Random House, 2010.

Urbinati, Nadia. *Democracy Disfigured: Opinion, Truth, and the People*. Cambridge, MA: Harvard University Press, 2014.

———. "Unpolitical Democracy." *Political Theory* 38, no. 1 (2010): 65–92.

Vecsey, George. *Baseball: A History of America's Favorite Game*. Modern Library Chronicles. New York: Modern Library, 2008.

"Vin Scully's Greatest Calls: Hank Aaron's Historic 715th Home Run." April 8, 2016. www.usatoday.com/story/sports/mlb/2016/04/08/vin-scully-calls-hank-aaron-historic-715th-home-run-babe-ruth/82799928

"The Vocabularist: Are Fans Fanatical or Fanciful?" *BBC News Magazine Monitor*. September 22, 2015. www.bbc.com/news/blogs-magazine-monitor-34298659

Voegelin, Eric. *The New Science of Politics: An Introduction*. Chicago: University of Chicago Press, 1987.

———. "The Origins of Scientism." *Social Research* 15, no. 4 (1948): 462–94.

Voigt, David Quentin. *America through Baseball*. Chicago: Nelson-Hall, 1976.

Wagner, James. "After a Long Lull, Protesting Is Taking Hold across Baseball." *New York Times*. August 28, 2020.

Waldron, Jeremy. "The Wisdom of the Multitude: Some Reflections on Book 3, Chapter 11 of Aristotle's Politics." *Political Theory* 23, no. 4 (1995): 563–84.

Walzer, Michael. *Spheres of Justice: A Defense of Pluralism and Equality*. New York: Basic Books, 1983.

Weaver, Bill L. "The Black Press and the Assault on Proffesional Baseball's 'Color Line,' October, 1945–April, 1947." *The Atlanta University Review of Race and Culture* 40, no. 4 (1979): 303–17.

Weber, Max. *The Theory of Social and Economic Organization.* Translated by A. M. Henderson. Edited by Talcott Parsons. New York: Oxford University Press, 1947.

Wendel, Tim. *Summer of '68: The Season That Changed Baseball–and America–Forever.* Cambridge, MA: Da Capo Press, 2012.

White, G. Edward. *Creating the National Pastime: Baseball Transforms Itself, 1903–1953.* Princeton, NJ: Princeton University Press, 1996.

Whitman, Cedric Hubbell. *Homer and the Heroic Tradition.* Cambridge, MA: Harvard University Press, 1958.

Wilhalme, Matt. "Mo'ne Davis Helps Set Little League World Series TV Record for ESPN." *Los Angeles Times.* August 21, 2014.

Wolin, Sheldon S. "Democracy, Difference and Re-Cognition." *Political Theory* 21, no. 3 (1993): 464–83.

———. "Fugitive Democracy." *Constellations* 1, no. 1 (1994).

———. "The Liberal/Democratic Divide. On Rawl's Political Liberalism." *Political Theory* 24, no. 1 (1996): 97–119.

———. "Norm and Form: The Constitutionalizing of Democracy." In *Athenian Political Thought and the Reconstruction of American Democracy,* edited by J. Peter Euben, John R. Wallach, and Josiah Ober. Ithaca, NY: Cornell University Press, 1994.

———. *Politics and Vision: Continuity and Innovation in Western Political Thought.* Expanded ed. Princeton, NJ: Princeton University Press, 2004.

Wootton, David. *The Essential Federalist and Anti-Federalist Papers.* Indianapolis: Hackett, 2003.

Xenophon. *Scripta Minora, with an English Translation.* Translated by Edgar Cardew Marchant. London: W. Heinemann & G.P. Putnam's sons, 1925.

Young, Iris Marion. *On Female Body Experience "Throwing Like a Girl" and Other Essays.* Studies in Feminist Philosophy. New York: Oxford University Press, 2005.

Young, Michael Dunlop. *The Rise of the Meritocracy, 1870–2033: An Essay on Education and Equality.* London: Thames and Hudson, 1958.

Zeigler, Cyd. "Billy Bean Hired by Major League Baseball as Ambassador for Inclusion, Will Lead Gay Inclusion Program" (2014). www.outsports.com/2014/7/15/5898727/billy-bean-gay-baseball-mlb

Zirin, Dave. "Victory! USA Women's Hockey Team Just Won Their Strike." March 29, 2017. www.thenation.com/article/victory-usa-womens-hockey-team-just-won-their-strike

INDEX